FORWAR

CW00696403

While visiting my friend Dorothy Bowles at t
we were talking about the necessity of re|
Church. The cost of this was estimated to k
were discussing how we could raise the m......, ...,
work. I mentioned that I could do a sponsored walk to pay for the repairs and
suggested to Dorothy I would climb Snowdon. She was shocked at my idea
but I was deadly serious! I explained to her about my past adventures in my
scouting days with the Venture Scouts and she felt I should write a book on
my experiences. This was how the very first seeds were sown regarding me
writing my life story and also how the sponsored walks for charity began!
Ironically, the repairs were never carried out to the organ but my first
sponsored walk was for Callow Hill Church to raise part of the money required
to provide new toilet facilities, a vestry and modernised kitchen at the grand
age of 86!

It evolved, therefore, to celebrate my birthdays, for several years I have
marked the occasion with charity walks every other year to raise much needed
funds for meaningful causes. Due to my life-long affinity with scouting and
love of the outdoors, which took me to many places such as Scotland,
Switzerland and Wales where my passion for mountaineering has been
regularly pursued, it seemed fitting to choose Snowdon as the venue as it is
the nearest challenge I can accomplish in one day!

On my first climb in my 86th year I was accompanied by my friend Damien
Chance from West Bromwich and we raised £1,561 for Callow Hill Church. On
my second, in my 88th year, the proceeds of £2,116 were shared between
Bewdley Methodist Church (£1,200 for the provision of a lift and building
alterations) and Bewdley Scouts and Guides (£650 for their Gangshow at
Bewdley High School) and the remainder to Callow Hill Church. My next
fundraising exercise in my 90th year raised £6,714 to provide a Paxman Hair
loss System for the Millbrook Suite at Kidderminster Hospital to arrest hair loss
for cancer patients undergoing chemotherapy.

In order to reach the total of £6,714 we spent many months visiting homes
and businesses in Bewdley, Kidderminster, Stourport, Bliss Gate, Far Forest,
Heightington, Pound Green, Arley, Abberley and Callow Hill. My daughter Des,
friend Andrea Clarke and myself spent many hours collecting the donations
and this proved to be more difficult than climbing Snowdon itself! The
previous two sponsored walks I carried out with the support of ex 3rd Bewdley
Scouts: Peter Johnson, Andrew Franklin, David Thomas and his friend Al
Callen who originated from Snowdonia and had two knee replacements not
long before the ascent!

I climbed Snowdon again on 29th July, 2011, in my 92nd year with Damien and Andrea and we had a wonderful day with weather perfect for the climb. The purpose was to raise funds for the Help for Heroes charity and this was possibly my very best walk to date! A total of £3,420 was raised for this cause and if I am sufficiently fit, although my daughter Des is very concerned at this idea, I plan to do it all again this year with Damien and Andrea in aid of the Air Ambulance which again, is a very worthwhile cause.

In an effort to maintain physical fitness to prepare for the climb I generally aim to walk between 4 to 16 miles on a Saturday morning. It was at about the time when I had completed my second charity walk I heard from my sister Florrie my friend Andrea (from our time at Brintons) had been very ill and I went to visit her. She was amazed at what I had done and desperately wanted to get fit again. I took her for very small walks at first, around a mile in length along the old Wyre Forest railway track. Over the months we built this up until we reached 14 miles and she often joins me on my Saturday morning hikes.

During the course of our walks following the varied routes around Bewdley many memories have been ignited from my distant past and I have taken this opportunity to explain the history of the local area to Andrea which has proved to be very useful to us both when compiling this book on my life story. On our return we write up all the notes to compile my book. As Des says, Andrea is her adopted sister and we are all getting along so well it really does feel that I have two daughters! Andrea also attends church with me at both Abberley and Bewdley and I enjoy her company.

Allen Birch

Bewdley Born & Bred
1st Printed October 2012
Published by Design Direct
Copyright © Allen Birch

BEWDLEY BORN AND BRED BY ALLEN BIRCH

C O N T E N T S

BEWDLEY BORN AND BRED
by
ALLEN BIRCH

INTRODUCTION

Firstly, I will begin my book with a little slice of Bewdley's ancient history. The town dates back to Saxon times and the earliest settlement recorded was at Wribbenhall or "Gurbehale" as it was known, which formed part of the ancient parish of Kidderminster and was mentioned in the Domesday Book (1086). In the year 1300, when the portion west of the Severn came into the possession of the great historic family of the Mortimers, its owners, impressed by its beauty, gave it the French name "*Beaulieu*" meaning "*the beautiful place*" (in latin *Bellus Locus*). The great antiquary Camden, after mentioning that the name originates from its most pleasant situation, uses these words of praise:

"Delicium rerum Bellus Locus undique floret
Fronde coronatus Virianae tempora sylvae"

Translated by Bishop Gibson this means:

"Fair seated Bewdley, a delightful town,
Which Wyre's tall oaks with shady branches crown"

Another settlement grew up on the opposite side of the river above the flood plain which is where the town centre is now located. Saint Annes Church and Bewdley Bridge are possibly the most famous landmarks in the town. Historically there have been a total of three bridges built since mediaeval times; the first in 1447. The previous bridge comprised of five pointed stone arches, one of which originally supported a stone gatehouse and a sanctuary chapel but one of the arches had been damaged by the Royalists in 1644 necessitating being rebuilt in timber.

Bewdley Bridge was in a dilapidated state when in 1795 a great flood swept it down the Severn and destroyed the majority of the structure. The current bridge replaced the one destroyed during those floods. Thomas Telford (then Surveyor of Public Works in Shropshire) designed the current 8.2m wide three-span masonry bridge which was constructed in 1798 by John Simpson of Shrewsbury and the total cost was £11,000 which included buying the land each side of the bridge. Parts of a 15th century bridge were rediscovered in 2004 during the process of excavations to install the flood alleviation scheme we have today.

Thomas Telford also designed the Toll House on the bridge but sadly this was demolished in 1960 and all that now remains to commemorate this is a plaque set into the paving and one remaining stone was installed in the foundations of Bewdley Rowing Club in around 1962. From Severnside South and Severnside North there was an extensive range of quays. On the opposite bank is Wribbenhall which had wharves and warehouses and this was originally a separate village to Bewdley. Wribbenhall is certainly as old as Bewdley and was often referred to as "the Christian Shore." It was recorded in the Domesday Book as being part of the manor of Kidderminster.

There were many famous people over time with Bewdley connections way before our famous Prime Minister of three times, Stanley Baldwin who was born in Lower Park on 3rd August, 1867, an only child to Alfred and Louise and more detail on this family is covered later in the book. Many of these are summarised as follows:–

Prince Edward (later King Edward V), was born in 1470 to Edward IV of England and Elizabeth Woodville within Westminster Abbey where his mother had sought sanctuary from the Lancastrians who had temporarily removed his Father, the Yorkist, from power as part of the Wars of the Roses. He was created Prince of Wales in June 1471 and in 1473 was established at Ludlow Castle on the Welsh Marshes.

The Prince of Wales lived in Bewdley until he became King of England on 9th April 1483. His reign was dominated by the influence of his Uncle, Richard, Duke of Gloucester who succeeded him as Richard III along with his brother Richard of Shrewsbury, Duke of York. Edward was one of the Princes in the Tower who disappeared after being sent (for their own safety) to the Tower of London. Responsibility for their deaths is widely ascribed to Richard III but the actual events remain controversial. Along with Edward VIII, Empress Matilda and Lady Jane Grey, Edward V is one of the only four English monarchs since the Norman Conquest never to have been crowned. If, as seems likely, he died before his 15th birthday, he is the shortest lived monarch in English history. His great nephew Edward VI died in his 16th year.

Mary Sidney (later Mary Herbert), Countess of Pembroke was born at Tickenhill on 27th October, 1561, daughter of Sir Henry Sidney K.G. Lord–Lieutenant of Ireland, who died in Bewdley in 1584. Sir Henry was also Lord President of the Marshes of Wales and as such Tickenhill and Ludlow Castle were his official residences. Incidentally, Henry VII built the Palace of Tickenhill for Prince Arthur who, in 1477, married Catherine of Aragon. In 1502 Arthur died and Henry VIII repaired the property for his daughter Princess Mary.

William Thynne, editor of Chaucer's Works and Clerk of the Kitchen in the household of Henry VIII. On 20th August, 1528 he became Bailiff of Bewdley plus keeper of the park and passed away in 1546.

Arthur Massinger, Father of the famous Philip Massinger (1583 to 1640) was one of the most scholarly and powerful dramatists of his day. Mr Massinger was educated at St Alban Hall, Oxford (as was his son), was a Member of Parliament and was attached to the household of Henry Herbert, 2nd Earl of Pembroke, who recommended him in 1587 for the office of examiner in the Court of the Marshes. He died in 1603.

Sir Ralph Clare (1589 to 1670) was an English courtier and politician who sat in the House of Commons. Caldwall Tower in Castle Road, Kidderminster is all that remains of the castle of Sir Ralph, a leading Royalist. He was a devoted servant of Charles I and Charles II, was jailed after the Battle of Worcester and later banished. After the restoration he returned to the country and is buried near Kidderminster. The three storey building has a colourful history with close connections to the Gunpowder Plot and to Geoffrey Chaucer.

Sir Henry Herbert, (1595–1673), son of Richard Herbert of Montgomery Castle, became Master of the Revels to both King Charles I and King Charles II in 1641. Herbert was the Great Uncle of the Hon. Henry Herbert and the youngest of a brilliant family. After he married a city widow he purchased the mastership of the revels with a salary of £500 per annum for £3,000 and in 1627 he acquired the Manor of Ribbesford. He and his brother sought political neutrality but without success. He was plundered by both sides and early in 1644 a Cavalier officer blew open the gates and doors of Ribbesford with gunpowder, regarded him as a traitor and carried him off by force to sit in the Oxford Parliament. His last speech was in the debate on relief for *"tender consciences"* on 14th February, 1673. He died on 27th April and was buried at St. Paul's, Covent Garden.

John Tombes was born in Bewdley in 1603 and was educated at Bewdley Grammar School. He became a great opponent of infant baptism and disputed with Richard Baxter on this subject on New Year's Day 1649, in Bewdley Church, from nine in the morning to five o'clock in the evening. He was preacher of The Temple in London and one of Cromwell's "Triers" which was a national body set up to vet all new clergy. He afterwards conformed to the Church of England and died at Salisbury in 1676.

Sir Charles Compton, born in 1623 was son of Spencer Lord Compton and grandson of William the Earl of Northampton and was thought to have been born at Tickenhill. He was baptised on 25th November, 1624 in the old chapel there and is recorded to have fought in the battles of Edgehill, Hopton Heath and his chief exploit was the taking of Beeston Castle in Cheshire, where six men disguised as butchers and bakers surprised the garrison in their beds. After the Restoration he was advanced by the King to a position of trust but a fall from his horse in Northampton caused his untimely death.

Rev. Henry Oasland (1625 to 1703) was educated at Bewdley and Trinity College, Cambridge (MA 165). In 1650 he was elected Minister of Bewdley where he was a friend of Richard Baxter. At this time he was described as "the most lively, fervent and moving Preacher in all the Country" but after the Restoration he was arrested on suspicion of being implicated in the Packington's Plot, although was soon released. In 1662 he was ejected from Bewdley. After the Toleration Act he preached regularly until his death. In 1660 he married a Miss Maxwell of Bewdley with whom he produced two sons, Edward and Henry. His son became the Rev. Edward Oasland, Pastor of the Presbyterian Chapel of Bewdley. The Rev. Henry Oasland's printed works were The Dead Pastor Yet Speaking and The Christian's Daily Walk.

Rev. John Boraston was prebendary of Hereford and Rector of Ribbesford for 58 years, spanning from 1630 to 1688. He passed away 29th December, 1688 aged 85 and his grave is at Ribbesford Church.

Richard Morton, M.D., (1637–1698) son of the minister of St. Annes Church, Bewdley became very well known in the medical profession and was President of the Royal College of Physicians in 1696.

Richard Willis was born 17th January, 1664, the son of a tanner in Bewdley. He laid the first stone of the famous church in St. Martin's–in–the–Fields, Trafalgar Square, and preached the first sermon on behalf of the Society for the Propagation of the Gospel. He passed away 11th July, 1845 aged 69 and was buried at Ribbesford.

Sir Thomas Lyttleton, 4th Baronet (1686–1751) was the eldest son of Sir Charles Lyttleton, 3rd Baronet and inherited his family estates in Frankley, Halesowen, Hagley and Upper Arley on his death in 1716. He married Christian in 1708, daughter of Sir Richard Temple, 3rd Baronet of Stowe. Her brother, Sir Richard Temple, 4th Baronet was created Viscount Cobham. Sir Thomas represented Bewdley and was elected as one of the Members of Parliament for Worcestershire in 1721 and served until 1734. He then represented Camelford until 1741. He held office as one of the Lords of the Admiralty from 1727–1741. On his death his title passed to his younger brother, the 3rd Baronet. The Lyttleton coat of arms is displayed on the Town Hall which was built in 1808 as the late Lord Cobham was the last High Steward of Bewdley.

Sir Edward Winnington was born February 28[th,] 1728. He lived at Stanford Court and was Lord of the Manor and proprietor of the parish of Stanford (which was between Worcester and Tenbury). This gentleman was created Baronet in 1755 and sat as a Conservative Member of Parliament for Bewdley from 1761 to 1774. He died in 1791 when he was succeeded by Sir Edward Winnington, 2nd Baronet, his only son.

Rev. Edward Baugh MA (1759 to 1795) was Rector of Ribbesford and was presented to the position in 1765 by Lord Powis. He passed away, however, 20th May, 1795.

Rev. John Cawood was born 18th March, 1775 in Matlock, Derbyshire. His parents were poor and he had very little formal education in childhood but when he reached the age of 18 he was engaged in the service of Rev. Cursham in Sutton-in-Ashfield, Nottinghamshire. In 1797, after a period of three years study under Cursham, he entered St Edmund Hall at Oxford and graduated in 1801. He lived in High Street, Bewdley and became Curate of Ribbesford and Dowles churches and Incumbent of St. Annes Chapel of Ease in Bewdley. He died 7th November, 1852 in Bewdley and during his lifetime wrote 17 hymns.

Peter Prattenton, M.B., born in 1776, became the noted antiquary whose collections on Worcestershire and Bewdley in particular are now owned by The Society of Antiquaries in London. He died on 11th July, 1845, aged 69 years and was buried at Ribbesford.

George Jorden was a self-taught naturalist who knew every inch of the Wyre Forest and collected specimens of all plants for his *"Flora Bellus Locus"* which is now held in the Worcester Museum. He passed away at the age of 88 years in 1871.

Rev. J. G. Breay was born on 9th April, 1796 in Plymouth. He placed himself under the tuition of Rev. John Cawood of Bewdley (whom I have covered earlier in this text) and sadly passed away in his 44th year.

George Griffith served his first clerkship in a corn merchants' office in Bewdley. He sat for Bewdley in 1796 until his death.

Canon Hugh Stowell (1799–1865). In 1801 he gave £3,000 towards the building of Bewdley Bridge and in 1814 he was appointed Minister of St.Annes Church.
Edward Baugh of Wribbenhall (1801 to 1870) was a local fossil collector

and part of his collection was purchased by the National History Museum in March, 1860.

Edward Field, Bishop of Newfoundland was born at Worcester 7th June, 1801 and was educated for several years at Bewdley School, moving to Rugby in 1814. In Christmas 1827 he was ordained a Priest of the Church of England and became Second Anglican Bishop of Newfoundland in 1844-76. He passed away on June 8th, 1876,

John Medley, First Anglican Bishop of Fredericton and metropolitan of Canada was born in Chelsea 19th December, 1804. Sadly his Father died while he was very young and his Mother wanted him to become a Clergyman from the outset. She decided to send him to school early as she felt he needed to be in the company of other boys. He attended Bewdley School and was also educated at Wadham College, Oxford. The Bishop had many amusing stories to relate of his school life at Bewdley, Bristol and Chobham and was active in the English ecclesiological movement which stressed the improvement of church music and architecture, spending 47 years building up the church physically and spiritually. He stayed in office until his death in 1892 and it is noted Gladstone said of him "His was the wisest head that wore a mitre."

Dr. John Beddoe, F.R.S., was born in Bewdley on 21st September, 1826. He originally trained in law but qualified as M.D. in Edinburgh in 1851 and in 1889 he was elected President of the Anthropological Society of Great Britain. He was an accomplished and popular physician but his heart was given to the anthropological study of man and ethnology for which he gained a European reputation. He passed away 19th July, 1911.

Frances Ridley Havergal, born 14th December, 1836 was a famous religious poet and hymn writer. Her Father was Curate of Astley Church. I have written about this lady in greater detail under the chapter of Winterdyne where she spent a considerable amount of her time. She passed away at the age of 42 on 3rd June, 1879.

Rev. John Venn (short for Donald A. Venn) was born in Kingston-upon-Hull, Yorkshire on 4th August, 1843. This man became a Priest in 1859 and was involved with Dowles Church. He was also a famous logician and philosopher, introducing the Venn diagram in 1881 which is used in many fields such as probability, logic and computer science. He was instrumental in campaigning for prison reform and the abolition of slavery and cruel sports and passed away on 4th April, 1923 at the age of 88 years.

MY CHILDHOOD

I was born at Number 35 High Street, Bewdley on 9th December, 1919 and my parents were William James Birch and Elizabeth Helen Birch (nee Weston of Wribbenhall). I was one of four children: a sister Florence Elizabeth (whom we called Florrie) was the first born, in Spencer Avenue, Wribbenhall on 23rd April 1914; my brother Jeffrey John was born 19th December, 1922 at 35 High Street, followed by the youngest called Stanley who was born at Winterdyne on 19th May, 1925.

Next door lived my paternal grandparents, Allen grandfather, whom I was named after, was a coal merchant. Grandad used to buy a railway truckload of coal at a time filling the bags of coal at the station and then loaded them onto a dray before delivering them to the houses in Bewdley.

Granny Weston and I with Floss

I well remember the horse he used called Drummer which was jet–black in colour and was stabled in Lax Lane, at the rear of Stanley Baldwin's birthplace in Lower Park.

I recall Granny and Grandad Birch walking along High Street every Monday and Thursday evening at around 6 pm to visit the Garden Cinema which was

situated over the bridge. It was always referred to as the Picture House in those days and the site of this is now Bridge House offices. On the corner of the bridge was a sweet shop where most people called before visiting the pictures and the owners were Mr and Mrs Gale. The building itself was the old toll house although this has since been taken down by those I believed at the time were 'the vandals' of Bewdley Town Council! The Gale family later moved to the Mug House in Severnside North. Bill Gale, the son, was in the 2nd Bewdley Scouts and Florrie, the daughter, was a teacher in Class 2 of Lax Lane School.

My school photograph age 10

In the summer when the coal business was quiet Grandad used to buy the fruit on the trees from Beeches Farm which was situated in Light Lane and owned by Mr Price. He would pick the cherries and damsons and then take them to Gardners Meadow to Mr R Jackson the Headmaster at Lax Lane School who was also a wholesale dealer. He employed a man by the name of Mr Darkes (also lived in Lax Lane) whose job was to weigh the fruit into baskets which would later be delivered to the station to then be taken by train and sold at Birmingham market.

There was an open area at the back of the row of houses where I was born in High Street which was a communal yard to service all 7 houses from No.35 to 41. In the yard was a wash-house and there was a rota to allow each of the houses a specific time to do their washing. The water was collected from a pump in the middle of the yard which provided all the 7 homes with water for cooking and washing. There was also a block of toilets covering all our houses, including a double with one seat for a child and another for an adult to sit beside! Underneath the toilets was a brook which came from Park Pools, carrying on down Lax Lane to the river Severn, so in effect, everything put down the toilet made its way straight into the river.

I have often thought since about the pump on the yard supplying water as this was situated close to the brook, so the water could not have been very clean! At the back of the toilet was an ash-pit where all the homes placed the ashes from their fires. Obviously, this would have needed to be cleaned out from time to time but I do not remember when or who was responsible for this. All of the cooking was carried out on the open fire in the living room and the pantry was also used as a kitchen. Bathing was carried out in a tin bath in front of the fire in the living room.

Next to my Grandmother's house was No.37 High Street which was a grocers shop owned by Mr and Mrs Gardener. Mrs Gardener (the daughter of Mr Owen, the owner of the shop on the corner of Load Street and High Street) also owned all the houses in our block and ran the shop whilst her husband worked in a local carpet factory as a designer. They had a son named John who was the same age as me (born 22nd December, 1919) and we became good friends for a number of years.

My family moved from High Street when I was 5 years old as my Dad was provided with a home over the stables at Winterdyne House nearby, where he worked as a Coachman. John continued to visit and we played together in the fields and woods surrounding the house. There will be frequent references to my time spent with John during my early years in this book.

School Days at Lax Lane School

I started at Lax Lane School at the age of 5 and my first teacher at that time was the junior Miss Newell. There were two Newell sisters, the elder being the Head Teacher of the juniors who taught the six year olds.

At the age of 7 I moved to Class 1, taught by Miss Joiner who lived with her Mother in High Street. During my early working days while I was an apprentice at Coldricks she moved to the last council house built on Cleobury Road and I recall carrying out repairs to the property for the local council. She later moved to the first bungalow in Pewterers Alley. This was so called as pewter goods were made in the very old building on the right hand side of the walkway.

I then attended Class 2 with Miss Florence Gale who lived at the Toll House on Bewdley Bridge where her family used to run a sweet shop although as previously explained, this was sadly demolished in the 1960's. I remember everyone calling there on their way to the pictures at the Garden Cinema where Bridge House is now situated. It was a very small house and space must have been very limited for a family!

Class 3 was led by Mrs Knock who lived in High Street next to the old Grammar School. Her husband I remember was an engineer in one of the car factories in Birmingham and must have had an influential job as he was always very smartly dressed. They had a son named Jim and a daughter by the name of Molly and later in life I used to go riding with her and her friend named Nora Powis at Sandbourne Stables. Molly was well known for walking around carrying a live monkey on her shoulder and always dressed rather outlandishly!

Class 4 was taught by Mr Joe Bates. He was a very stern teacher and most of the children feared him as his discipline was very extreme! He ran the school football team but it has to be said he was considerably more patient on the football field and went to great lengths to explain the rules of football! Bob Jackson, the Headmaster, also took an interest in the school football team and as he was a Wolverhampton Wanderers supporter he made the school colours the same as his favourite team, black and gold.

During my time in the school team we played for the Charles Austin Cup at Aggborough. In the semi-final we used the Kidderminster Harriers practice pitch and the final was played on the actual Harriers Football Ground. The

practice ground was later used to build Kidderminster College but this has since been demolished to make way for a housing estate.

In the final we played against Stourport School and won 6–0! Members of the team I can recall were:– Alf Jackson, Bill Coss, Jim Coles, Jack Darkes, Vic Fryer, Ted Miles, a lad with the surname of Millward (whose parents owned a vegetable business on the corner of Dog Lane), myself and the goalkeeper was named Harry Fowler. We also played in the Bridgnorth Cup and were runners up in that competition because we lost in the final match. We also played Broseley but we lost that game also and I well remember as I was suffering dreadful toothache my mother made me wear a scarf wrapped around my mouth and I was none too pleased! My Uncle Cyril and Dad always came to watch us in these matches.

Joe Bates also ran the gardening class and the school had the use of two allotment plots (which were owned by Mrs Sturt of Winterdyne) situated along the riverside. We had to learn about digging, planting and weeding and grew all types of vegetables but I do not know what happened to them. I imagine the teachers used them!

There was a school room in Dog Lane which took the form of a wooden shed situated where the car park for Bewdley Medical Centre is now. This was used to teach woodwork for the boys (which was led by Mr Morgan) and we also sometimes did tin work when I recall making such items as cake tins and brush and comb boxes. We learnt to draw plans of the items we were to make and I well remember Mr Morgan being a very hard task master. On one occasion we were asked to use a chisel to apply a design to

the top of the brush and comb box and unfortunately I made the mistake of using the chisel the wrong way round. The result was I was never to make a mistake again having incurred the wrath of Mr Morgan for not carrying out his exact instructions.

The girls obviously did not have any involvement with Mr Morgan as this was men's work and were taught either Laundry or Cookery instead. My cousin, Gladys Birch, has told me of a very amusing account of her experience during one of these lessons. She was having Laundry class during which pupils were told to take certain items in to wash, for instance a shirt or blouse and the teacher would also take several items of her own and pass these onto each pupil to wash. Gladys was given a pair of very large winceyette bloomers to wash which she refused and was most indignant that people should wash their own knickers! The teacher insisted she should do as she was told or be reported to the Headmaster, Mr Jackson. She ardently refused and the following day was called to speak to him and when she explained what she had refused to do he agreed with her wholeheartedly and admitted he too would have objected to being asked to carry out such an unpleasant task!

Class 5 and 6 were taught together by Mr Charlie Alberts. He lodged in the property in High Street called the Bailiffs House and in my opinion he was the very best teacher – strict but fair in his approach. I remember he used to provide jam jars with blotting paper inside and we planted these with kidney beans. These were placed in the school windows which were set very high in the wall and strings were placed from the jar to the top of the window for the beans to climb up. Also on the allotment in the school plot was a rain gauge

Lax Lane School boys football team

and Mr Alberts used to send one of the boys to collect any rainfall each day whereby it was measured and the level recorded in the log book. It was in this room that I can remember there was a coal fire as the heating source. I can still visualise Mr Alberts standing in front of this to keep warm! From this class we used to go on to play football and Mr Alberts did not agree with this as he said we would never earn a living from it. I wonder what he would think about the amount footballers can earn today!

I was chosen for the school team and we used to practice at 3pm until 4pm on Tuesdays and Thursdays so we were late finishing. The class times were 9am until 12 noon for dinner and afternoon sessions were from 1.30pm until 3.40pm unless we stayed late for some reason. On Wednesdays we used to play what was called the *early closing team* which consisted of youths working in shops. Two of these players I recall were Frank Ashcroft and Les College.

Class 7 was the final year and this was taught by Bob Jackson. I do not have very clear memories of this time but I do recall also in this class was Mike Young, Harold Jones, Joan Breakwell, Maud Brettle, Mary Marcus, Edna Evans, Doris Breakwell and Gladys Timms who became my wife. Also Betty Reynolds, Gerald Clee, Ida Wigan, Sydney Wigan her brother, Cliff Lancet, Ruth Gitting, Alf Jackson, Fred Moule, Harry Purcell, Derek Parmenter, Marjorie Bond, Jim Tolley, Jack Darkes and Vera Darkes.

I recall each day when I came home from school for lunch at 12 noon I always called to see Granny Birch in High Street on my way to Winterdyne and she prepared me a piece of bread and cheese to eat. This tasted delicious as it was always a fresh cob loaf with a thick crust baked at Catchems End by Coopers the Bakers, situated where the Fish and Chip Shop currently stands.

Now I will share a few of my memories of my school friends whilst I attended Lax Lane. Firstly, Mike Young buying Gladys Timms a box of milk tray chocolates for her birthday on May 5th and she later told me she gave them away to her other girlfriends because she was not happy to be receiving gifts from him! I also well remember Gerald Clee as he was the person responsible for me joining the Ribbesford church choir and later you will read of my happy memories of choir practice at Mr Stevenson's home under the heading of Severnside South. Also, I recall Harold Jones, a fellow pupil living in Lax Lane who had a pet jackdaw which used to sit on the school roof waiting for him to finish school at 12 noon and 3.40pm and as Harold came out of school the bird would immediately take up its position on his shoulder!

WINTERDYNE ESTATE

House and Grounds

The stables and living quarters   *Winterdyne House today*

Winterdyne House was built in 1760 by Sir Edward Winnington and in my childhood the estate was owned by Mrs Napier George Sturt. Mrs Sturt was widowed before moving to Winterdyne, her late husband being a famous explorer in Australia in the time of Captain Cook. She lived there with her daughter Miss Katharine Sturt and also had a son by the name of Geoffrey living in Oxfordshire who often visited with his wife and three sons Anthony, Phillip and Evelyn. I lived here with my family in the stables until I joined the army in 1941 and my parents remained there until the 1950's when the estate was sold, as after Mrs Sturt passed away her daughter left for Oxfordshire to be with the rest of the family. My time spent at Winterdyne was extremely happy; my childhood was idyllic as my family were given total freedom in the grounds and the Sturts were kind and generous people.

We moved from High Street to nearby Winterdyne in September 1924 as my Dad was provided with a home over the stables there when he was appointed to the position of Coachman. John Gardiner (my childhood friend from High Street) continued to visit after and we played together in the fields and woods surrounding Winterdyne House. Unfortunately I do not remember actually leaving High Street, however, as I was just approaching 5 at the time and had only just started school. Dad's wages in those days were £2.1.0 but deductions were made from this for rent and coal. I have in my possession Mrs Sturt's wages book and it is interesting to note an entry for a Mr John Pudner (who was Dad's predecessor). On 5th January, 1918 his wages amounted to £1.5.0. per week and he left employment at Winterdyne on 29th April, 1918 after almost 16 years service. He moved to Lax Lane and opened a sweet shop where the children used to call on their way to school. I can remember buying sweets from there myself!

As I grew older my Mother would give me a shopping list to leave with Mrs Gardener (John's Mother) at her shop in High Street and this I would deliver twice a week on my way to Lax Lane School. Mrs Gardener would put up the groceries ready for me to carry home to Winterdyne in my school lunch hour and I believe Mother used to visit the shop every Saturday to settle the bill. There are several differences I remember to how we shop today. The sugar arrived in one hundred weight sacks which Mrs Gardener would weigh out into 1 or 2lb neatly folded blue paper bags. She also kept a side of bacon which was sliced by hand in whichever quantity was needed. The sweets were in jars on the counter and she would weigh these out mostly at a penny's worth at a time! There were several types of biscuits in tins. We mostly bought arrowroot and these are still available but tinned food was few and far between as we mostly ate fresh in those days.

John always had a weeks' holiday with his parents at Weston Super-Mare each year and we were always pleased to see each other when he returned home! He attended the Grammar School in Hartlebury and as such had more homework to do so we had less time together but John and I remained good friends. Eventually he found a girlfriend by the name of Margaret Timmis, daughter of Tom Timmis, the butcher at the very top of Load Street.

Mrs Sturt recognised my keen interest in farming and nature and offered to send me to Grammar School but Mother did not allow this as she considered it unfair as my parents could not afford to do the same for my siblings. Just before War broke out John joined the Territorial Army. When the War started he was posted to France but unfortunately he was reported missing at Dunkirk and was never seen again so I do not know exactly what happened to him. He has a grave stone at Ribbesford Church where his baby sister and parents were buried. I always pause and reflect as I pass through the churchyard on my Saturday morning walks.

Going back to my life at Winterdyne, walking to the top of Red Hill we arrive at Winterdyne Lodge on the left-hand side. This was occupied by Mr Joe Bond the Cowman when I was young and after he passed on it was lived in Mr Ciss Alberts the Gardener and his family. In my childhood this road was obviously much quieter with only horse-drawn vehicles but due to increased motor traffic in recent times the main approach to Winterdyne House has been changed. The main entrance used to be directly onto the road opposite the lane to Ribbesford Church. In those days this lane was known as Church Carriage Road and was used by the hearse, drawn by two black horses, owned by Mr Riley Coles who lived in Stourport Road.

Mr Coles also used to take out the fire vehicle to attend to local fires. People getting married at Ribbesford would also have to use this route to the Church. The only wedding I can remember as a youth was Dr Bob Miles' celebrations and when he left church we formed a guard of honour when I was in the Scouts.

This no longer exists as an access road to the Church and now presents as a field on the right-hand side of Red Hill but in my youth there was a large white gate with a very rough drive, owned by a Mr Scott and his family who also kept Ribbesford Farm. Along this track towards

Dr. Bob Miles' Wedding

the farm was a cherry orchard, together with a cottage lived in by Mr and Mrs Yarnold (a Cowman at Ribbesford Farm) and their daughter Kathy.

Returning to the field on the right-hand side of Red Hill, opposite Winterdyne Lodge, Bewdley football team used to play here and the players used to change underneath the large yew tree which is still present. There was also a brick building which was formerly a pig sty and a toilet for the Lodge (which in effect meant the residents of the Lodge had to walk across the road in order to use the toilet!). Next to this here was a large area of ground which was split into two parts and Redcliffe Bungalow has since been built on here by Mr Jack James who was a grocer based in Load Street. This land provided a garden for the Lodge and the other half was for the use of the groom at Winterdyne, which of course was my Dad! I used to help him dig this throughout my childhood in order to plant potatoes but the ground was not very good as the large holly hedge next to the path took a great deal of the goodness out of the soil. Also, at the bottom of our garden were several egg plum trees but these did not do very well either as there was a row of elm trees in the hedgerow drawing the nutrients from the land.

Reverting back to The Lodge at Winterdyne now, as you passed through the large white gate leading to the driveway of the main house there was a large Rhododendron bush to the left of the Lodge and a Beech tree. We were told by Joe Bond that during strong winds the roots of the Beech tree used to physically move the quarry tiles in the floor of The Lodge! Beside the Lodge was a field called The Little Lawn which was separated from the driveway leading to the main house by an iron-railed fence on either side. On the right-hand side of the driveway was what was then known as The Big Lawn which had a wicket gate opposite the Lodge where the staff used to go to work on the farm and gardens.

About two years after we moved to Winterdyne Mrs Sturt decided to buy a pony for her three grandchildren (her son Mr Geoffrey's children) called Anthony, Phillip and Evelyn. The pony she asked Dad to buy was chestnut with a black patch on one hind leg, approximately 14 hands high and he also bought a trap with it. The pony spent a great deal of time with me as Dad started to teach me to ride – I was just over 7 years old then and would get up early before going to school at Lax Lane. I used to groom Tommy and clean him out each morning and after school in the afternoon it was my job to exercise him. Soon after, another hunter was bought named Morley, and later a grey called Clymore, to enable Dad to teach all of Mrs Sturt's grandchildren to ride and go hunting when they visited Winterdyne. Clymore could get very temperamental and was therefore not an easy ride at times but was very good in the hunting field.

Tommy   *Philip riding Morley in front of Winterdyne*   *Dad on Clymore*

We used to play on the Little Lawn quite often and I would cross it to look out for John Gardiner coming up Red Hill to visit me! There is also a photograph of John stood with my mother at the top end of the new drive. I will explain the significance of the new drive later in this chapter. When I grew older, after I had started work we used to play cricket with some of my friends and Dad on The Little Lawn. I bought bats, pads and wickets from the shop in The Butts, Kidderminster, together with a book in which we kept scores. We played against Carpet Trades in Chester Road South and I recall two of the players in the opposing team were brothers attending Lax Lane School and their surname was Bishop. The Captain at that time I believe was Cliff Bishop.

Mother with John Gardiner

Standing at the top of the current driveway the road split into four different ways. The first was on the left leading down to the stables, the next was the old drive passing by what were our living quarters at the stables. Parallel with that was the new drive used by carriages leaving the main house and lastly the road used by vehicles going to the farm. Mrs Sturt decided to have the new drive constructed as there was insufficient room for two carriages to pass safely in both directions simultaneously. The area in front of the drive is where a number of my photographs have been taken. The old drive had thick shrubbery on both sides and at the beginning of this there used to be a Scotch Pine tree with massive fir cones but this has since been removed. One of these trees remains on the far side of The Little Lawn. There was also a number of shrubs and trees of various kinds bordering the main driveway, including the Acacia trees which are still on both sides of this drive today. Ladder rungs used to be constructed from Acacia wood as it was very strong, yet flexible.

Taking the old drive down to the stables was a wall on the right, about eight feet high, which surrounded our garden and followed completely around to the stable yard. In front of the wall my Dad stored all the timber cut down from the trees for drying out before being taken to the woodshed to be chopped into logs for burning in the house. Later I kept my ferret and fowl in the garden where we also grew our own vegetables and Mother used to dry her washing in this area. The garden wall and barn has now been demolished and the area has been filled in and grassed over. Passing by the rear of our living quarters above the stables, my bedroom window faced the driveway leading to the main house, there used to be a very large Cedar tree approximately eight feet from the window but this has since been removed.

Carrying on towards the main house was also a shrubbery and further Acacia trees which still remain. The shrubs have been removed exposing the wall which formed part of the coachhouse and there was also a chimney set into this wall which went down to a fireplace in the coach house below but I do not remember this ever being used in my time. This brings us to the front of the main house where there was a large area for carriages to turn and stand outside for guests leaving and arriving at the Main Entrance. When the weather was fine Mrs Sturt used to sit in a basket chair on the lawns in front of the house overlooking the Big Lawn and was always dressed in black.

In front of the lawns were two grass tennis courts and I remember Ciss Alberts (also known as Jack) mowing them. At the facade of Winterdyne, underneath the right-hand chimney stack can be seen the bell which was rung by the House Boy (for whom Dad was responsible), or in his absence, Dad would have to ring this to call all the staff to work at 8 am and again at 1pm. There is a Copper Beach tree on the edge of the big lawn and I recall finding a partridge's nest underneath this tree when I was about 12 years old. I was rather surprised at this as they are usually very difficult to spot. There were four or five eggs in it nestling in the long grass which had survived the lawns being cut! The big lawn had cattle grazing on it in my childhood and they often used to lie under the five trees in the middle of this for shade.

I also recall a number of Cedar trees on the lawns in front of the main house, one of which had blown down after a serious gale. This was written about by Frances Ridley Havergal, a relation of the Shaw family who lived at Winterdyne previous to Mrs Sturt. Miss Ridley Havergal was a famous English religious poet and composer of hymns born at Astley on December 14th, 1836, and was the daughter of Reverend W. H. Havergal. She frequently stayed at Winterdyne and there is a commemorative plaque erected by the current owners on one of the fallen cedar trees.

The poem reads;–

O cedar tree of Winterdyne,
The shading guardian of our peaceful home,
How much we loved thee!
Thy boughs in summer seemed to cool the air
For those who sat beneath. In stormy winds
We loved to see how bravely thou didst stand,
Nor thought that thou couldst fall.

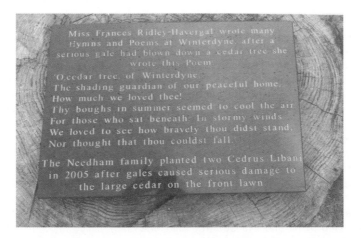

She wrote so many hymns, some actually at Winterdyne, notably "Tell It Out Among The Heathen" in April, 1872. One snowy morning when she was unable to attend church she asked for her prayer book in bed so she could follow the service. She read "Tell it out among the heathen that the Lord is King" and said to her brother "what a splendid first line and then the words and music came rushing in to me. There it is, all written out." With copperplate neatness she had quickly composed all the words, harmonies and music. Her first book was published in 1869 but sadly she did not enjoy very good health and latterly suffered from several bouts of typhoid. She tragically lost her sight and at the age of 42, on 3rd June, 1879 in Caswell Bay on the Gower Peninsular she died as a result of peritonitis.

Reverting to the main house now, the level of the lawn at the back of the house was a great deal higher in my childhood as on the ground floor (which was the servants quarters) the lawn height blocked three-quarters of the view from the windows so the servants could not see anything outside from any of the rooms on this level. There were five floors in total. The basement housed the Scullery/Boiler Room and on the ground floor were the Kitchen, the Staff Room, Miss Dyer's Sewing Room/Silver and Oil Lamp Store, Wine Cellar and Food store.

The first floor was the Main Entrance and Hallway with Mrs Sturt's Study forming the right-hand bay (Dad had to visit this room at 10 am daily to take his orders from Mrs Sturt personally). The Flower Room was in the left-hand bay and this was where all the vases for the house were kept and all the flower arrangements were created in this room. The Music Room and Library were combined and Miss Katharine Sturt entertained her guests in this area which often took the form of concerts and piano   recitals   and   I remember Dr Bob Miles and his three sisters used to attend and take part in these events, including Miss Tangye (a retired lady who lived in High Street). From this room there are double doors into the hall which were for privacy as servants could not listen to private conversations through two doors. The code to the servants was that if the inside door was closed the party was not to be disturbed! Also on this level was the Dining Room/Sitting Room where the family always took their meals, including guests when they were visiting.

On the second floor, firstly taking the front rooms, there were three bedrooms for the grandchildren Anthony, Phillip and Evelyn, On the opposite side of the house overlooking the rear garden (where it is possible to see right across the woods to the river) was Mrs Sturt's bedroom and next door to this was the sleeping quarters of Miss Hudson, Ladies Maid and Nurse as Mrs Sturt suffered ill health in later years. The following room was occupied by Mr and Mrs Geoffrey Sturt when they visited and next to this was the Bathroom. There was also a guest bedroom on this floor.

On the third floor was Miss Katharine Sturt's Drawing Room which had panoramic views overlooking Blackstone and the river. There was a connecting door to Miss Sturt's Bedroom with Miss Dyer in the room next to this as Ladies Maid (who was later replaced by Miss Hudson) and this was both their Bedroom and Workroom. Across the corridor were the servant's bedrooms overlooking the Big Lawn. The first one was for the Cook, Miss Potter and the second was for the Head Housemaid called Lizzie James with Miss Sturt's Maids in the next room by the names of Mollie Morris and Jean Smith. The Parlour Maid's Bedroom was the last room on this level and she was called Ida Baldwin in my childhood.

The outdoor staff during the time I lived at Winterdyne were: Mr. William Birch (my Dad) who was Groom, Bert Bond who started as House Boy, was later moved to the position of Gardener and Charles Jones took his place as House Boy (he later married my sister Florrie). The Cowman was Joe Bond, followed by Wilf Birch and Ciss Alberts was a Gardener as was Cyril Birch and William Brookes (known as Bill). The first Head Gardiner was Mr Bennett but he left to be replaced by Mr Sheward. There were also three members of temporary staff called Mr Gittins, Mr Jim Davies and Mr Parmenter. It took a staff of around 20 to keep Winterdyne running smoothly.

Returning to the stable block, there were two stables through a large doorway on the left-hand side. In the corner of this room, behind the door, was a chute from the bin situated in the room above where the oats were stored to feed the horses. The oats and bran were delivered in 2cwt sacks by 'Jim' from Clarke and Cranes of Stourport and the oats were hoisted up to the first floor via a pulley on the outside wall of the stables. On the end wall was a bin containing bran on the left—hand side and on the right we used to mix the chaff and bran together for the horses feed.

Linley was in the left—hand stable (previously Tommy was kept here until he was sold and replaced by Linley) and Rona the carriage horse was on the right (Rona replaced Rudge due to retirement). Timmy the cat lived in this stable during the night—time, when we would shut her in the stables to catch the rats which often came up the drain. She was very skilled at killing the rats and mice and during daytime was free to roam, often spending time with Mother in the living quarters.

I recall one day when we were clipping Linley he reared up and for many years there was an indentation mark in the wall where the tip of the horseshoe struck but this is no longer visible! He just clipped Dad's head in the process but fortunately the injury was not serious. One day while I was riding Tommy across the Big Lawn, he took off across the field, jumped over a bed of nettles and threw me off in the process. I landed in the nettle bed and was totally shocked and in pain but Dad made me get straight back on.

In the corner of each stable was a hay rack for the horses daytime feed. In the floor was a drain to take the urine away and straw was used for bedding. Sheathes of straw were then left upright around the edges of the stable to prevent the horses from lying against the cold walls. When we cleaned them out the soiled bedding was put onto a wheelbarrow and taken to the Little Lawn for compost. Once the manure was well rotted down it was taken across the Big Lawn where Dad ploughed it in to where the mangles were planted as feed for the cattle.

There was a ventilation shaft going from the stables out through the roof, passing through what was my Sister's bedroom above. This can be seen as a white tower structure on the top of the roof, resembling a dove cote. The door to the staircase provided access to our living quarters above the stables. We had a horse shoe as a door knocker and this is still in my possession today. Climbing the stairs, we reached a landing and the living quarters consisted of one bedroom for me, a large one for Florrie and the boys, a further large bedroom for Mother and Dad and a living room. In this room was a table where we took all our meals together and a fireplace with an oven and open fire for cooking purposes. We all took our baths in an oval shaped tin bath in front of the fire in this room.

I used to get up at six in the morning to light the fires for Mother to enable her to prepare breakfast. At the far end of the living room was the piano which Florrie used to play and I carried out my violin practice in this room. On the left hand side was a long shelf about 5 feet above the floor where Mother kept her ornaments and Florrie and myself also used to store our music sheets on this. On the opposite wall were two windows which used to look over the stable yard.

My parents decided they would convert the scullery into a dining kitchen and we had a stove installed in this room for cooking purposes. Alongside this was a brown sink where we washed ourselves and the dishes after meals. At the far end of this room was the pantry with a wooden partition dividing the room into two. The window from the dining room looked over the drive to the main house. The room where Florrie, Stan and Jeff slept was quite large and it was therefore easy to divide it into two separate areas. The bin for the oats was also located in this room and each room was lit with oil lamps. The main living room had a large lamp with glass dome and the other rooms had hurricane lamps which we could carry around with us where required.

The stable yard was also used for playing football and Dad, his brother Cyril, Jeff and I used to play together. We also played cricket in this area and used the coach house doors as the wickets. One day, while playing cricket I knocked the ball and it went straight through the living room window! I broke several of the windows in the garage doors playing football on various occasions and Mr Bert Hancox was brought in to repair them. I was expected to pay for some of these breakages but fortunately Mr Hancox never charged very much! Also in the yard was a slope up to the drive level in cobble stones and Dad took two rows of these cobbles out and replaced them with brickwork to make it a smoother ride for the carriages to travel over.

Next door to our entrance was the Saddle room which had a fireplace at the far end where we boiled the linseed until it formed a jelly which was then mixed with warm water and fed to the horses when they returned from hunting to keep them in good condition. In front of this fireplace I used to dress the chickens for the table. Between the doorway to our staircase and the Saddle room door was a window and a wooden bench was situated beneath it. When Harry Gillam, the local baker delivered the five or six loaves twice per week, he would place them on this bench and a member of my family would collect them and take the bread to Mother upstairs.

On the left wall of the Saddle room the harnesses and bridals were stored on hangers. On the right was a blanket horse and over the top of these were the saddles. We also had a dartboard in the Saddle room and for our amusement used to box in this room also. The recess in the top left-hand corner of this room formed the underneath of the stairs to the living quarters which had a cupboard on the left and a window opening into a passage which led to a doorway in the stable yard. This enabled any leaves and debris to be cleaned out and allowed a little more light into the room but this no longer exists.

There was a large chest underneath the saddles in which we used to keep all cleaning materials, medicines for the animals and drenches. A drench consisted of a cow's horn with a hole in the narrow end and a handle the opposite end. The hole was sealed with a stopper while it was filled with medicine and the horn was placed in the roof of the animal's mouth in order to administer the treatment. The horses tongue was pulled out to the side of the mouth in order to insert the drench and the horn was placed at the back of the tongue so the medicine went straight down the throat. A "twitch" was attached to the upper lip of the horse to control the head of the animal. This was a piece of rope looped around a stick and the loop was attached to the top lip of the animal and tightened to control the movement of the animal's head.

The door next to the Saddle room on the right-hand side of the entrance to the stable block contained another two stables and hay store built by Dad. One was for Clymore on the left which was separated by a wooden partition and Morley was stabled on the right. These were called "loose boxes." The hay was kept in front of the back wall and the chaff-cutter was kept in here to chop the hay into 1" lengths to feed to the horses. I do not recall very much about actually building the stables as I was at school during the daytime but I do know he used two trees felled by Dad from Winterdyne Woods, which had been trimmed down for the uprights, to provide a partition between the two stables.

On the right hand side of the stables was a passageway leading to our toilet and wash house. The toilet had a high level flush tank and there were doors on both sides – one to enter and the other led into an open space where the waste pipe came down from our kitchen to the main drain. This drain then ran across the stable yard where it picked up other drains on the way, including those from the main house which passed through the shrubbery down to the wood and into a pit in the Severn Meadows by the river. This pit had to be pumped out with a hand pump and I remember it had a large wheel which had to be manually turned to pump the waste out into the field. The area around the pump I well remember was a massive bed of stinging nettles!

During the time Dad was responsible for caring for the horses at Winterdyne he was promoted to the position of Chauffeur/Groom and it was decided he should take driving lessons at Austin Longbridge works. Mrs Sturt bought an Austin 16 so he could take Miss Katharine for drives. I was allowed to go with him on one occasion and I remember the instructor telling Dad to drive at 60 miles per hour which I shall never forget as it seemed out of this world to travel at such speed in those days! Whilst still on the subject of driving, Dad had to take Miss Katharine out on regular shopping trips and also deliver her to the station for her holidays in Oxfordshire. These trips were always a source of great stress as she would only allow him to drive at 16 miles an hour and this caused many differences. I well remember one occasion when he stopped the car and promptly told her to drive herself! Mrs Sturt had words with them both on this matter and they developed a mutual tolerance of one another afterwards but Miss Katharine still forced him to drive slowly!

Reverting back to the wash house where Mother did the family washing, there was a brick–built structure housing a metal boiler in the corner with a window looking over the garden to provide light. When Mother completed the task of washing the clothes she had to carry the basket a considerable distance across the stable yard into the garden where the lines were kept to dry the washing.   In my childhood there was a barn on the right– hand side of the stables which was turned into a coachouse to store the carriages after Mrs Sturt purchased the Austin 16. When we began storing the carriages in this barn, the old coachouse was then turned into a garage for the car.

On one occasion, Mr Geoffrey arrived from London and parked his car next to Dad's in the garage but during the night hours there was a fire which damaged both cars and destroyed the roof of the building in the process. The fire brigade was called to control the blaze and afterwards it was necessary to erect a completely new roof. A couple of years later, the Peat House situated next to the garage caught fire and also had to have a new roof constructed. I believe some of the ash from the fires stored in the first bunker could have blown across and started to smoulder, possibly for several days before being noticed and a fire resulted. I was only a small boy at the time but I remember this vividly.

Dad built a wall about 3 feet high in front of the main 8 foot high wall bordering the stable yard which was filled with soil and we grew kidney beans in this area. There was a set of double doors on the opposite side of this wall which were secured each night with a bar across, slotting into two iron brackets. At the end of this wall was a barrel which was used as Rover's dog kennel (our cross Wire–Haired Terrier). Beyond the barn was our garden behind the 8 foot brick wall.

To the right—hand side of the double doors was an entry leading down to the main house. In this area was a door on the right leading back into the stable yard and a little further along was another door on the left—hand side leading into the woods up a set of steps. Next to the doorway were the bunkers which continued down as far as the main house. There was a pair of gates beside the first bunker which were locked every night at 10 pm as all the staff had to be back for this time. Obviously, the boys had developed a way of overcoming this problem when they were distracted by the girls in the laundry. They would climb the roof, arriving at the entry, making their way to the laundry for illicit meetings and the reverse to make their way back home, either walking or riding a bicycle!

Reverting back to the function of the bunkers now, the first was used for storing ashes from the fires in the house, the remainder being used for storing peat blocks for burning, surplus coal stores, coke for the boiler in the scullery and storage for other household uses. At the back of the coachouse (which later became the garage for the car) was a door beside the gate where the bulk of the peat blocks were stored to be used as fuel for the main house. This was collected in a basket by the houseboy and carried to the various rooms in the house where it was needed for the fires.

Next to the peat house was the timber store and there were a series of window shaped openings at the front for daylight. Dad brought the timber he had cut down from Ribbesford Woods here. When the weather was wet the gardeners would come and spend their time cutting the wood into manageable logs. These were again collected in baskets by the houseboy and were taken to the house for burning on the fires. Next to this building was another small wood store where the houseboy would split some of the logs into sticks for kindling. Other duties he had to carry out were sharpening knives, cleaning shoes and any other jobs the cook required him to do. When he had completed the house duties he would report to the stables to assist Dad.

The coal stores were next door and Mrs Sturt used to buy the fuel in truck loads which had to be collected by Dad from the Goods Yard at Bewdley station by cart. He would take Rona to the station, load up with coal and deliver this to Winterdyne but as Red Hill was too steep for Rona to pull the weight up on her own we would use Grandad Birch's horse called Drummer to "tush" which was the expression used to assist another horse to pull the weight. Sometimes there would be three or four in a team if heavy weights were being pulled, as in the case of whole tree trunks being removed from the forest for instance. Jim Davies (who worked for Grandad) usually helped to deliver the load to the Lodge and then Dad would bring it along to the door in the entry by the stables. It would then have to be wheel—barrowed by the gardeners up to the coal house to be stored.

Adjoining the coalhouse, at the very end of these buildings, was the laundry and this included the toilets for the indoor staff. The gardener's tools were also kept in the laundry and I still have in my possession the oak garden seat which was stored in this area. When I visited Winterdyne with the current owner, he believed the laundry had once been a Blacksmith's Shop but I cannot remember there ever being a Blacksmith's hearth so it must have been before my time. After the washing was completed, it was taken to the drying green within the grounds to hang on wire lines. Dad also used these lines to hang the carpets at spring-cleaning time and beat them with cane carpet beaters to remove the dirt. The carpets were then pulled across the morning dew on the grass of the Little Lawn face down to freshen the pile before returning them to the house.

Here I am riding Morley at Trimpley House

Dad's job was to look after the two horses named Rudge and Tommy the carriage horse. As previously explained, Rudge was later replaced by Rona. Tommy was retired and turned out onto the Big Lawn to graze where he remained until he died around the age of 30 to 40 years. Rudge was originally chosen to draw the carriages – one was an open top called a Victoria which was used to take Mrs Sturt for a drive up Light Lane each day (weather permitting) as far as the Gospel Oak Tree. My Dad told me this was so called as it was where druids used to preach the gospel although sadly it has since been cut down as it became unsafe.

I used to ride with Mrs Sturt and Dad when I was on holiday from school and I always found Mrs Sturt to be a very nice lady. Her daughter, Katharine, used to take holidays in Oxfordshire as they had relatives and friends living in that area. Dad had to take her to Bewdley Station to catch the train in the other carriage called a Landau which was designed for a pair of horses and during the school holidays I was allowed to go with them. On the journey back from the station Dad used to let me take the reins to drive them home and I felt incredibly proud to be driving a carriage and pair!

The other work Dad had to do was to plough one small field in order to plant mangles each year and these were used to feed the cattle in the wintertime. In the spring he used to chain-harrow the fields which were used for hay making. Dad was also responsible for maintaining the hot water boiler for Winterdyne House which was located in The Scullery. It was stoked-up twice a day and I sometimes helped if he couldn't manage at night as it only needed filling with coke and then the boiler had to be closed down each night.

When I returned home from school in the afternoons I used to exercise the two hunters, afterwards grooming them thoroughly before our teatime. I had to make a good job as Dad often inspected my work to make sure they were clean as if the mud was not totally removed he told me they would suffer from mud rash. This was done during the wintertime and after the hay had been made the horses were turned out into the fields until September.

After tea I used to help Dad to bed the horses down for the night then stoke the water boiler in the House and we generally finished the days duties around 8 pm. Dad was given an extra 10/- per week for the extra work I was covering and he took me to the Midland Bank on Severnside South to see Mr Perrin the Bank Manager, who provided me with a savings box to collect my earnings which could only be opened by the bank! Most of the money I earned was put in the box by Mother, which held 10/- notes, half crowns (then called 2/- pieces) and sixpenny pieces. I do not remember there being a place for pennies. This is how I started saving and the practice has served me well throughout my life!

Here I am stood beside Linley

At this point I was beginning to develop an interest in other things. I used to visit Ribbesford Church regularly as I was in the choir there and also played football as I was a member of the school team. I became involved with cricket with other members of my family and we would play on the little lawn within Winterdyne grounds. Mike Young, Harry Purcell, Les Evans, my brother Jeff, Dad, Frank Ashcraft and myself all played sport together.

The next horse we purchased was Linley and as Dad was driving at this time I went in the car with Bill Coldrick, one of the builders of Bewdley who was a relation of the owners of Linley. We had to travel to the Bridgnorth area to a farm and after Dad agreed to buy the horse the farmer brought out the home—made wine. I was given a glass of this, which I proceeded to drink, but it made me feel ill all the way home. I will say, as a result of this experience I have been a tea—total ever since! With Linley safely installed at Winterdyne, this gave us a total of three hunters for the grandchildren to ride.

At this point it was decided that Tommy the pony would now be sold, which naturally made me very upset as I had become so attached to him and Rona was purchased for both hunting and pulling the carriage at Mrs Sturt's request. The reason she specifically wanted the roan colouring was due to the fact that whilst her late husband was in the desert in Australia, a roan horse survived some very harsh conditions and she would never forget the bravery shown by the animal at the time.

All of the hunters were now set up for the boys' use during the holidays. When they went hunting Dad and myself used to ride to their Meets which started at 11 am; sometimes they were held at The Cat at Enville and other times in Droitwich or Quatt near Bridgnorth and the boys were driven to the hunt in the car, either by their Mother or Father. I recall as we were riding along the Bridgnorth Road on our way to the Meet at Quatt, on the left hand—side were several fields which housed a large flock of totally black sheep and each time I pass this area now I always remember this!

After the hunt moved off we were brought back by car and upon completion of the days hunting the boys rode the horses back home. We would then have to groom them down which was very hard work as the mud on the legs and undersides had mostly dried on, often taking in excess of an hour to complete. The horses were then given a drink of linseed oil and water to condition the coat. We boiled the linseed for several hours in a large pot on the Saddle Room fire until it resembled jelly. It was then mixed with warm water which we collected from the main House.

A feed of bran and chaff was then given to them – the chaff in the hay was cut up on the chaff cutter into short lengths. This cutter consisted of a big wheel with two large blades attached which had to be kept very sharp and these were manually turned by one person and another was needed to feed the hay into an open box about six feet in length. The hay was pushed through a series of rollers before the blades cut it into small pieces. It was important the hay was forced through very tightly in order to cut it into short lengths as if it was allowed through loosely the cuts would be in lengths too long for the horses to eat. My sister, Florrie, sometimes helped me and other times John Gardiner if he was visiting but the task of actually feeding the machine was always mine!

When we took the horses to the Meets I mostly rode Linley but he was a very hard ride, continually pulling, so if we went to Enville or Droitwich my arms used to feel as if they would drop off by the time I arrived! He was more of a racing horse than a hunter, to the extent that as soon as someone mounted him he wanted to be away and was very difficult to hold back. When he was being clipped he was an absolute terror. In order to have his head clipped we had to fit a twitch to his top lip to control him and even then he would rear up! I rode Clymore on occasions and led Morley but that was not an easy task either as Clymore would often shy at different obstacles. Dad was therefore afraid that I might lose Morley and we would have a difficult task trying to catch her again!

Dad allowed me a day off school when the Meet was at Trimpley so that I could have a few hours hunting over the Devil Spadeful area on the Rifle Range. The hounds which hunted this area were the Albrighton and Woodland Pack and I remember a person by the name of Mr Butcher who lived at Beau Castle, Longbank, Bewdley was the Master of the Hounds. Bob Powell was the Head Huntsman at the time and a person by the name of Harry was the Whipper In. The kennels were on the Kidderminster/Stourbridge Road and are still there today but I do not know much about them now.

Of course, purchasing the hunters resulted in a great deal more work to do. I had to groom two more horses and clean them out before attending school each day which meant I needed to get up at 6 am. My sister Florrie had to catch the bus in Bewdley at 7 am each week-day morning to work in a factory and for several years I followed the routine of walking with Mother and Florrie down to Lower Park as Red Hill was very dark.

Mr Bourne was responsible for controlling the two gas street lamps on Red Hill. He would carry a pole with a hook attached which he would use to pull the chain in the gas lamp in order to put the lights on or off. There was a continual pilot light running and as soon as he pulled the chain down to allow the gas to flow, the pilot light would ignite the gas light. It is interesting to note the groove which was channelled out to house the gas pipe feeding the light is still in situ in the rock face at the side of the path at the top of Red Hill. This also fed the gas to Mr Humpherson's house situated on the top of the rocks at Red Hill but sadly this property has since been demolished.

When I used to ride around the lawn exercising the horses our dog named Rover would chase around with me cutting the corners to keep up with us. In the middle of the lawn Dad and I had a jump on which we used to practice and at weekends we used to go up Light Lane to Heightington to exercise the horses. On the left-hand side was a shed where Arthur Stokes from Lax

Lane kept some pigs. It was always a major job to persuade Clymore to pass as she did not like the smell of them! On the opposite side of the road lived Mr and Mrs Leek who were a very colourful couple and I will go into greater detail to explain this under the chapter on Light Lane. Once we had passed the pig shed we would continue around Heightington and back along under Ribbesford Woods, now known as the Switchback, passing a Lido on the left-hand side at that time.

The site of the Lido was later turned into a public house called the Woodman but this is now a private dwelling. I went swimming several times with my Uncle Cyril there but the water was very cold so it was not a very enjoyable experience. The fields on the opposite side to the Lido were called the Dirty Meadows which went down to the river Severn. It is now a football pitch belonging to Bewdley Town Football Club but the field in those days was full of horses and ponies owned by the Knackerman from Kidderminster. He used to buy up all the old horses and ponies and also collected the dead animals around the district. These animals were then supplied as food for the Albrighton and Woodland hounds and also the Worcestershire Pack.

Other times we went up Light Lane and over Stagborough which brought us out at Coney Green Farm, owned by a Mr Crump. We then made our way back along the Switchback towards home which took us approximately two hours to complete our ride before arriving back at Winterdyne to groom the horses. On other occasions, when we rode over the Devils Spadeful (then known as Spittleful) we would meet up with a groom from Stourport and have a race across the Spadeful, finishing in front of the Rifle Range targets. It was here where Dad took a fall and broke his collarbone resulting in him taking to his bed for several days.

The Spadeful was also used as a training area by the young Albrighton and Woodland Hounds. They used to meet at Spring Grove House as at this time Major Webb was Master of the Pack, having taken over from Mr Butcher of Beau Castle. They always met in September, the first part of the hunting season, at 6am, which was called the 'cubbing season' and the hounds moved down to the wood and thicket area at the side of the farm where there was also a railway embankment. One year when I was working at Spring Grove Stables at least twelve cubs were killed. The hounds had quite a number of young dogs in the pack and it was good training for them. In those days I enjoyed a good days hunting but now my feelings regarding the killing of foxes has changed somewhat.

Winterdyne Farm

In the summertime Dad arranged for the grass to be cut for haymaking. Mrs Sturt always insisted the cutting was started on 21st June so Dad made arrangements for Mr. Tommy Gardener, a local coal merchant, to start cutting that day each year. The only exception was if 21st fell on a Sunday which meant the process had to be delayed until the Monday as Sunday was deemed as the day of rest. Two days after the grass had been cut Dad would use a tedder, a horse-drawn machine to turn the grass and place in rows for the wind and sun to dry it out naturally. The staff would then turn it with pitchforks, also relying on numerous outside helpers to complete the task as quickly as possible. The people involved in this were Bert Bond, the Houseboy, Wilf Birch (second cousin to Dad) and he was the Cowman, Jack Alberts and Bill Brookes who were both Gardeners. In addition help was sought from Wilf's wife called Gladys and sometimes Mr Bennett the head gardener plus two extra people from High Street by the name of Messrs Gittins and Breakwell. The cook would make jugs of real lemonade for everyone in the fields to drink as it was very thirsty work.

After the hay was gathered Dad would go around with the horse-rake putting all the loose hay that had been left behind in the field onto the dray to take to the ricks (the name given to the storage area for the winter feed). The tools used in haymaking were a pitch-fork for loading the dray and also putting the hay onto the ricks; a smaller fork was used for turning the hay and a wooden rake, approximately 4 foot wide with of series of wooden pegs about 6 inches long, spaced 3 to 4 inches apart was used to gather up the loose hay which was dropped when loading the dray. The hay-making process would last around one month, depending upon the weather. We always had some good times during this season, especially helping to drink the lemonade which had been specially made for the working staff at Winterdyne! When the haymaking was over Dad would put the horses into the fields to graze for the summer months and this would also provide more room for the cattle to graze in the pastures previously used for growing the grass for hay.

When the time arrived for the hay to be taken from the fields to the ricks the horse and dray was loaded with the hay for the farmyard. It was Wilf Birch's job to build the ricks and Bert Bond would help him. The ricks were shaped like a cottage with a pitched roof. The centre was called a chimney, which was a wooden structure approximately 2 to 3 feet square and 4 to 6 feet long. As the rick was being built, the box forming the chimney was pulled up and the space remaining would be filled with loose hay to prevent the hay from overheating and setting fire.

During wintertime, partridge were also caught for our own use. I helped Dad catch them with a long net, usually on a dark, misty night, which was important because the low visibility would help as on bright, moonlit evenings, the birds would simply fly away. The partridge used to visit the Big Lawn at Winterdyne to roost. They would huddle together to keep warm, so we would take this opportunity to spread the long net in line with the birds and run with it where they were roosting, keeping the net tight so it went over the top of the birds. As they flew up into the net you could hear them strike it immediately. The trap was then dropped and we would make a dash to catch any of the birds trapped underneath, usually catching one or two partridge at a time.

I also had an interest in the cattle and would go down to the farm at milking time with John and Jeff to watch Wilf milk the cows and he would always give us some to drink straight from the cow. We always enjoyed this treat and I vividly remember the froth on the top of the milk created by Wilf milking directly into the cup! He also had two calves to feed as they were kept for about two months before going to market. Dad had to take them by horse and trap to Kidderminster Livestock Market when they were two or three months old. Sometimes I would go with him if I was on holiday from school.

Wilf would take the milk up to the Dairy at Winterdyne House, carrying it on a yoke. This was a piece of wood shaped to fit across the shoulders with two hooked chains on either side and a can suspended from each. The milk was put into large enamel pans; about 3 feet in diameter to enable it to settle and these were placed on a cold quarry tiled slab in the Dairy for about 12 hours. The cream was then skimmed off the top by the cook to make butter.

I remember the cook using a wooden churn with a handle into which she poured the cream which she repeatedly turned until the cream solidified. This mass would have been salted and then she would make it into half pound blocks and small single portion sized balls to be used in the main house. The remainder of the milk was used in the house and some was sold. My family had 2 pints of full-cream milk per day, which cost a halfpenny per pint and three local school children called Ruth Gittins, Derek Parmenter and Betsy Reynolds used to fetch some for their parents each day after school.

The groceries were delivered to Winterdyne by Mr Griffiths from their shop in High Street and the fish was brought every Tuesday by Simpsons the Fishmonger situated in Mill Street, Kidderminster. A wagon (driven by Mr Wigan from the Great Western Railway at Bewdley Station) used to deliver each week and I recall these delivering the tea in large tea chests. Once empty the boxes would be stripped down and the wood was used for many different carpentry jobs. The meat was delivered on horseback by one of the men working for Tommy Timmis, the butcher in Load Street. His horses were kept in the fields at Patchetts Hill Farm (Dowles area nowadays) and sometimes I used to ride them.

Wilf and his wife Gladys and family lived in the farmhouse overlooking the farmyard at Winterdyne. Uncle Wilf was responsible for looking after the poultry and all the food waste from Winterdyne House was brought here by the Houseboy for feeding them. There were about a dozen Gallinis (guinea fowl) which roosted in the trees at night and they were excellent watch dogs! If anything ventured in the area of the farmyard they would instantly chatter thus warning the remainder of the poultry to be on their guard. Nature is a wonderful thing.

Uncle Wilf would kill the birds after fattening and his wife dressed them in the open shed at the rear of their cottage ready for the table at Winterdyne House. The hens would lay reliably for two to three years and the method for ageing the birds would be colour coded rings applied to their legs from about four months old at which point they would be capable of laying. After three years they would be used for the table and were known as 'Boilers' but mainly the cockerels were used for Winterdyne House and sometimes the guinea fowl on request.

Adjoining Wilf's cottage was a fruit store for supplying Winterdyne during the winter months and there was a doorway in the back wall which led to an Ice House used for keeping foodstuffs cool, which was set into the rock beyond. There was a sandstone wall running along the back of what was Wilf's home and farm buildings. I recall climbing down these rocks to gain access to the fruit store to scrump apples when I was a young lad! As with the stables, there was a narrow passageway separating the rear of these buildings from the rock in order to prevent the rooms from becoming damp.

Next to the fruit store was a brick building forming the fowl shed. Approximately 100 hens and cockerels were housed in here and the eggs supplied Winterdyne House. We were allowed a dozen each week which I had to fetch from the farm. There were two sheds for the birds to go in at night and they were left to roam at will in the farmyard during the day. Wilf also had to feed the cockerels up for use in the main house and these were kept in the area in front of Mr Bennett's bungalow, the Head Gardiner. This bungalow was built in the early twenties by Hunts Builders from Bewdley before I moved to Winterdyne. Facing the front of the bungalow, to the left was an oak tree on the South Bank with a profusion of blackberry bushes. In this area I used to catch quite a number of rabbits with my ferret's help and occasionally gave one to Mr Bennett if I had caught several!

Wilf kept an incubator for hatching the eggs in his kitchen and explained to me how this worked. An oil lamp was kept inside the incubator to provide warmth and his wife would turn the eggs every day and damp them down by sprinkling water over them. This was important to prevent the shells from becoming too hard for the chick to break when hatching. This process was important as it mocks the hens' action of turning the eggs in the nest to keep the chick mobile in preparation for hatching and takes around 21 days.

When the chicks hatched they were fed with finely ground corn for a week or two and kept in the kitchen, later being moved to small runs with a broody hen in the farmyard once they were large enough to be fed on normal sized corn. The natural way of the hen hatching her own eggs in a nest box or a nest outside (the amount was usually 10 to 12 eggs) would involve her sitting on the eggs for 21 days. She would then bring the chicks into the farmyard and they would be put into small runs with the hen. She would then tend to her chicks in safety as often the cockerels would peck at them. With the knowledge I gained from Wilf I kept chickens of my own in my parents' garden for a number of years and still have them to this day!

Another of Wilf's jobs was to tend the bee hives all the year round which were placed on the land in front of the Summer House overlooking Blackstone. In May the swarms of drones and worker bees would appear surrounding the queen and these would be caught by Wilf and introduced into the hives. By the next day the bees would be working normally, collecting pollen and nectar to mix together to build the wax combs to house the eggs and also repair the damaged combs. There was a saying *"a swarm of bees in May is worth a load of hay; a swarm of bees in June is worth a silver spoon; a swarm of bees in July is not worth a fly!"*

By the end of the summer, around September time, the bees would have filled all the honeycombs with honey which could then be extracted by cutting off the tops of the sealed combs with a sharp knife and placing the frames into an extractor. This was spun at great speed to remove most of the honey and if there was any honey left in the frames these would be placed back in the hives where the bees would repair any damage to the combs. The bees at this point would be fed with sugar and water to replace the honey extracted for human consumption. Before the winter, they would turn this into honey to feed themselves throughout the cold months. Once the weather started to get warmer again, the entire cycle would restart.

On the subject of bees, I have kept them myself for a number of years in hives at The Glen. On one particular occasion I received a call from Neville Williams the local Police Officer who had discovered a swarm under one of the benches by the Bandstand in Bewdley. He knew I kept bees (Neville was a personal friend) and asked me to remove them. I knocked them into a cardboard box, placed a bag over the top and turned the box upside down and propped the box slightly open to allow the worker bees to return to the swarm.

I had to wait for the bees to settle before I could take them home and during this time I was approached by a woman who tried to sit on the bench. I obviously alerted her to the problem to which she gave the amusing reply "that's s funny place to keep bees!". She gave me the length of her tongue but I just quietly set about the business of moving them safely. Eric Bishop came and collected me, together with the contained bees in his open-top sports car and I returned home and settled them into a hive. I kept them for many years but one winter lost them all to a nationwide disease, although during the summer for many years a swarm came back to one of the hives, they entirely died off and I have not kept them for five years or more.

At the side of Wilf's house was a flight of steps leading up to a steep bank (please see picture). These led to the kitchen gardens which were situated on both sides of the steps. There were Bramley apple trees on the left-hand side of the steps and at the rear of the trees was a strawberry bed. On the right-hand side was Wilf's shed and the vegetable patch behind. At the rear of the shed where the poultry were killed was another flight of steps and path leading to a doorway which eventually led into Winterdyne grounds.

At the top of the steps, to the right, was the greenhouse and to the left was a door leading to a pathway to the main house and across the fields. There was another door beyond the greenhouse which provided an additional route to the main house and rose gardens. There is a cart track which led from the farm through the Big Lawn up to the main driveway at Winterdyne House. At the side of the door by the greenhouse was a large Quince tree which was used by the cook in the main house for making Quince Jelly. There were many medicinal benefits to eating Quince. In Medieval times, Europeans believed this fruit aided the digestion and prepared them frequently as an accompaniment with meats. The English called this combination *chardeqynce* which is believed to have meant 'flesh of

Quince'. Reverting back to the greenhouse, the first section was for growing plants and flowers and the remainder housed grape vines, both for use at Winterdyne. Behind the greenhouse was a brick–built potting shed where the gardeners worked and there was a door out of this which led to a path to the main house and grounds. In front of the potting shed was a series of three cold frames in which cucumbers were grown and small seedlings were started off in these to prepare them for planting in the vegetable gardens.

Previous to construction of the Bewdley By–pass, an area known as the South Bank region stretched from the hedge in front of Mr Bennett's bungalow right up to Dark Lane. There was a gateway in front of the area where the cockerels were kept which led to the South Bank. This area was sectioned off with an iron railing fence and housed the main vegetable gardens. I saw my first calf being born here when I was alone, around the age of 12, and vividly remember it was completely white but unfortunately when the cow calved she delivered it against the iron railings. As she was lying down the calf was badly damaged at birth and had to be put down. Continuing along the cart track on the South Bank approximately 200 yards along was a bull pen. This consisted of a brick–built area with two sheds and an open space in front which was another foal yard. In my day the hay and straw was kept in this area for cattle feed and this building still exists today, albeit in ruins.

Carrying on past the bull pen was a gate which led into Dark Lane. The South Bank was split into two halves with a valley between and was approximately 30 yards from The Big Lawn. On the left of the bull pen were two oak trees and a couple of blackberry bushes where I used to gather several pounds of fruit from which my Mother would make jam. It was in this area, when I was about 12 years old I recall seeing two Ordnance Surveyors. As with any inquisitive young child I approached them and asked what they were doing! They told me they were merely surveying the area but on reflection this must have been early information gathering for Bewdley By–pass as this is exactly where it was positioned many years later. Had Mrs Sturt been aware of their presence they would certainly have been ordered off her land in no uncertain terms as she was immensely protective of her property!

I often walked Winterdyne Estate with Dad who acted as Bailiff and if I was alone often assumed Dad's role. There was many an occasion when visitors found their way into the grounds, usually courting couples frequenting isolated areas under the hedgerows, but if alone I took little notice of them as at 12 years of age I had no idea of their intentions! In the next field was Blackstone which was situated by the river, opposite Blackstone Rocks and this was rented by Mr Scott from Ribbesford Farm.

Each day he used to bring his cattle across the road in Dark Lane through a gate beside South Bank gate for milking. They would graze here until milking time at 4 pm and he would turn them out at night in the field belonging to the farm, alternating between the two for fresh grazing. Blackstone had a sandy beach, very much like the seaside and often people would cross over the ford to reach the fields opposite which belonged to the Richie brothers of Blackstone Farm. There was quite a number of very small fish at Blackstone, including salmon. One day, I found a salmon which the otters had killed in the field as I walked through. Sadly it was not in a fit condition to eat as this had been left for some time, I assume because it had been disturbed and dropped its catch. Miss Katharine Sturt used to take Stan, Jeff and myself down to the Blackstone beach to have a tea party when we were young and this would have been prepared by the cook and placed in a basket to carry it safely to our picnic area.

Winterdyne Grounds and Woodlands

I would now like to talk about the wonderful grounds I was fortunate to have access to around the estate as it was my home. These, of course, were on private ground owned by Mrs Sturt and as such were not accessible to the public and it remains strictly private ground today. They formed such a huge part of my life at Winterdyne I felt compelled to share these experiences with the reader. During the process of writing this book the current owner afforded Andrea Clarke and I the opportunity of rediscovering all my childhood haunts around Winterdyne grounds which took several days as it is now very overgrown. This brought back many, many fond memories and I have used the route we discovered in writing about the numerous areas of interest.

Leaving the stable yard now, which was where our living quarters were situated, there used to be a doorway leading to a flight of steps. This in turn led to a pathway running around the rear of Winterdyne House to the right and to the left was the route to the shrubbery leading to the Rose Garden where Mrs Sturt often took a walk in good weather. There was another shrubbery directly in front of the stable yard with a Mountain Ash tree where the blackbirds used to feed off the berries in the autumn and also a number of Golden Chain and Laurel bushes. On the right of the path was part of Winterdyne woodland which contained many different types of tree, for instance Beech, Larch and Sycamore. In front of the stable yard was a path leading down a further flight of steps which led to a second route around the grounds. On the side of the pathway was another Beech tree which my brother Jeff used to frequently climb. I recall one day he was seen by Miss Katharine while up the tree and from this point she gave him the title

"Monkey Mischief" and referred to him by this nickname thereafter!

Continuing along this route there is a large Scotch Fir tree and we often played around this when I was a child. Just past this on the right-hand side is a Lime tree and to the left was a single Beech which still remains today. In this area was a large number of Beech trees and in the wintertime the Wood-Pigeons used to come in large numbers to feed on the beech nuts. There was one particular Beech tree which had a small hole 3 to 4 inches in diameter and every year the Starlings would return to nest in there and some would also build their home in the roof above our living room window. The mess and noise caused by the young ones demanding food was tremendous! There was also a large Oak opposite the tree in which the Starlings nested (today this has a chain across the 'V' to prevent the main trunk from splitting and John, Jeff and myself often played around this area as Mother could keep an eye on us from the living room window!

Progressing now to the Drying Green where the laundry was brought from the House in wicker baskets to hang out to dry until this task was later delegated to Miss Phillips in High Street. (I have drawn reference to this later in this book where I have explained in detail the residents in High Street). Some of the trees are now missing to what I remember in my youth but a number of the Chestnut trees are still there, where Gladys and myself used to sit overlooking the river. This area of The Severn used to be called Deep Splunts and was where Bewdley people used to go swimming. The school has now been built close to this point and the area is currently used for canoeing activities.

We continue along this path until reaching Rosehill and this is where the second path continues around the woodland. Carrying on along this path, on the left-hand side there are various types of trees and one large area of Rhododendron bushes with magnificent blooms. We have walked this route recently and a picture of me in front of a particularly beautiful specimen is included in this book, together with a close-up of one of the blooms. There was a rabbit warren underneath this Rhododendron bush and I regularly used to catch rabbits at this point. I would panch these (remove the internal parts) before taking them to Mother. After panching them I would push a hole with a knife in one rear leg, forcing the other through the hole, forming a loop and cross their rear legs in which was pushed a stick to carry a number of them back home.

Past the Rhododendron bush, 50 to 100 yards towards the cliff face, we would turn right which would take us approximately 200 yards to The Look Out Cave and in front of this was an area railed off where you could look over the River Severn. The cave itself had a quarry floor and I believe this must have been for the soldiers on duty (possibly in Cromwell's time) to keep watch over the river to enable them to have somewhere to stand in the dry. Continuing on along the path for approximately 50 yards, this brings us to another cutting into the rock which was known as The Hermits Cave. There was an area made in the rock to form a bed for the Hermit to rest and the entire ceiling and walls were plastered with pieces of glass and shells set in to provide reflective light.

On the left—hand side was a serving hatch with an iron frame which formed a hatchway to serve the Hermit his food. I always imagine the entrance would have been blocked off with lumps of stone as there are no signs of previous fixings. I was told by my Dad the reason for the Hermit being there was that the gentleman who owned Winterdyne at the time had an accident in High Street while riding in his coach. Apparently, the coach knocked someone down and the person was sadly killed. A court case ensued where the gentleman was sentenced to 7 years imprisonment so to prevent him from going to prison he paid a person to serve his time for him in the Hermit's Cave.

We carry on along the path which takes various turns and eventually meets with the route coming down from the Stables. We pass the drain which comes down from the main house and stables and turn along the cliff face (a sheer drop) down to the fields below. About two or three hundred yards along we turn right and on the left—hand side is another footpath which goes down to the fields below and has a doorway with a large beech tree at the side. This door was always locked for some reason unknown to me. We continue along the footpath passing a large Rhododendron bush with another footpath coming down from the main house. This was always unused and there was usually briars and grass to break through so I always carried Gladys on my back to return her home and prevent her from laddering her stockings! After crossing this stretch of pathway, on the right-hand side was a 30-40 feet sheer rock face and set into this was a lead plaque where a dog had once been buried in the ground below. This read:

> "Through the oaks and beeches, looking down,
> On the winding valley and the quaint old town;
> Where ivy green at the red rock grows,
> And silvery Severn swiftly flows,
> With an extra sparkle, and glitter and shine,
> Under the woods at Winterdyne.
> Here lies an honest dog, "Bravo" by name,
> Who for nine years retrieved his master's game,
> Through cover dense or stubble bare,
> With nose unerring he tracked the wounded hare."

This plaque had been damaged in my youth as I recall seeing knife marks where part had been lifted to show the rock behind, but today the plaque has been totally removed by vandals sadly, possibly believing the dog was buried behind when it was in fact laid to rest in the ground below. I was very sad to find there is unfortunately nothing left to commemorate this spot now.

Walking along approximately 20 yards we turned right and on the left-hand side was a steep slope with trees and Laurel bushes. To the right was a rock face with trees and shrubs and we continued along this path for 200-300 yards until we arrived at yet another cave cut approximately 3 feet deep into the rock with a wooden slatted seat inside. This is where Gladys and I shared some very happy moments together.

Gladys at 20

After leaving the cave and walking 100 yards we entered what was known as The Battery. In my youth the footpath used to pass right through The Battery and on the right-hand side were the ammunition departments, with the outlook on the left providing views over the river – one directly facing the river, one facing upward and the other down river. These were so positioned for the guns to be fired over The Severn in the event of intruders but I have never witnessed an actual gun in this area in my lifetime as they were moved to Sudbury to be used for the great battle.

Continuing another 50 yards along the pathway to the point where it divides. One leading to Winterdyne House and the other to what was known as the

Summerhouse. Approximately 100 yards before arriving at the Summerhouse there is a path which goes down to the fields by the river. Andrea and I rediscovered this path during our research for the book and this section had changed beyond belief. In my childhood it was possible to look up and see The Battery (which dates back to the Cromwell era) but sadly this is in ruins now. It was in this area that a number of jackdaws used to build their nests in the ruins of The Battery or on the rocks themselves.

A little further down the bank was a rabbit warren where I recall a fox had once made its lair having had several cubs and I had previously witnessed them playing while walking along the path above where it divides between Winterdyne and The Summerhouse. I believe I would have been about 13 years old at the time. The fox had been killing the chickens at the farm so I waited for the vixen to return to her cubs above the warren at 4 am. I heard the baying and she came across and stood in the middle of the field when I shot her with a 12 bore gun.

Several days later the cubs were wandering about and I was told Bert Bond had seen one of them in Light Lane. In those days the fox was regarded as a dreadful nuisance but nowadays I have respect for them to the extent that I have nightly visits from a fox living in the area of the Severn Valley Railway lines and make a point of leaving scraps of food for it each evening. I often hear the dog and vixen barking on The Maypole beside my home around the months of December and January, particularly when they are mating in February time. The dog barks once and the vixen twice when calling and answering one another. The cubs are usually born around April or May time.

Reverting back to the top of the main path now, this led to The Summerhouse where Mrs Sturt's grandchildren used to play as children when they came to Winterdyne on holiday. In front of The Summerhouse was where my Uncle Wilf kept his bees after the children had grown-up and I have explained about the beekeeping activities earlier in this book. Carrying on the pathway at the back of The Summerhouse, the one route leads down to the farm and the other, straight ahead to Winterdyne House. On this path leading back to Winterdyne was a gate on the right which led back into the Rose Gardens and on both sides of these was an orchard with apple trees on the left (one of the trees had very nice applies so I used to go scrumping to sample them!) and on the right was a selection of fruit trees, including damsons, more apples and one pear tree. Further along was another gate which led you to Winterdyne House and this is the path which Mrs Sturt used to walk down to visit the Rose Gardens. One day I saw her and walked around the garden with her and she talked to me about all the various types of roses.

Referring back to the path which leads to the farm, this passes beside the bungalow built by Hunts on the left, then progressing through the gate with the vegetable gardens on the left and around 200 yards on we arrive at the area previously explained   as 'the bull pen' and this leads through the gate to Dark Lane. The new by-pass and bridge we have today was in-fact built upon the vegetable gardens and part of the South Bank.

View from Winterdyne looking towards High Street
with St. Annes in the distance

I would now like to revert back to the Bewdley path which continues along Rosehill to the point where there is a magnificent view over what used to be the allotments, now the Bewdley Cricket Ground. To the left is a bird's eye view of High Street with Saint Anne's Church tower ahead and Lower Park leading to Red Hill. Also visible from this viewpoint is Gardener's Meadow which in my youth was Bewdley Comrades Football Pitch and Tommy Gardner's Timber Yard. From this point Dad and I used to stand and watch the football matches. On the left hand-side is shrubbery, consisting of Laurel bushes, Sycamore trees and a Crab Apple with very large fruit which I remember tasted repulsive!   Walking up towards Winterdyne Lodge there is a gate which still exists, coming off Rosehill, and opposite there used to be an iron ladder stile to enable people to pass across The Little Lawn in my childhood.

Continuing along with The Little Lawn on the left is an area of dense shrubbery (which has always been so) and blackbirds and thrushes used to nest in this area. There is a Scotch Fir tree which still exists to this day that bears extremely large fir cones. The grey squirrels feast on the seeds of these cones now but in my day Winterdyne hosted a large number of red squirrels around the grounds and there were no grey ones in those days.

One day I found a Hedge Sparrow's nest in the nearby holly and hawthorn hedge around Rosehill which contained several eggs and on the first day there was one Cuckoo egg and four Sparrow's eggs. On the second day I noticed another Cuckoo's egg had been laid and I advised Miss Katharine Sturt about this as it was unusual and she was very interested. A few days later when I visited, one of the Cuckoo eggs was missing and several days after; all the eggs had been destroyed. I do not know whether this had been Magpies or Jackdaws eating them but we were both very upset.

It is interesting to note what happens to a nest selected by the cuckoo. They always choose a small bird's nest in which to lay their eggs and they lay their own egg and remove one of the existing eggs so the original bird believes it is still rearing its own clutch. Cuckoos never rear their own young and when they lay additional eggs it will always be in a different nest. Hedge Sparrows and other small birds usually lay five eggs and when the young chicks begin to hatch, as the Cuckoo chick is born with a hollow at the back of the neck it will wriggle around the nest until one of the other chicks or eggs fall into the hollow and the cuckoo chick then pushes it out over the top of the nest until there is only the Cuckoo left.

The adopted parents have the thankless task of feeding the Cuckoo which grows large in relation to their own species and as such takes a great deal of feeding. This would go on for four or five weeks before the Cuckoo is ready to leave the nest. Even then, the adopted parents will still feed it for a few weeks after the Cuckoo takes flight. The mature cuckoos leave this country in July and make for Africa (where they remain until returning here in April) and the young ones leave at the end of August. They also always return to the area in which they were born.

The Sturt family were very good to us and I remember Miss Catharine, in particular, spent a great deal of time entertaining us. She was always very interested in my activities, particularly regarding birds and bought me two books on this very subject in 1931. The first was regarding Woodland and Wayside and the second was Seabirds, both entitled The Birds of The British Isles and Their Eggs by T.A. Coward and I still treasure these to this day.

Walking further along past the Scotch Fir Tree there is a section of Beech and Oak trees and I recall us all playing in this area, climbing the trees as young boys do! There was one particular Beech tree which had a very thick and long, level branch protruding and we always made a beeline for this! On the opposite side, the path forms the end of the field at Rosehill.

There used to be an iron railing which formed the boundary of Red Hill and another fence which continued up to Winterdyne grounds. These joined a wooded area of Oaks, Firs and Sycamore and beyond this along the edge of Red Hill rock were a number of Oak trees, some of which are still visible today. On the opposite side of the footpath are more shrubs right up to the boundary of The Little Lawn. This footpath continues along to a wicket gate beside The Lodge and within this boundary was a tank which supplied the water from Park Farm for the cattle to drink.

Dad (far right) during a visit to Stroud
after Miss Katharine left Winterdyne

The End of My Time at Winterdyne

Mrs Sturt died during the latter part of the war and it was thought losing her grandson Phillip (of whom she was very fond) whilst in action in Italy as a Regular Army Officer, brought about her demise. She had hoped he would return to Winterdyne to live and take over ownership of the Estate and also develop Racing Stables which would have been built on the Little Lawn. Dad was to groom and train the racehorses and I would have eventually helped Dad when I was old enough. Sadly, due to the untimely death of Philip, however, these plans never came to fruition otherwise I doubt I would have ever left Winterdyne and my life would have been completely different.

In Mrs Sturt's time at Winterdyne the Estate comprised of the house and grounds (including the farm), the riverside fields, Bewdley Allotments, Rosehill, the house on the bend at the bottom of Red Hill (now named Lower Lodge) and the house   at the top of Red Hill on the right-hand side occupied by Mr Humpherson (later demolished). Also, the bungalow since built by Jack James called Redcliffe was also part of the Estate as was Bewdley Park, Blackstone Field and Severn Meadows. It covered a very large area of land but this was later divided into various sections and sold. I often think about Winterdyne with great affection and wonder which path my life would have followed if Philip had survived and the Racing Stables had gone ahead, as to have been involved with this project would certainly have realised my dream to train racehorses. However, this was not to be! Miss Katharine, upon the death of her mother, left Winterdyne to live in Stroud and Dad stayed on a short while, making several journeys to her new home to help her settle in. Afterwards, Geoffrey, son of Mrs Sturt, bought a house in Hurcott Road for Mother and Dad to rent and Dad took up a position in Mortons Carpet Works in New Road, later moving to Brintons. My parents eventually purchased the property in Hurcott Road from Geoffrey before purchasing a piece of land in Spencer Avenue where I built my parents a bungalow.

Winterdyne estate was then sold and bought by Quakers who turned it into a nursing home. It was then later sold to Mr and Mrs David Needham in around 2002 and they have worked tirelessly to restore it to its former glory. I would like to take this opportunity to acknowledge with thanks the kind help given by David and his wife in allowing Andrea and I access to their wonderful home and grounds. This proved to be a very useful exercise as it brought back so many special memories which I feel privileged to be able to share with you in this book.

RIBBESFORD WOODS

During the time I was at school (the exact date I cannot recall) the oak trees were cut down in Ribbesford Woods, which follow the course of the Switchback Road. After the trees were felled they were pulled out of the woods to the side of the road by a team of horses supplied by Mr Tommy Gardner who also provided the timber wagons and horses to take them down to the fields by the river Severn, just off Lax Lane. The trees were left to dry out for about a year before being cut up for further use. Mr Gardner, who was also a Coal Merchant, lived at No.28 Severnside South with stables at the rear where he kept his horses.

After the trees were cut down they were trimmed with an axe and the trunks were cut up into manageable sizes ready to be put on the wagons. A large quantity of the brash (the thinner branches of the trees) was gathered up mainly by women from around Bewdley – particularly from High Street and Lax Lane. I knew some of them, especially Mrs Hayden and Mrs Perks who both lived in Lax Lane and there was also an old man from High Street involved in this work by the name of Bill Ashcraft (who I recall walked with a severe limp) plus many others. They gathered all the brash into bundles and carried them on their heads back home for lighting their fires and heating the houses as most people could not afford to buy coal.

In my childhood the lighting in people's homes was mostly by oil lamps. Others had gas lighting as there was obviously no electricity at the time. In fact my first experience of electricity was at my Granny Weston's in Kidderminster who was one of the first people to have it installed. I recall the excitement of being allowed to switch this on in her living room as we only had oil lamps for lighting at this time. It was quite a special moment!

After all the trees had been cut down the butts were pulled out and sold for fire wood. Mrs Sturt was one person who bought these and I remember Dad used to travel down with the horse and dray with Bert Bond to take them to Winterdyne to burn in the house where the heating method consisted of wooden logs and peat. Any timber required for wood burning in the house resulted in Dad cutting down a tree, chopping it up and these were put into the log shed as previously mentioned, for the gardeners to cut into smaller logs when the weather prevented them from doing their work outside.

Once all the trees were removed from Ribbesford several young oak trees were planted to replace them and these are still here today. One part of the wood which I believe was owned by Mr Crump of Coney Green Farm was planted with Spruce and Larch trees but a large number of these were cut down around the year 2000 and some are still being felled currently. The area of Ribbesford Woods entered from Light Lane is now used by motorcyclists and mountain bikers in the forestry area.

LIGHT LANE LEADING UP TO HEIGHTINGTON

Turning into Light Lane from Red Hill, on the right-hand side there was a garden and house owned by Mrs Sturt of Winterdyne which was lived in by Mr Humpherson a surveyor for Bewdley town. This property was occupied in later years by Wilfred Birch from Winterdyne Farm but has since been demolished.

On the opposite side of the road was a further two gardens also belonging to Winterdyne. One was for the coachman i.e. my Father and the other was for the gardener living in the lodge. Further along the lane it crosses the pathway from Bewdley to Ribbesford Church and about one hundred yards on the right-hand side there was a small holding consisting of two fields and a damson orchard belonging to Charlie Ife, formerly from High Street.

When he made his hay in the summer my friend John Gardener used to go and help Mr Ife when he came home from school. Mr Ife was rather a colourful character and I recall him raising his caravan off the floor so he could turn the wheels round once a year to enable him to live in the van without paying rates! Next to the caravan was a tin barn where he kept his hay for the cattle and this remains today. As my Father and I rode along Light Lane on horseback, I remember he kept his sheepdog in this barn and the dog would push his head through the shuttered door, barking madly at anyone who dared to pass! For drinking water for his own personal use he unofficially tapped into the water main that came from a well at Park Farm which supplied Winterdyne and Kateshill and this well can still be seen today. The water supply pipe, however, which was of lead construction, was removed when Bewdley By–Pass road was built.

About one hundred yards past Charlie Ife's on the left was a tin shed which contained pigs owned by Arthur and Albert Stokes from Lax Lane. Just a short distance further up Light Lane lived Mr and Mrs Leek. She was a farmer's daughter and he was a bricklayer. Mr Leek owned a white Morgan car which he drove at terrific speed in those days and when he turned from Red Hill to Light Lane he used to go several feet up the bank to execute the turn! One day he had an accident and lost his leg in the process. I am not sure where this occurred but it had no effect on his driving. The last time I saw him was in Kidderminster Hospital while I was visiting a friend. I had a few words with him but he was very poorly and died shortly afterwards.

There is a lane leading to Park Farm off Light Lane which was owned by the Wilkes family. There are two drives side by side and the left–hand driveway leads to Haye Farm owned by a Mr Bray when I was a lad. I can remember seeing him quite a few times and he would chat to Dad when we were riding along the lane. He left the farm while I was still at Lax Lane School and set up a small–holding on the Cleobury Road where the remainder of his family still live to this day although Mr Bray passed away some time ago.

After Mr Bray left the farm it was taken over by Mr Goodman and his family, whose daughter used to keep horses and Charles Jones, who helped Dad at times at Winterdyne was given the job of caring for them. In the grounds of the farm was a cork tree and to my knowledge it is the only one in this country but I have no idea if it is still there. The family had a new house built on part of the farmland which immediately bordered Light Lane and this still remains today. The Goodmans had a wooden building constructed for the Guides to meet as their daughter was District Commissioner of Guides. This is now used as living quarters and its outward appearance has not changed from the original. The family have since moved to Abberley where they run a famous goose farm.

On the opposite side is the Beeches Farm which was owned by a Mr Price when I was young. Mr Price kept mostly store cattle for fattening and I recall him telling Dad he was able to cure the dreaded foot and mouth disease which was and still is regarded as an incurable problem in farming but I do not have any further knowledge on this. Also on the farm was both a cherry and damson orchard and as I mentioned earlier, my grandfather used to buy and pick the fruit to sell on.

One day I remember going up to the Beeches Farm and walking along Light Lane. When we arrived as far as the seat which used to be in the avenue leading to Ribbesford Church, there used to be an Elm tree with a rabbit burrow underneath. We saw a rabbit enter the burrow and therefore netted the rabbit holes and put the ferret down one of them. We were astounded to witness rats coming out of the holes before the rabbit entered one of the nets and it seemed unbelievable for both animals to be living closely together! The nets I have mentioned were used on each of the rabbit holes before the ferret was put in the burrow, with the aim of catching the rabbits as they tried to make their escape from the ferret.

Continuing with my memories of rabbiting, the other practice my Uncle Cyril would follow on a Saturday was to put wires down in the Fourteen Acre Field at Beeches Farm during the day on the tracks the rabbits made when they were running through the grass. Cyril would put his wires down on the runs and these consisted of a loop attached to a strong string which in turn was tied to a wooden peg. The peg was then driven into the ground so that when the rabbit was caught in the loop he was unable to break free. The loop was held at the right height by a wooden stick, split at the top to enable the wire to be pushed in. The stick was then knocked into the ground and all that was needed was patience to wait for the rabbit to approach! As the rabbits only came out in the evening, Cyril would then revisit all the wires to collect those that had been caught before taking them home for food.

Mr Jack Wadeley purchased the farm afterwards and passed his bakery business in High Street onto his family. After he moved to the farm Mr Wadeley started a poultry business, having two or three large poultry houses built quite near to the house. He also had quite a number of bee hives which he placed around the fields around Light Lane and sold the produce locally as there was a big demand for beeswax, besides the honey.

Mr Wadeley also planted a cherry orchard in the Fourteen Acre Field. Afterwards, Mr and Mrs Wadeley (senior) handed the responsibility of the farm over to their son, John who continued with producing poultry and bee-keeping, exactly as his father had done before him. John was also a member of the Bewdley Cricket Club and I recall was rather a good cricketer but sadly he died in middle age so Mrs Wadeley, John's widow, continued to run the farm. Although she kept a few poultry, the farm soon began to run down and she left soon afterwards. The new people who purchased the farm have done a considerable amount of work since with extensive installation of new fencing around the border of the property. A wooden bungalow has been built in the middle of the field, the old house has been demolished and while walking past I have noticed the new owners also keep a few sheep.

Moving further along Light Lane now, we arrive at Horse Hill Farm which was owned by Mr Chapman who kept a large dairy herd. When my Dad was young he worked for him helping with the milking. I do not think he stayed long as the wages in farming at the time were very poor. Mr Styles purchased this farm from the Chapmans and turned it into a pig farm where he kept pedigree pigs for which he was well-known throughout the country. This has since been run-down as a farm and once again the farm buildings have been turned into dwellings, although some of the fields are still worked for crops and a few paddocks have horses and ponies on them for riding purposes.

Further along the lane on the left-hand side is a small cottage where the Bourne family lived. I believe Mr Bourne must have worked on the farms in the area. I remember one of his sons particularly well by the name of Bill as he was my age and went to Lax Lane School. There were other children, an elder brother called Jack who was a similar age to my sister Florrie and he was in the regular army before the War, stationed in India where he was involved with the fighting over the Khyber Pass. He later worked at Brintons in the Blacksmiths shop.

Going along Light Lane, approximately half a mile on the right-hand side is situated another farm which was known as Fernihoughs' Farm in my younger days. I do not have much knowledge of the farm itself but they had two sons around the same age as me. One day, the one son, while carrying a gun, tragically stumbled while climbing over the hedge and accidently shot and killed himself.

Continuing another mile or so along the lane on the left-hand side is another farm at the side of Gladderbrook which was owned by Mr Cope and this was called Brook Farm. Crossing the brook up the very steep bank there was another farm owned by Mr and Mrs Bert Bond and their son's named Dick, Bert and Harvey. Dick worked on the farm, Bert was house-lad at Winterdyne and Harvey worked on the weaving at Brintons. Mr Bond had a dairy herd and he and his wife milked the cows and with a horse and float delivered the milk around Bewdley as did his brother Bill (who is later mentioned under the heading of High Street).

One day, Mrs Bond, an extremely hard-working lady, was helping the horse to climb the steep bank by pushing the back of the float and something happened to cause the horse and float to travel backwards. Tragically, the float ran over Mrs Bond and killed her outright. Mr Bond was not making the journey into Bewdley with her at this time as he had been unwell for some while so this unfortunate accident happened while Mrs Bond was totally alone.

Reverting back to Chapman's Farm, on the opposite side of this is a lane leading up to Park Farm and also the school camp. Mr Chapman (the owner of Horsehill Farm) kindly gave some land and woods to the Smethwick Schools for the children to use for holidays. The children used to come down for two weeks at a time during the summer months. There was a house and school built on the land for rural education and when I was in the Scouts we sometimes went to visit in the evenings to play cricket with them. Now the education authority has taken over and it is run in a different way.

Down the lane near to the education centre was a stone built cottage owned by Mr Baker and his family. He did some farming to make a living and also had a horse and trap which he and his wife drove down to Bewdley daily to do their shopping and deliver eggs as they kept a few poultry. He also rented two fields along the riverside from Mrs Sturt at Winterdyne where he kept a small number of store cattle so I suppose this would have brought in a little more income.

When I was at school I sometimes walked along the riverside and pumped water from the river into the tank for the cattle as I often noticed they had nothing to drink. During the War he died and left two daughters; one I recall was named Addie (who later left to live in the Far Forest area) and a son called Johnny (who was a little backward) and although he stayed on at the cottage, it became very dilapidated during the time he lived alone so the school authorities purchased the cottage, dismantled it and built a small bungalow in its place where he lived until a short time ago. I do not know what happened to him afterwards.

Further along the lane was Park End Farm. I do not know much about this farm but the buildings have been converted into private dwellings. The last building is now lived in by David and Wendy Hinton and their daughter Carol. David is a very keen photographer and has been responsible for taking many of the historical shots throughout Bewdley for Ken Hobson, a local historian. I occasionally call to see them both when I am walking in the area and they always offer a welcome cup of tea. David has always been very generous in sponsorship of my different causes over the years.

BEWDLEY TOWN AND DISTRICT

Load Street

Load Street was named after the old word for ferry "lode." The street is unusually wide as it once served as a town marketplace.

The first business in Load Street, next to what was Owens grocers shop (currently a hairdresser) was the butchers owned by Tommy Timmis. He slaughtered the animals at the rear of his premises and delivered fresh meat to the local businesses and gentry. He was noted for providing the slowest service in serving the customers in his shop but this was tolerated as he was very humorous! The business next door (currently selling patchwork supplies) was his living quarters when I was a child.

The barbers shop was Pleveys Saddlery in my time. Leather goods have been manufactured in Bewdley since the 15th century. The plentiful supply of oak bark from the Wyre Forest used for dying and water from the Severn made it an ideal place for manufacturing. Many tanneries supplied leather to the town's leatherworks and some tan-yard owners became very wealthy and owned substantial properties in the town. Many items were produced including saddles, harnesses, shoes and boots and the gloves were made by women. My father and I purchased our saddles from this shop when at Winterdyne and took to them any leatherwork repairs that were needed.

Adjoining Pleveys was Bewdley Institute for scientific and literary study but previous to this it was a public house and coaching inn and the Red Rover called here from Birmingham. This was established in 1848 but the present building was erected in 1877 at a cost of approximately £1,000. It used to have a reading room which was open to the public by payment of 1d. Its President was Viscount Cobham and the Honourable Secretary was R. H. Whitcombe jnr. Esq., M.A. from Kateshill. In my youth it was used mostly for business people playing bagatelle.

Alan Lawson, Tailor traded from the next shop (now the fishing tackle shop) and I have had reasonably priced suits made here. His wife was named Maggie and she also helped in the shop and was a good friend of my wife. The following business was a cake shop, then Hemmingway's the Solicitors, who were responsible for the administration of the alms houses and was the only Solicitor in Bewdley until just after the War when another, named Mr Gorfangle, started up his own practice in the town.

The Brass Foundry, H.J. Exley was situated behind the shop called The Chocolate Box in Load Street. This building dates back to 1745 and is now the HSBC bank, formerly Midland Bank after it moved from Severnside South). Exley's bought their business in 1923 and it remained in their family until it closed in 1964 but the earliest brass foundry in Bewdley was established by the Bancks of Wigan in the year 1697 and the business was carried on by Messrs. G. T. Smith & Son which was noted for its manufacture of maslin kettles. These were so named as they were used for cooking maslin, which was a blend of grains, i.e. porridge. Production of brass weights was its main function and these were made from scrap brass for both the home and export market. The person I best remember here was Mr Moule who had a son named Fred the same age as me (who sadly has since passed on) and we went to school together.

The Chocolate Box was a shop and restaurant owned by Mr and Mrs Stowe and this was next to the Bewdley Post Office which closed in 1972. The old Post Office dates back to 1636 as during renovation works in 1965 when the rendering was removed from the façade of the building this date was revealed in the form of a carving onto one of the beams. Up until quite recently this property was used by Phipps and Pritchard Estate Agents but it is now the Kemp Hospice Shop.

The next property was owned by Mrs Broad who ran a haberdashery business selling clothes and knitting wool, but this was later demolished in the 1950's to create a passageway leading to the sorting office for the post depot. This was later moved to Kidderminster and the Post Office was moved to the rear of Preedy's (now Martin's), the only newsagent in the town.

We now arrive at what used to be the Fire Station situated underneath the Guild Hall, nowadays known as the Town Hall. The fire engine at the time was drawn by two black horses supplied by Mr. Riley Coles who lived in Stourport Road. The house still remains but the school has since been built upon the fields to the rear where he kept the horses. Mr Coles also owned a hearse which he used to transport the deceased on their final journey to either Ribbesford, Dowles or Wribbenhall churches. Sadly he was killed in a motor accident, together with his wife, on Blackstone bank when they were returning from holiday. The Fire Station was transferred to Dog Lane in 1960.

Next was the Town Hall, built in 1808 and renovated and enlarged in 1873, where all the court cases were held until 1989. The interior of the building contains some very interesting items such as the details of all the Mayors who have held office and also the original Latin charter, granted by Edward IV in 1472, together with others granted after this time and the two maces presented by Queen Anne which can be found in the Town Clerk's Office. This building now provides the entrance to Bewdley Museum and the house to the left, now called the Mayor's Parlour, was where the Police Sergeant lived and in my time the last one I remember was Sergeant Heath. This was where Bewdley Police Station was situated in my youth until it was moved to its current location in Wribbenhall.

To the rear of the entrance to Bewdley Museum lie The Shambles and the three Police Cells. The term The Shambles is believed to have come from the Anglo Saxon word *"Fleshamels"* meaning *"flesh shelf"* which described where butchers displayed their meat. The Shambles referred to the building in which animals were slaughtered and the meat was sold but in my time the slaughtering process was carried out by the local butchers at the rear of their premises. Both Lukie Needham and Mr Timmis in Load Street, Mr Palmer in Westbourne Street, Wribbenhall and Mr James in Welsh Gate also did this.

We then come to the Newsagents owned by the Shepherd family and later Mr Fred Harris, which is currently the Vantage Chemist. There were two Newsagents in Load Street at that time, the other being Mapps at the top end of the town, to the left of what used to be Cooks the Florist which is facing Saint Annes Church and is currently Bewdley Cutting Rooms, a hairdressers.

There is a passageway in Load Street which served as the rear entrance to the old Newsagents and also what was then a Wool Shop owned by Harry Bishop. In the first instance it was owned by his wife but she sadly passed away in childbirth although a surviving baby daughter was delivered. Harry then took responsibility for running the shop and bringing up his son by the name of Eric. His daughter was adopted as a small baby by his late wife's family. Eric, a retired school teacher, has since emigrated to Canada and I keep regular contact with him. Betty Bishop, Harry's Niece, went to work for Harry when she left school and remained with him for many years until she moved to Brintons working in the Print Room.

We have now reached No.8 Load Street which was Sid Green, a Butcher when I was young. He bought his meat in and never slaughtered on the premises. Sid used to supply the meat to Harry Bishop for the Scouts wherever they were camping in the summer. I recall one day when I was not able to go to camp, Harry suggested I took the meat up to them on the Sunday as I was working the previous Saturday at Brintons. The camp was at Rhyl, Wales and we travelled all the way there but when we arrived Harry suddenly remembered he had forgotten to put the meat in the boot of the car and despite our efforts, as there were no shops open in Wales on a Sunday, the Scouts had an alternative menu and Harry took the meat up the following day!

The next establishment was a garage owned by Mr Evans and his family. They had two petrol pumps on the edge of the pathway and at the side of the shop was an entrance where the cars could be driven to the rear for repairs to be carried out. The Town Clerk lived in the next house and this is the Council Office currently where the Council Tax is paid. Just after the war the appointed Town Clerk was called Mr Hales and he was also responsible for running the 5th Bewdley Scouts during Wartime.

Just beyond the next series of houses was The Dairy, owned by Mr John Thomas. This was previously situated on the Stourport Road, Bewdley, in between the Station entrance and Westbourne Street. In those days, he used to deliver with a horse and dray or trap and a gentleman by the name of Harrold Carter worked for him throughout his entire working life. Before he moved to Load Street I recall working on the Dairy by helping to tile all the walls in preparation for the opening of his shop and once he moved to Load Street the horse-drawn drays were replaced by motorised vehicles to deliver his produce. It was a very big business at that time. This is a kebab shop currently.

In my childhood, the Sandwich Shop we know today, next door to the Dairy, was an antique shop in the 1950's to 1960's. The following shop (currently an Ice Cream Parlour) was owned by the Crump Family and this brings us to Teddy Grays Sweet Shop on the corner of Load Street where it meets with Severnside South and this shop has been there for a very, very long time. In my early days it was a private dwelling but it was certainly Teddy Grays during Wartime and onwards.

Crossing the road now, beginning at the corner house where Load Street meets Severnside North, this was a private dwelling in my childhood up until I was in my 20's rather than a commercial property as it is currently. Adjoining this was a Fish & Chip Shop as it is today. I frequently stopped here with my friends Mike Young and Harry Purcell to buy chips wrapped in newspaper, which we took to the rails in Severnside North to eat, chat and watch the river.

The Angel public house is the next property in Load Street and I recall this black and white half-timbered building being knocked down and re-built further back to enable people to sit in the front as it did very good trade in the 1920's and 30's when the Birmingham people came to Bewdley on the trains and buses. The Angel was rebuilt in 1938. Historically, it was host to Charles I during the Civil War as Tickenhill was in a damaged state at the time and in the 18th century it had a fashionable Assembly Room where the Welsh actress Sarah Seddon (born 5th July, 1755 in Brecon and died 8th June, 1831) once played. She was the best known tragedienne of the 18th century.

Bewdley in those days was a very popular holiday destination and was extremely busy during weekends and public holidays. I have seen as many as six buses lined up at the side of the road on a Sunday evening to take the people back to their homes in the Birmingham area. The bus stop in those days was in exactly the same place as it is today and the first bus was introduced in approximately 1913 as I remember my Mother telling me how she always walked to her place of work in Kidderminster up until a short time after her marriage to my father when the bus service from Bewdley to Kidderminster began. Previous to this there was an omnibus service running to and from the George Hotel and the Railway Station in Bewdley and a capital service running daily at frequent intervals from the Royal Hotel and Black Boy Hotel to Kidderminster.

The next shop was a grocers shop (this is a discount hardware shop now) and adjoining this was a Tobacconist in my youth which was owned by a Miss Humpherson. She lived there alone, was a very popular person and everyone nicknamed her Shucky Humpherson. The word 'Shuck' was used in Bewdley quite frequently to address a female and I remember my own Father addressing my Mother in this way so it was obviously a term of endearment! The next establishment of note was Dr Bob Miles' Surgery and home. I do not remember very much about the actual Surgery as I can honestly say I never went to the doctors!

Dr. Bob had a spaniel dog by the name of Whisky as he was black and white. He used to bring him from home (in Lea Bank Avenue) to the surgery when he came to work in the morning and when Whisky decided he had had enough, he would take himself to the bus (which stopped outside the surgery) and hop on! Most of the drivers and conductors knew him and he would stay on the bus until it reached Lea Bank Avenue and the conductor would stop the bus for him to hop off! He carried on with this routine for several years and became quite a celebrity to the extent that I remember this being reported in the local paper. Later the surgery was transferred to Dog Lane as it is today.

The next shop was a sweet shop and during the War and just afterwards it was owned by the Butcher family who originated from Wharton Park Farm. Adjoining this was a Greengrocers owned by the Granger family and I went to school with their son. This was followed by a lock-up shop run by Daisy Bell selling sweets and ice-cream. Daisy was the daughter of Mrs Bell who also owned a sweet shop which I have talked about under High Street but this wooden structure was taken down to make way for the entrance to Dog Lane Car Park, possibly during the War or immediately afterwards.

We now arrive at Barclays Bank and this has always been there in my time followed by Mountfords, the Ironmongers, which is Timmis' today. Mountfords was the place everyone in the area visited to buy all their ironmongery. Hamiltons the Shoe Shop was next door and I went to school with their Son, John. The family later went to live on Bark Hill and the business was bought by Blunts until recent years but they too closed their Bewdley branch a few years ago. There are double doors leading to Saint Georges Hall which was used for all local events and I can vaguely remember there being one or two school concerts held there which were attended by Mr Frost, then the Mayor of Bewdley. Dances, Rummage Sales and Church Bazaars to raise money for different causes were all held in the hall.

I have helped the Methodist Church in High Street to raise funds from the Christmas Bazaars and Rummage Sales held in St Georges Hall. On one particular occasion I persuaded my daughter Des, albeit under protest, to walk up and down Load Street wearing a sandwich board to advertise the Bazaar. She dutifully did this for me but was none too pleased when she returned home having been assaulted by a passing dog relieving itself against the board. After that incident I didn't dare ask her to do this again! I have raised money for the Venture Scouts also by arranging a number of Dances and Frank Freeman used to come and run these for me in the hall. Gladys and Des would provide the refreshments on these occasions.

In addition, before the War boxing was held in St Georges Hall. This was where the Berwick family from Dowles Church used to box, trained by their Father (who was also Dowles Church Warden) and one of his sons held a British title. The Berwick family lived in a house in Dowles churchyard where they also did their boxing training. They owned a Blacksmiths shop in Wribbenhall on the corner joining Northwood Lane (called Rag Lane in my youth). I well remember   the family making their way to work each morning and returning at night in single file, walking behind one another along the riverside.   Mr Berwick followed by Mrs Berwick, then their backward son the rear. I never had reason to visit this Blacksmith as Spring Grove always used Tommy Ricketts in Ricketts Yard and Winterdyne passed all their work to Ralph Jones at the top of Dog Lane.

This now brings us to the George Hotel which dates back to the 15th century and was owned by Mr Cooper in my early life. The earliest written reference to the hotel was in 1609 and at that time the premises was officially known as *Saint George Inn*. In my youth The George was heavily patronised by business people, often arriving in their horse–drawn coaches which entered through the double doors to the yard at the rear. Here there was a Cooper who constructed barrels for the business and further open fronted coach–housing. Beyond this was a closed building which was converted into a factory during Wartime.

The front of the hotel was used for business meetings and all sorts of influential people met there. Very little has changed to the facade of this grand piece of Georgian architecture over the years and coach services to The Star in Worcester ran from here where the journey time was approximately 2 hours and 15 minutes. The builder I worked for, Mr Jack Coldrick, was one of the business people who regularly visited this venue, often at lunchtimes, and he would pick up trade in the process. I have transcribed an extract of an advert of their services from when I was a young boy:

THE "GEORGE" HOTEL
BEWDLEY
Old Family and Commercial Posting House
AND ST.GEORGE'S HALL
Stage and proscenium to seat 500.
Fully licensed for theatricals
WELL APPOINTED
COFFEE, COMMERCIAL, SMOKING & BILLIARD ROOMS
An ideal bowling green
WHOLESALE WINE AND SPIRIT DEPARTMENTS
Single bottles at wholesale price
Terrace and Arrangements for Private or Public Parties
with use of Meadow
BRAKES, WAGONETTES, LANDAUS AND DOG–CARTS FOR HIRE
WEDDINGS AND FUNERALS FURNISHED
Omnibus to and from the Station.
Parcels Agent for the GWR
EXCELLENT YARD AND STABLES
MONTHLY STOCK SALE HELD ON PREMISES: G H BANKS Auctioneer
MRS WOODWARD Proprietress

Harcombes the drapers and clothes shop was next door to the George and the owners employed two sisters with the surname of Toone (who lived at Catchems End) to serve in the shop up until it closed in the 1960's. The next premises were Styles the Chemist after the War and beside this is an alleyway called No Road which led through to Dog Lane. The wall of the shop building on the right forms the first part of the alleyway and immediately after the living quarters to the shop the owners kept a parrot which we enjoyed teasing on our way to carpentry lessons with the school.

Further up towards Dog Lane, on the left was a row of houses and Bill Clarke (a retired game-keeper who later worked for Coldricks Builders) lived in the first one. This is now known as 3, 4, 5 and 6 Hafren Court and was in fact three cottages in my youth. No.2 is an extension and was Bill Clarke's open yard on the left hand side. I recall while I was working at Coldricks, Bill Clarke was most excited one day when the state pension first started and he was given a pension of 10/- per week! At the end of No Road where it meets with Dog Lane, on the left hand side were the sheds and yard belonging to Woods the fishmonger, which I have covered in greater detail under the section on Dog Lane.

Reverting back to Load Street assuming you had not taken the turning named No Road was George's Shoe Shop, selling Kays Shoes and this is where the whole of my family used to purchase their footwear. Next door to this was an electrical shop run by John Davis selling radios and electrical goods. We took our radio batteries there to be re-charged periodically and these were very heavy to carry indeed. The next shop, now Co-op Undertakers, in my childhood was Wrensons, a grocer followed by Peckhams the bakers next door. They were also known as 'the midnight bakers' and baked their bread on the premises and the baker and his daughter delivered it during the evenings around the homes in Bewdley.

The predominant building in Load Street is St. Annes Church (built between 1745 and 1748 to a design by Thomas Woodward, a Stone Mason and quarry owner from Chipping Camden and commands the area in the centre at the very top of the town. While the present building dates back over 250 years, the tower dates back to 1695 when it was built on the west end of the chapel, perhaps to support the old wooden building until 1745 when the leading churchmen decided a more spacious and commanding stone edifice was required. The tower is some 87 feet high. There are 8 bells and a fire bell above the clock which was recast at the same time as the church bells in 1780 by Rudhalls of Gloucester. On the east side is the War Memorial commemorating the 75 Bewdley men who lost their lives in the First World War and 29 who sacrificed their lives for their country in World War 2.

Next to Peckhams in Load Street was Fosters the Chemist, then Trout's the Bakers (they had a son named Norris whom I met at Scouts and more of this will be mentioned under the chapter on Scouting). We now arrive at the Dry Cleaners followed by a greengrocers shop after the War and this is now the only bakery in Bewdley. Lukie Needham the Butchers follows who sold the venison out of the forest and I remember Dad used to buy a joint of this when it was in season and the deer were culled in the forest each year to keep the numbers under control. Deer over the number of 300 were destroyed for this purpose.

There was next an ironmongers shop owned by another Mr Mountford (no relation) followed by a small hairdressing salon owned by Mr Rogers. James' The Grocers was next door with a double fronted shop and there were at least three of the James family working there so it was quite a large business. Crawleys the Tinsmiths lived and traded next door, selling tin kettles, baths etc, including enamelware and this is now a Chinese Takeaway. The last shop in Load Street on this side of the road was Millwards the Greengrocer but when this shop was knocked down to widen the road the family went to live on Long Bank.

On the opposite side of the road, between Welsh Gate and Dowles Road was a fishmonger and greengrocer named Woods and this was where Harry Bishop worked. Woods also had a yard with a shed in Dog Lane where they stored the van they used to drive to Birmingham Market each morning to buy the fish and I have spoken about this later in my book under Dog Lane. On the left hand side of Woods was another public house, later to become a fish and chip shop but today it is known as the Welsh Gate Diner.

On the opposite side of the road to Millwards in Load Street was a double fronted shop providing the living accommodation and business premises of William Hunt the builders. This was originally a domestic dwelling. He had a large number of staff working for him and the family had several building businesses around Bewdley. It later became an MEB shop for paying domestic electricity bills and purchasing electrical goods. Next there was an alleyway between Hunts and Coldricks, two other local building firms, the latter was where I served my apprenticeship. Bill and Jack Coldrick were the two brothers in the business and Bill used the front section as an office to carry out estimates and general administration, including paying the wages. His brother Jack visited the sites and distributed the work to the men and their Aunt lived in the house. These premises were referred to as The Swan Yard in those days.

We now arrive at the situation of the Swan public house, previously a hotel, called the London Vaults. This brings us to No.36 which was a Tin–Smiths owned by the Watkins family. Years ago if you had a leak in a bowl or kettle it was repaired rather than replaced and Watkins did this or you could purchase the bolts and washers to do the repair yourself. With enamel bowls, kettles, saucepans etc if they became chipped they would be repaired with metal and leather washers with a bolt through and tightened. Next door there were several small shops and the last of these was Slaters (at the bottom of Park Lane) which sold grocery and sweets but this was later knocked down to widen Park Lane.

Crossing the road we arrive at the estate agency on the corner of Park Lane and in my childhood this was the Royal Hotel, (the main entrance being up the steps of The Zoo, computer repairs nowadays). There used to be a private dwelling next door and I believe the owner was a local school teacher but I do not recall her name as she did not teach at Lax Lane School. This, of course was Cooks the Florist until recently.

We have now arrived at the gentleman's hairdressers which used to be Mapps the Newsagents at the very top of Load Street which we have referred to earlier in the book and I have an amusing story to share with you. One day when Dad collected his daily paper from the newsagents his Airedale Terrier, called Floss, parted company with him when he called into Mapps. Floss took herself across the road to Timmis' the butcher and came out sporting links of sausages and my Father immediately made his way home in pursuit of the dog! Fred Hunt (a bricklayer at Brintons) lived in the private dwelling next door but this is a small shop selling cards and party goods now. The last house in Load Street where it meets High Street was a tobacconists and this is a Chinese takeaway business today.

High Street

High street, formerly known as Upper Street, is thought to have taken its name originally from its relative position above the river. Beginning at the point where High Street meets with Lax Lane (on the opposite side of the road to our family home at No.35) there was a coal yard with double doors on the corner and this is now a public car park. No.33 High Street was lived in by and Mr and Mrs Bill Bond and his three daughters. Edith and Winnie were much older than me and Marjorie, the youngest, was my age and we were in the same class at Lax Lane School together. Marjorie in later life married the late Harrold Simmonds, a carpet weaver at Brintons Limited where he was heavily involved with the Carpet Weavers Union. He later became a Councillor and was eventually made Mayor of Bewdley. Mr Bond ran a small holding in the area still known as Bewdley Park which was rented from Mrs Sturt at Winterdyne and this is covered in more detail later in this chapter when we arrive at Park Alley.

On the opposite side to our home at No.35, adjoining Mr Bond's home was The Pack Horse public house kept by Mrs Martin at that time. Later, her son William became the Landlord and it was as popular then as it is to this day. Three doors are visible from the front of the pub but it is apparent structural changes have taken place over the years. The first door from Lower Park end was the main entrance to the pub but this is no longer in use. The next door is also no longer used and the last door was the tradesmen's access in my youth, which is now a passageway leading to the main entrance.

The house attached to the other side of the Pub at No.29, now known as Sand Dollar, was occupied by Mr and Mrs Bill Ashcraft and their grandson by the name of George (who sadly later lost his life in the war). I understand their home was also originally a Public House as after the Ashcrafts passed on I worked there carrying out repairs and whilst removing some floorboards I found a number of old pennies which had possibly fallen down a hole in the boards while playing games of "pitch pennies"

Next to the Ashcraft's was an entry door on which is now inscribed Court No.2. The first house was lived in by the Ashcraft's daughter by the name of Lizzy but beforehand was occupied by Mr Hinton and his ginger-haired girlfriend who was much younger in years. He used to have a vegetable business delivering the produce to houses around Bewdley by horse and dray which he kept outside the Alms Houses in the daytime. George (who I mentioned earlier) was Lizzy's son born before she was married and was looked after by his grandparents next door. He was around the same age as me and we attended Lax Lane School together. She later married someone by the name of Mr. List from Far Forest area but during the time I knew of her she lived alone. The entry also led to four small terraced houses behind but these are now converted into two cottages known as Numbers 1 and 2 White Cottages. These are reputed to be in excess of 300 years old and can now only be approached from the car-park at the rear of The Pack Horse in Lax Lane. I only knew the kind old lady who lived in the first house and I recall she was profoundly deaf – I believe she was related to Alf Jackson who attended school at the same time as me. I remember when I was working on the houses in High Street she would often invite me down to her house at around 10 o'clock and ply me with a cup and tea and piece of pork pie which was delicious!

Reverting back to the houses at the top of the entry at 28 High Street was a house lived in by another Mr and Mrs Hinton and their large family (he was a brother of the vegetable delivery man). Mr Hinton did not work to my knowledge and they were very poor. Mrs Hinton was a very pleasant, though timid lady and worked extremely hard caring for such a large family.

Mr Charlie Ife lived at No.27 for a few years but later moved to a caravan on a small holding which is covered in detail under my chapter entitled Light Lane. The Old Bewdley Grammar School was founded by William Monnox in 1591 and was refounded in 1606 by James I. It was rebuilt on the present site in 1865 at which time its administration was reorganised by the Court of Chancery. A valuable and extensive library of around 1500 volumes was presented to the school by the Rev. Thomas Wigan in 1819. In my time this building has never been used as a school as it closed in 1912. It was built in 1861 on land previously occupied by the Blue Bell Inn. The school was used by the Free French Army during the War. I recall it being used as the headquarters for 2nd Bewdley Scouts and as a member of this troop, we built the heather huts for Eastnor Park Jamboree inside there with the help of Dr Bob Miles who was Scoutmaster at the time but this was before the War. I have covered Eastnor Park Jamboree separately in greater detail later under the chapter on Scouting. After the War it was used by Bewdley Guides (as now) and June Sweet was the leader at the time.

We now arrive at No.26, which was a large house lived in by Mr and Mrs Knock (Mrs Knock was a teacher at Lax Lane School). The name of the residents occupying the next large house at No.25 was Dr Castle and his wife and daughter plus a friend's child whose parents were living in India and they held the surgery from their home. Historically, this was a timber framed house but was re-fronted in 1780 by Samuel Skey whose chemical works outside Bewdley brought him wealth. He founded the original Bewdley Bank here in 1760 situated in Lower Park opposite The Rectory. We now approach Skey House at No.24 but I believe there is no reference to suggest Samuel Skey ever occupied this house. In my childhood this property was lived in by Miss Gabb and a lodger by the name of Mr Brown. Miss Gabb raised canaries and I purchased one of these at a cost of 10/- when I was about 14 years of age. She was an Aunt to the Bullock sisters who lived in St. Annes House.

The following house, No.23, was occupied by Miss Joiner (the teacher at Lax Lane School) and her Mother, and No.22 next door was lived in by Mr and Mrs Gillam and their three sons. There was Sid, the oldest, who became a Special Constable in the Police Force and later married Vera Darkes from my schooldays who lived along the riverside. Next was Harry who married Mrs Wadely's sister from the Bakers in High Street and he later moved to the Bakers Shop as mentioned a little further on in this chapter. Lastly, the youngest was Harold who worked at Brintons in the Design Room.

There was another alleyway leading off High Street at No.21 and it was necessary to go down a series of steps which led to the Ashcroft's house. I have already mentioned Frank under my football days while at Lax Lane School and he had a sister by the name of Edith who was a regular member of the congregation of Ribbesford Church. I do not remember the occupants of No.20 High Street but at No.19 lived a Mrs Moule who sometimes did dressmaking for people. Next we reach No.18 called The Old Bakehouse belonging to Jack Potter. He and his wife had a daughter a little older than me by the name of Jean and used to deliver the bread from a basket on his arm to the local people.

The College family lived at No.17 and their son Les worked at the Grocery Shop "Thomas Evans" at the corner of Load Street and High Street. The neighbouring property was No.16, a sweet and grocery shop owned by Mr and Mrs Bell and family. Mrs Bell was a very motherly type of person and when I left school I would call in for a bottle of Tizer with my friends Mike Young, Harry Purcell, Les Evans and Jim Tolley after we had been to church on Sunday evenings. We would play her up a little and she enjoyed every minute of it! Mrs Bell made her own ice-cream and her son Colin rode an ice-cream bicycle to Severnside and the field by Blackstone Rock to sell the ice-cream to visitors and fishermen. The fields now have been turned into a public picnic area and this was owned by Mrs Sturt in those days.

We now arrive at No.15, another greengrocers shop followed by No.14. a private dwelling lived in by a Mr and Mrs Tolley. After came the Wesleyan Church which dates back to 1795, now known as the Methodist Church of which my late wife Gladys became a member in 1953 for the rest of her life. Although not a member, I have also been very involved with this church with raising funds and carrying out maintenance work in the past but now regularly attend for worship, together with Abberley Church and Callow Hill Methodist and I will go into more detail later on this in this book under the heading 'My Places of Worship'. At the front of the Church there is a gas lamp at the top of the steps and the name "Wesleyan Church" is etched onto the glass Some 40 years ago I recall repairing the damage and restoring it to its former glory! It is interesting to note the organ originated from Kinlet Hall and was purchased during the 1970's.

Underneath Bewdley Methodist Church, approached by a gateway on the left hand side, are steps which used to lead down to the living quarters where the caretakers Mr and Mrs Parmenter and family lived. At the bottom of the steps, under the archway is a small courtyard and on the far right is a door which leads to the toilets and old schoolroom. The vestry is also off the schoolroom and there is flight of stairs leading up to the church. I can remember it was on the pathway outside the church where I last saw my good friend John Gardiner as he had joined the Territorial Army and was due to be posted to France. He went missing at Dunkirk and was never to be seen again.

This brings us to the entrance of Jubilee Gardens which in my childhood formed part of Redthorne House and gardens. There were two coach houses close to the road to the right-hand side of the house which have since been removed and fronted by two very grand, large iron gates which were later removed from the facade. This house was originally built in 1765 for William Prattinton, one of the richest merchants of Bewdley who imported goods from the West Indies to sell to his customers throughout the Midlands. It was occupied by two sisters in my time who ran it as a guest house but I do not recall their names and never saw very much of them. There was a large garden at the rear which is now car-parking and part of Queen Elizabeth II Jubilee Gardens. These were opened in 1978 in an area which since medieval times has been used for gardens, brickyards and tanneries. Evidence of the tanning pits has often been found during building works in the area. During the Tudor period Bewdley had as many as 12 tanneries, the last closed in 1928 and was taken over by Williams, a timber business in Severnside South.

We now approach No.10 High Street, accommodated by the Lester Family. Mr and Mrs Lester, their daughter named Connie, a further daughter named Phyllis (who later moved to take up the position of housemaid at the Rectory) and a son called Bill who joined the navy as a regular before the War started. The neighbouring property is No.9 High Street, lived in by Mr Bert Hancocks and his family which bears a plaque stating "Church House" dated 1650. It has an extremely tiny door with windows set very low and the ground floor rooms are below the level of the pavement. Mr Hancocks was a plumber, painter, decorator and sign writer. Two of the people he had working for him were Vic Whitmore (the son of the dentist in Wribbenhall) and Dick Keightley his apprentice (the son of the caretaker at Lax Lane School). I was an apprentice at the same time as Dick and I was sometimes sent by my employer, Coldricks, to help out with the painting.

The Church Meeting House is No.8 High Street and this is where all the Church of England churches held their meetings. It was also a dwelling house but I cannot recall the name of the occupants. There was one family I knew in the houses beyond the Meeting House at No.6 and that was Mr and Mrs Harold Bowkett, one of the local postmen who frequently delivered the mail to Winterdyne when we lived there.

No.4 High Street was a private dwelling in my day but is now an unoccupied double-fronted shop. Then there was a coach house belonging to the

Bakers Shop and it was owned in my time for a short while by Mr Hayden, a baker, but he sold it on to Jack Wadely and his wife who ran the shop with the help of her step-sister Edith. In time, Jack moved to the Beeches Farm in Light Lane with his family and I have expanded upon this later in the book. Edith married Harry Gillam and they took over the running of the bakery business. I recall Harry was known as "The Midnight Baker" as he used to deliver all hours of the night. Harold, his brother, worked in the Design Room at Brintons and he was also a member of Ribbesford Church Choir which I have detailed later in my experiences whilst I was a choirboy. I vividly remember helping him to make the dough for the bread and the baking of pikelets on a Friday night. There is a passageway leading down to the rear of Evans' shop on the left hand side and the Bakehouse on the right hand side.

This brings us to the end of High Street where the grocers shop sat on the corner and this is now a hairdressers. It was originally owned by the Owens family who were the parents of Mrs Gardiner from 37 High Street. Historically, pack horses went as far as Wales delivering goods from here. I do not remember any of this family with exception to Mrs Gardiner but the family name 'Thomas Owens' can still be seen set in mosaic into the entrance step. They sold the shop to Mr and Mrs Griffiths, who improved the business greatly and they used to deliver locally, including to Winterdyne House once each week. In my youth it was owned by Mr and Mrs Evans. I recall they had a live-in servant who came from Kinlet originally. Mr and Mrs Evans had two sons, Colin and Les and we were in the Scouts together. Les had a billiard table in a room at the back of the shop where we all used to meet. Sometimes we were joined by Dorothy Broad, a niece of Jack Wadeley (who kept the Bakers) and another girlfriend of Dorothy but I only remember her surname Miss "Quick" and I recall she came from George Street in Kidderminster.

On the opposite side of the road to the hairdressers was situated the Talbot Public House which was owned by Fred Bishop at that time and was both his home and business. There was an entry on the right-hand side of the pub to provide access to the rear yard where he brewed his own beer on the premises as did a number of the public houses in Bewdley at that time. His daughter named Sheila I will write more about later in the book as she was involved with the Guides and also worked at Brintons Limited. I worked on this property carrying out various repairs whilst an apprentice at Coldricks.

Returning in the direction of Lower Park, the next business was a Greengrocer which is now the left-hand window section and main entrance of the Talbot Public House. The shop was owned by Fred Potter and his wife and they had a daughter named Rosemary. Fred's wife was a sister to

Gladys Birch, wife of Wilf Birch, Cowman at Winterdyne. The next house, No.70, was a private dwelling belonging to Miss Phillips who looked after the laundry at Winterdyne. She also ran a dressmaking business from home and my late wife had several outfits made there.

This brings us to the Bailiffs House which dates back as far as 1607 and this structure was built by Thomas Boulston in 1610. It is a fine example of timber framing and this style is typical in Worcestershire and the border counties. In 1606 the town of Bewdley was granted a charter by King James I and the office of the Town Bailiff was created at that time with a committee of burgesses to oversee municipal administration. The header panel over the door is inscribed 1610. Thomas Boulston was 1st Bailiff of Bewdley and lived there until his death when he was buried at Ribbesford on 17th October, 1621. Today this is a commercial property but when I was a child it was a private house occupied by Charlie Alberts, the School Teacher at Lax Lane.

The next property, currently Marion Evans, Solicitors, bears a plaque stating it was formerly 67 High Street and was restored in 1981 by J.T. Gwilllam, Builder. In my youth it was a private house lived in by the Eades family, followed by a Tailors Shop at No.66 High Street which was a private house owned by Mr and Mrs Simmonds. Mr Simmonds ran a tailoring business from home where he used to make the Grooms' suits for Dad while at Winterdyne. It later became a cake shop and restaurant run by Mrs Simmonds and this was where my wife and I had our wedding reception in 1943! There is an entrance leading to the home of my friend Peter Johnson at No.65 which provided the entry to the living quarters of the Simmonds family on the left and the entrance to the old restaurant and cake shop at No.66 was on the right.

The next dwelling, sadly now very run down, has blue double doors and bears a plaque of the business A.J. Domone and Son, a photo-stencil and screen process service. When I was young this was the residence of Horace Gordon who was a very jovial person. He was both the local milkman on a small scale and also ran a gentleman's hairdressers from the premises.

We now arrive at a long wall and piece of open ground with a rather dilapidated building to the right which used to be the old work house and also a horn manufacturer. To the left is the Catholic Church, formerly an early Presbyterian Meeting House established around 1696. It was rebuilt in 1778 and the meeting house closed in 1894. An old document describes the chapel as "an excellent building bearing evidence of erection by a wealthy congregation." Amongst its wealthy members would have been William Prattinton, the brothers Kenrick and Samuel Skey.

The long wall along High Street was one continual course in times past but a driveway has been made to provide parking for the church which is next to the house built during the time I was an apprentice at Coldricks by Mr Bishop and his son, for his parents. (Very soon afterwards he built a similar style house for his son in Kidderminster Road). The church in High Street situated behind the house was purchased by Mr Bishop and used to store building materials.

The next large Georgian property at No.63 was owned by the Howells family. Wing Commander Howell was heavily involved with scouting at the time, holding the position of Chairman of Bewdley District Scouts and he hosted most of the district meetings from his home. In 1945 the house and land were purchased by Wing Commander Howell, a Catholic who was keen to see the restoration of the church and it became a Roman Catholic place of worship in 1953. Upon the passing of the builder's widow it was possible in 1951 to purchase the chapel by Birmingham Archdiocese and it was reopened upon completion on 8th September, 1953.

This brings us to the large Georgian property known as The Manor House with an archway to the side leading to lawns in my childhood but this is now a car park and other dwellings at the rear. This house, built in 1870, was used by influential people at the time but unfortunately I have very little knowledge of its residents. This has since been turned into flats. We then arrive at the passageway leading to Bewdley Baptist Church at the rear (built in 1764) and on the left Bewdley Baptist Church House, the home of the Caretaker and in the 1950's my friend Don Williams lived here when he and his wife Hilda were first married. Next, at No.54 there is a very old half timbered black and white house which was frequented by Jack Carter and his wife and they also had a very large family.

Where there is a large opening there used to be a Fish and Chip Shop, however, this was demolished by Hunts the builders to make way for the garden at the rear where they built four very small terraced houses and this is now known as Burltons Terrace. The first house (No.2) was occupied by June Postings (formerly Sweet) and her husband Harry. June was in the Girl Guides, eventually becoming District Commissioner several years later. Harry Postings sadly lost a leg during the Second World War and was a weaver at Brintons. Their neighbours at No.3 were Cyril (my Uncle) and his wife Helen Birch and their daughter Judith, all of whom worked for the Post Office and next-door lived the Perks family. I do not recall who lived in the last house.

Back into the main street, the first house past the opening at No.55A was June Sweet's parents' home and next to this lived the Parmenter family at

No.55 – these were also linked with the Breakwell family at No.55 who lived at the rear which had to be approached by an entry. A little further along the road was a private house (No.49) owned by Jack Brown, a Carpenter and he used to work all around Bewdley and on occasions I worked with him while at Coldricks. I well remember carrying out repairs on the roof of Winterdyne House with Jack – he was responsible for replacing some of the old timbers while my colleague and I repaired the slates and Bert Hancocks carried out the repairs required to the lead work.

At No.51 there lived another Carpenter called Mr Brown who also worked with Jack and they may have been related. The next house along High Street was occupied by the Cartwright family and I recall the daughter frequently sitting in the front bay window as I passed by, often with my friend Mike Young, who nicknamed her Poker-nose! I believe the family later moved to Dowles Road, Bewdley. There was an entry leading to the properties in The Park, one of which is a black and white half timbered house and this was the home of the Page family. Their son, Sam Page, was in the choir at Ribbesford Church at the same time as myself and later became the organist. They also had a daughter named Reenie who had to wear callipers as she was born with a medical problem. She was a friendly, cheerful person despite her disability.

The following house at No.47 on the left-hand side of the alleyway was lived in by the Sanders family; husband, wife and two grown-up children. I do not recall the name of their next door neighbours but the forthcoming house in the row belonged to another extension of the Parmenter family. Mr Parmenter, you may recall, worked part-time at Winterdyne doing various odd jobs. His children were named Derek and Edna. I went to school at the same time as Derek and our paths crossed again during our working life at Brintons. I seem to remember his sister sadly passed away whilst very young.

My Uncle Sam Birch lived next door but No.44 is now one dwelling. Numbers 44 and 45 are considered to be among the oldest houses in Bewdley. You will possibly recall Uncle Sam's name being mentioned in the chapter on Sandbourne Estate where he worked as Head Gardener. Sam Birch was Father to Wilf Birch who was the Cowman at Winterdyne. It is interesting to note the 18th century brick front of this row of houses conceals a late medieval hall house. Smoke blackened timbers were found in the roof during past reconstruction work and this is regarded as possibly one of the oldest buildings in the town. All medieval towns' development land was valuable; therefore building often took place at right-angles to the street with tenements and gardens running behind the houses and shop-fronts. Evidence of this is illustrated in High Street in particular.

We now arrive at the Burltons Alms Houses which were used by the local poor when they became old. This section of alms houses were given by Thomas Cooke, son of Richard Cooke who died 22nd January 1693 at the age of 19. The building was completed by Mr. Thomas Burlton and Mr. Samuel Slade (then Justice of Bewdley). They were restored in 1860 by Rev. Joseph Crane MA and James Tart, Mayor. These were run by Hemmingway's, the Solicitors in Load Street who were responsible for all the maintenance of these properties and John Thomas was the Solicitor's Clerk who ran all of the Bewdley charities in those days. I often worked on many of these while at Coldricks carrying out repair–work. There were three lots of Alms Houses in Bewdley: one row in Lower Park for married families, one set in Park Lane which were mainly for ladies living alone and the Burltons alms houses in High Street for the aged.

This brings us to No.42 High Street called The Old Surgery which was owned by Doctor Hubert Miles who ran the practice from the side of his home. He was the head of the Boys Brigade in my Father's time and became head of the Scouting movement in Bewdley when it first began. Dr Miles and his wife had five children, the eldest was a son who I recall was sent to Canada and returned to Bewdley on several occasions but I do not know what became of him. He also had three daughters, Mary, Katherine and one further daughter, all of whom married and left the district. Lastly, his son Bob (who was one of the Scout Masters in 2nd Bewdley Scouts) followed in his Father's footsteps and became a Doctor.

Dr. Bob Miles junior married a lady from South Africa at Ribbesford Church and while I was in the Scouts we formed the guard of honour for them when they left church. Dr Bob junior and his wife had two daughters called Margaret and Elizabeth. He was very well liked in Bewdley and worked for a short while in his Father's practice, then moved to Load Street and worked for a good many years at the surgery in Dog Lane until his untimely death. During the time St. Georges Hall was being renovated (Dr Miles was the main person responsible for this work) sadly collapsed and died in the Hall and I was asked to be bearer along with other Scouts at his funeral at Ribbesford Church.

My late wife Gladys (nee Timms) was housekeeper and receptionist at the surgery and in the course of her work she became a well known face to all the local residents in Bewdley. It was during her time here I recall on one occasion calling with a number of other Scouts selling programmes in connection with the Coronation of George VI. This would have been during 1937 while I was employed at Spring Grove Stables. Another person who worked with Gladys at that time was Jack Bough who did the gardening duties and if the weather was wet he helped in the house. He was also one of the 2nd Bewdley Scouts and in later years he became chauffeur to Doctor Hubert Miles. I can remember the garage being built for Dr Miles' vehicle in Lax Lane while I was still at school and this still remains today, next to the Boys Entrance to the school playground.

Walking up Park Alley towards Bewdley Park, the first house called Park Cottage was lived in by Mr and Mrs Lancet and their son Cliff, who later became a Weaver at Brintons Limited. Joined to their house was part of the Convalescent Home which was previously the home's Tool Room with a games room over the top. During the War I helped to build a brick air-raid shelter in the Tool Room while on leave from the army when I was based at Ditton Priors. After the War the Old Pals purchased this building which they used for playing games of cards etc. They generally met once a week and once a month they had a special tea provided free by Harry Bishop, Nancy Baker and my late wife Gladys, which was very popular. After I constructed the new Scout Headquarters I then built new toilets for the Old Pals. There also used to be an iron staircase leading up to the games room providing a fire escape which I installed, together with an iron gate fitted at the same time as cutting through the wall, to provide an entrance to the property. This building has since been converted to a private dwelling.

Reverting back to the actual Convalescent Home which was opened in 1893, this was provided for people within 50 miles of the Birmingham area requiring rest and recuperation. Further along the lane from Lower Park, on the left-hand side of the alleyway is the old main entrance to St. Annes House which could also be approached via the lane from where Lower Park meets Red Hill. This was the home of the Bullock sisters whom I have written about previously in this book. The garden opposite belonged to the Convalescent Home and part of this was sold off to the British Legion to enable them to build their Headquarters but this has since been taken over by the 1st Bewdley Scouts. Past the facade of the Convalescent Home, taking the path on the right-hand side brings us to the rear of what used to be the Page's family home, a very old black and white half-timbered house which I have covered previously under High Street.

There is a footpath running at the end of Park Alley, through Bewdley Park, leading down towards Ribbesford Church. The footpath in those days was maintained by Bewdley Council and the man responsible for its upkeep was Mr White. The Park has one field on the left-hand side which is made up of a distinctive large tump of earth and is called The Round Hill. This has an oak tree which was nicknamed The Monkey Tree and was so called as it was popular with the local children from High Street and Lax Lane for climbing and playing games. This was a favourite place for them to play after school, weekends and during holiday time and is still there to this day.

There is a field with a footpath opposite the monkey tree which leads to Cannon Hall and a bridge over the brook. In this field there were cowsheds where Mr Bond milked his herd and there was a pump in the field providing water to clean the sheds. Drinking water for the cattle was a fenced off area which incorporated part of the water fed by the Golden Valley Pools. Mr Bond owned approximately 8 to 10 cows for milking and Arthur Stokes from Lax Lane used to carry out the cleaning of the cowsheds and milk churns here whilst Mr Bond delivered milk to the houses in Lax Lane and High Street. He had a truck with two churns and he used a pint ladle to measure the milk into people's containers when he went around the streets. This cart, known as a milk pram, is currently exhibited at Hartlebury County Museum. Mr Bond also rented the Cherry Orchard situated next to Red Hill from Mr Whitcombe at Kateshill House who was a Solicitor in Bewdley. Mr Bond also employed Mr Taylor from Lax Lane (nicknamed Tucker Taylor) to mind and pick the cherries for him.

Reverting back to the field by the cowsheds, on the left–hand side of the field was The Snuff Mill. This was fed by the Golden Valley Pools which provided the power to work the mill producing snuff. Also, in this brook in my youth there was trout in this area and as a young boy I would tickle them and catch them to eat. By tickling them, the fish were attracted by the heat of your hand and this made it quite easy to rapidly toss them out of the water onto the bank once they hovered above your hand.

Continuing now with the remainder of High Street we arrive at No.41 which was the home of the Bond family and their neighbours, Mr and Mrs Gittins and their daughter Ruth lived next door. This adjoins No.39 High Street which was lived in by a Cobbler who repaired shoes from home. My Auntie Emma lived at No.38 with my Uncle Bill and I recall her being very old when I was a child. Mr and Mrs Gardiner who owned the grocery shop lived in No.37 (easily recognisable by the two bay windows) being the parents of my friend John, whom I have described in detail at the very beginning of my book.

The next houses were my grandparents at No.36 and our family home at No.35 High Street (up until I was 5 years of age when we moved to Winterdyne). Next door to us at No.34 is the last house in High Street (which is double–fronted and faced opposite Lax Lane. This was occupied by the Homer family and after the war Bill Purcell, his wife Freda and their son Charles lived there. Bill was the Manager at Williams Sawmill on Severnside South. He was also the Mayor of Bewdley in the 1950's and was involved with supplying items for the 3rd Bewdley Scouts headquarters in Spencer Avenue. I will go into greater detail on this under the chapter on Scouting.

Lax Lane

Lax Lane takes its name from the Danish word "Lax" meaning salmon which was fished nearby at Lax Lane ford. I have not seen salmon fished here personally but I witnessed several otters in my youth. Snuff Mill Brook runs from The Park, through the garden of the house owned by the Bullocks in Park Alley, then through the Rectory and under Lax Lane where it is culverted. This then leads to the ancient ford which is believed to have been used to cross the river before the medieval bridge was built in 1447. We will begin on the very corner where High Street meets Lax Lane. There was a pair of double doors leading to a coal yard on the left when I was a child. Next to this was a very old black and white timbered house which was occupied by the Danby family but at some point after the War ended this was demolished to make way for the car park and the entrance to the cottages behind.

The first house in this row to the right of the access to the car park used to be the home of Mr and Mrs Bennett (now No.3). All the cottages in this row were tiny places in my childhood but it appears that a number of them are now two cottages converted into one larger one and therefore have two doors to their frontage. This is certainly the case with Numbers 3, 6 and 8. During the process of writing this book I have spoken to the current owner of No.3 who advises me this property could be one of the oldest houses in Bewdley town and tests are being carried out by laser on the roof timbers to verify this. No.3 still has what is reputed to be an elm tree strengthening the beam for the first floor, which has since been cased in.

Next door was the home of the Perks family at No.4 Lax Lane but of course 3 and what used to be No.4 are now one dwelling. No.5, currently named Beggars Roost, used to be lived in by Mr and Mrs Pudner and this was their home and a sweet shop then. Mr Pudner came from Winterdyne estate where he was employed as a Coachman. Next door at No.6 lived the Gillam family, whose daughter had polio and used to lie in an invalid basket placed on the pavement under their window in fine weather. We used to stop and talk to her on our way to school and several years later she managed to learn to walk. I worked in this house later in life, as with many houses in Bewdley, carrying out various repairs such as roofing etc, where the timber rafters and purlins came directly out of the Wyre Forest to be used for reconstruction work on the properties. These were in a very crude state in that while the top and bottom of the sapling was axed level so they sat flat (allowing the tiling lath and the lath for plastering underneath to be fixed) the remaining area sometimes still had the bark attached.

While I worked at Coldrick's I actually witnessed the use of a telegraph pole in this property to prop up the sagging beam of the bedroom floor. I believe Mr Gillam worked for the post office in those days and this is possibly where he obtained the telegraph pole! Mr and Mrs Bond lived next door at what was No.7 and I recall Mr Dick Bond worked for Worcestershire Council on the roads. One day while he was bending–down cleaning the drain out on the corner of Lower Park and Red Hill, I was coming down the hill at terrific speed on my bike and brushed past him as I went by! I did not stop and, of course, he reported this to my Dad who chastised me. This is not the only occasion I was in trouble for such pursuits. I was reported once again to my Dad for dangerous cycling by the two Miss Westley sisters who lived in the house facing towards Red Hill! Another Mr and Mrs Bond lived next door (currently part of No.8) but they were no relation to Dick.

The Stokes brothers, Arthur and Albert lived in the right hand half of cottage No.8 and were general handymen. Arthur Stokes used to work for Bill Bond and made the cider at the bottom of Red Hill. The brothers also kept the pig sties in Light Lane which is where Albert spent most of his time. When I was a baby in arms my Mother handed me to Arthur Stokes, whereupon I disgraced myself upon him and my parents reminded me of this on many occasions, much to my embarrassment. I also recall Arthur was very fond of his drink and I watched him many times come rolling out of the Pack Horse and stagger down to his home in Lax Lane!

Mr and Mrs Aden lived at No.10 and I recall their son, Bill, with whom I attended Lax Lane School, was sadly killed in the War. The next properties were called Florentine Terrace which was laid back from the road. I did not know any of its occupants but I remember my sister Florrie was friends with an auburn–haired girl who lived there. She married one of the carpenters from Brintons. Next we arrive at No.20 of the terraced houses and this was a sweet shop run by Mr Millward, followed by Harold Jones and Fred Perry who lived with their relations at No.23. Fred was in the choir at Ribbesford Church and Harold, as mentioned under my schooldays at Lax Lane, owned a jackdaw which patiently waited on the school roof until he came out at lunchtimes and at the end of school. The bird would fly down onto his shoulder and accompany him all the way home, which caused a great deal of interest with the local schoolchildren! The jackdaw possibly came from Winterdyne Woods as there were a number of them nesting on the rocks there. What was known as "The Battery" at Winterdyne was also a nesting ground for them and as I always had an interest in birds I would frequently visit these places.

We now arrive at Mr and Mrs Keightley and family who lived at No.27. When I worked at Spring Grove I bought some eggs from there for "sitting" in order to raise my own chickens. After this I wanted a cockerel to put with the hens and Mr and Mrs Keightley kept Buff Rocks and sold me one of these. After then their daughter Hazel repeatedly enquired after the bird! Next door (at No.28) lived the Perks family. This property is now called Laxford House and I am told candle making used to take place in the attic room and apparently the scorch marks from lighting the candles can still be seen on the ceiling!

Immediately after Laxford House is an opening which led to two cottages in my youth. I recall fellow choir boy from Ribbesford Church lived in one of these by the name of Gerald Clee. At No.31 lived Bessie Parsons and her son Tom. Bessie used to deliver vegetables around the houses on a wheelbarrow and her son Tom joined the Grenadier Guards. The neighbouring property belonged to the Darkes family at No.32 and Sam Darkes worked for Bobby Jackson in his fruit business. Next door (at No.33) lived Mr White who was a window cleaner and also the person who pasted the advertising posters on to the billboards throughout the town. I recall watching him on my way to or from school with a brush attached to a long handle to paste the walls on which he applied the posters, usually in Lax Lane. I did not know the occupants of the remaining couple of houses until we reach the corner property belonging to the Faulkner family which I have referred to under the section on Severnside South.

Crossing Lax Lane now to the opposite side we have the large black and white house with ornately shaped gables which was occupied by Bobbie Jackson the school master and his family. This was aptly called School House (but is now named Severn Bank House) and Lax Lane ford, referred to earlier in this chapter, is located at the section of the river immediately opposite the house. Additionally, at the bottom of Lax Lane is the culvert where the otters used to hide and the large area in front of the school house was where the pack horses came from Wales to deliver wool. Before the bridges were built they used to cross the ford at this point to reach Wribbenhall.

At the rear of School House (where a large detached garage has since been constructed) were the sheds housing the fruit business which was run by Sam Darkes with the help of the local school children. At this time, the area now occupied by the Gardners Meadow development housed the school football field and the surface car park to the side was the storage area for the trees brought in from the forest by Tommy Gardner. His orchard and garden were situated next to the school wall.

Mr Jackson organised a bonfire on 5th November each year for the local people and this was situated in the middle of the open area in front of the school house. I went once or twice with my Father but I was never very fond of such occasions. Next to the school house was the playground for girls and infants, the boundary wall of which still carries the vertical marks caused by the partitions in the girls' toilets, since demolished.

From the girls entrance is a long corridor. On the left was the girls cloakroom and on the right-hand side was the infants classroom, followed by classroom No.1 (7 year olds), then No.5 (11 and 12 year olds), No.3 (9 year olds), No.2 (8 year olds) and then No.4 (for 10 year olds). The last class was No.7 on the left, which you entered when you reached the age of 13. At the age of 14 you left full-time education in those days.

From the boys entrance now in Lax Lane, on the right-hand side was the coalhouse and Class No.4 was opposite. There was a building next to the coalhouse where the inks were mixed which consisted of water and dye and this was used to fill all the inkwells set into the desks in the classrooms. The following building on the right was the boys toilets which led directly onto the playground surrounded by the boundary wall which separated the school yard from Tommy Gardners garden and orchard.

Entering the school via the boys entrance, on the right was the cloakroom and on the left was class 4. In the cloakroom were the boys washbasins which were used for washing out the painting utensils and also the Horlicks was made here and sold to the children at 1d per cup. Next to this was Class 7. The school is now the home of Bewdley Brewery, a pottery works and art and photographic studio.

The next building is the garage which was constructed by Hunts Builders for Dr Miles Senior. I was still at school when this was built and it was a single garage originally but this has since been extended to accommodate two cars. We now arrive at the site of an opening to Pritchard's coal yard but this is no longer present as it has been replaced by the British Red Cross building. The boundary wall of this used to be a two-storey shed in times past. It was very high and it was on this wall Mr. White used to paste the large advertising posters. At No.44 was the home of Mr and Mrs Pritchard the Coal Merchants and this is now owned by Mr Ashcraft, a local builder.

This now brings us to what was my Granddad's yard and stables in which he kept his horse and donkey. This was formerly part of the grounds to Lower Park House where Stanley Baldwin was born as was the coach house with the large opening onto Lax Lane, now used as a garage. Lower Park House was owned by the Yardley family in my childhood.

Lower Park

Lower Park is on the edge of what used to be a Royal Park. It begins at The Rectory, built in 1760 (on the right-hand side of the road) and No.15 Lower Park House, where Stanley Baldwin was born (on the left) which I have covered in more detail later in this chapter. The Rectory was given to St.Annes Church by a Mrs Fortiscue but the church sold this property when it became too costly to maintain. This was the home of Reverend Raymond Hollis and his sister who was the District Commissioner of Guides in my childhood. They had two members of live-in staff; Nellie Mynard was the Cook and Phyllis Lester was the House Maid. There was also a part-time gardener by the name of Mr Carter. Gladys was friendly with Nellie and Phyllis and used to pop down for a chat some mornings when Mrs Miles went out.

There were a number of functions held at the Rectory, one of which was the Garden Party for Lax Lane School in June of each year where the older children aged 12 to 14 years used to perform plays on the lawn and all the parents attended. In the grounds they used to have different stalls such as rolling the hoop and tombola and this was always very much looked forward to by the local people. There are two large garages, previously coach houses, belonging to the Rectory at the bottom of Red Hill and I recall the Reverend's sister standing in the middle of the road to stop the traffic when he needed to take his car out. It is a very dangerous corner to this day and has been the source of many accidents.

The Reverend Hollis was Rector for Bewdley, Ribbesford, Button Oak and Long Bank churches. He eventually married Kitty Williamson who was a very strong churchgoer but when he retired they moved away from the district. After the Reverend passed away, however, Kitty returned to Bewdley and the last I remember she moved to a flat on Hales Park before she sadly passed away. Kitty was a very pleasant person and I recall when Jake, her Father, passed away she gave me all his drawing equipment which I still have in my possession to this day. I will always be grateful to Jake for the advice and support he gave me when I started my building career at Brintons.

Beyond the coach houses, the house facing Red Hill belonged to Mrs Sturt of Winterdyne and the two Wesley sisters lived there. The elder sister was an organist at St Annes Church and played at our wedding. During the war, my late wife purchased a three piece suite while I was in the army and the Wesley sisters kindly stored it for us until we had a place of our own. This house was originally a public house, well before my time, called the Rose and Crown. On the left-hand side of this was a coach house and this is now a private dwelling.

There was a great deal of history attached to this area, particularly Kateshill and it is interesting to note both Winterdyne and Kateshill belonged to Ticknell Manor originally, which had very strong royal connections, being the home of Arthur, Prince of Wales (Son of Henry VII and Queen Elizabeth). A sweet chestnut tree, known locally as 'Bewdley's Sweet Chestnut' was planted in the grounds of what is now Kateshill House, built around 1740. It has been suggested that the tree was planted to commemorate Prince Arthur's Wedding to Catherine of Aragon, Princess of Spain on 14th November, 1501. It is also said that the hill above Kateshill was named after Catherine (in the shortened version of her name) and the Georgian Manor was aptly named having been later built on this land. In my youth this property was occupied by the Whitcomb family, local Solicitors.

At the rear of the coach house to what was previously The Rose and Crown was an adjoining brick-built shed used by Bill Bond for storing his cider press and other associated items. He would make the cider outside and store the collected juice and perry in barrels to ferment in here. The fruit was placed in layers on matting resembling coconut mats and was pressed on a cider press. The juice ran out into the barrels and was then left to ferment until it was ready for drinking and it was rumoured dead rats were thrown into the cider to aid the fermenting process. Sometimes, on our way home from school Arthur Stokes would give us a drink of the fruit juice which I believe was perry and I remember it was very sweet!

Taking the pathway on the right-hand side can be found a pair of double gates and a driveway leading down to St. Annes House which was owned by the Bullock Sisters, Dorothy and Phyllis. They had a large orchard of cherries and hazelnuts called 'filberts' which were generous in size and to gather them they would shake the trees when the nuts were ripe and then collect them from the ground. These were favoured as they were larger than the ordinary hazel nuts and were sold to the locals. After I left school I went to work for the Bullock Sisters during evenings and weekends as my Uncle Cyril Birch used to do part-time gardening for them, besides being a Postman in Bewdley. He had also, of course, previously been a gardener at Winterdyne. I helped him pick the cherries when they were ripe and these were later sold to Mr Jackson, the Headmaster at Lax Lane School. I have mentioned more about this earlier in my book.

The house opposite our home at No.15 was called Lower Park House. This is situated on the corner where Lax Lane joins Lower Park and was where in 1867 Stanley Baldwin (the local Conservative Member of Parliament for three times from 1908 until 1937) was born. Rumour has it when he was born he was tossed into the air and during the process his head hit the ceiling! He later became Prime Minister and on 8th August 1925 he was awarded Freedom of the Borough, 1st Freeman of Bewdley. He is best remembered for handling the General Strike in 1926 and the abdication crisis of 1936 when Edward VIII gave up his throne because Baldwin told him it would be unacceptable to marry American divorcee, Mrs Simpson, and still remain King.

I can remember Dad talking about Stanley Baldwin and the Election. Bewdley was a very strong Conservative area in those days so the Election was a very big day although I was too young to remember it personally. Dad was always very interesting to listen to when he shared talk about Bewdley history and I recall him repeating the chant everyone shouted when he was elected into parliament:

> *"Vote, vote for Stanley Baldwin*
> *He is the man*
> *We'll have him if we can*
> *So vote, vote for Stanley Baldwin"*

In 1927 he visited Canada with Prince Edward and Prince George and during this commonwealth tour a mountain was named after him 'Mount Stanley Baldwin'. He retired from politics in 1937 and was made Earl Baldwin of Bewdley. He and his wife Lucy moved to Astley Court near Stourport on Severn where they lived until he passed away in his sleep on 14th December, 1947 and his ashes were buried at Worcester Cathedral. Astley Court was later passed to his son where he lived for some time but this was later sold and turned into a nursing home.

Reverting back to Stanley Baldwin's birthplace, the family who occupied this in my childhood was called Yardley. Next door, at No.14, now known as Bank House, is currently a Guest House and as its name suggests this was a Bank historically, founded by Samuel Skey in 1760. This name is mentioned many times in Bewdley history and it can get a little confusing as there were three of them! I have no recollection of the owners of the following house until we reach the Sayers Alms Houses and my Granddad Birch moved into No.11 after my Grandmother passed away. In 1625 Samuel Sayers endowed these almshouses and therefore they were aptly named after him. In the late 1970's they were restored under the chairmanship of Councillor Mrs F. S. Pritchard MBE.

In my childhood there was an alleyway along here leading to the Quakers' Meeting House (built in 1706) which was the only entrance to the church until well after the War but it is no longer used today as there is now a large driveway leading to this further along the road. The Alms Houses were for married couples but the names of the occupants are very vague now, although the last one I remember was lived in by Bigum Bishop. Obviously, this was a nickname and I can say he was a very large man! I recall seeing him on my way to and from school each day and he would always lean over the stable door of his home smoking a pipe. This man had a brother who lived in Lax Lane who was also a very large gentleman.

Next to the Alms Houses was No.7 Lower Park, lived in by Mr and Mrs Eric Bishop and his family. When I lived at Winterdyne the family living there (or visitors to their home) played jazz which was a completely new style of music to me at the time and I remember it being very loud as we walked by and for some distance away! After the Bishops home at No.6 there lived the Stone family; the son was named Weedon and they had a daughter who was a friend of my sister Florrie. This house bears a commemorative plaque of the Bewdley Civic Society marking the birthplace of Captain G.T. Smith-Clarke MI MECHE FRAS, Chief Engineer of Alvis Limited, Automobile and Medical Engineer 1884-1960.

It is interesting to note these last two houses historically used to be one large Georgian residence occupied by Reverend George Browne MacDonald, a Wesleyan Minister and his family. His four daughters had notable connections through marriage. The first to marry was Georgiana (a Painter) to Sir Edward Coley Burne-Jones the famous Pre-Raphaelite Artist and Designer in 1860. The eldest daughter, Alice, married the art teacher John Kipling in 1865. They were engaged at Rudyard Lake in Leek, Staffordshire and this was how their son, the famous Author and Poet Rudyard Kipling, earned his name. Alice shared a joint wedding with her sister Agnes who married the Artist Sir Edward John Poynter. Lastly, his daughter Louisa married the ironmaster and Conservative MP Alfred Baldwin in 1866 and was the mother of Prime Minister Stanley Baldwin. Rudyard and Stanley Baldwin were, therefore, Burne-Jones' nephews. Alfred Baldwin provided the funds to build All Saints Church, Wilden and Burne-Jones created 14 designs for the windows between the period 1902 to 1914 which were dedicated to the MacDonald, Burne-Jones and Baldwin families.

We now arrive at a smaller house occupied by the Hobbs family. Behind the houses is the Quaker Meeting House which has been there since 1691 making it one of Bewdley's oldest religious foundations and the old churchyard lies to the rear. I attended one service here with Renault Beakbane, the Stourport District Commissioner of the Scouts in the 1960's. There were many renowned Quaker names who worshipped here besides Beakbane, such as Parker, Sturge and Derby. It was here in 1718 that Mary, wife of the first Abraham Darby was buried having passed away suddenly while visiting friends in Bewdley, sadly just a few months after her husband.

On the right-hand side of the drive leading to the Quaker Meeting House there is a detached property where two spinsters lived in my childhood. I used to pass by here as a short cut when I lived at Winterdyne and I well remember these ladies shouting at my brother Geoff and myself (and sometimes John Gardiner) for using this route! Originally, it was a road which formed part of Winterdyne Estate so they really did not have valid grounds for stopping us from using this route but they steadfastly protected the territory! In those days there were no further properties along here, but since the war one or two have been built in this area. On the entrance of this road is a house which belonged to Winterdyne and in those days it was rented to the Vicarage family.

Bewdley Allotments and Gardners Meadow

Taking the track that leads to Bewdley Cricket Club (and in my childhood Winterdyne Farm) we arrive at the changing rooms and clubhouse of the Cricket Club. On the opposite side of the lane is Rosehill which belonged to Winterdyne and in my childhood was rented to Harry James, the local odd-job man and chimney sweep who also worked at Kateshill as a gardener. He kept several store cattle and four geese and this field used to be full of rabbits. When I was young I used to catch the rabbits here for food and on occasions he would complain to my Father about this. I did not get into serious trouble but Dad did tell me not to venture on his land again! Before the War Mrs Sturt sold the bottom parcel of this land on Rosehill to Mr Bobby Jackson (the retired School Headmaster) on which he had a house built and this can clearly be seen from the road ascending Red Hill today.

There is a pathway alongside the cricket field which leads to the river and used to be the old tow-path. At the end of this route the right-hand turn leads to Ribbesford and if the left-hand route is followed it goes towards Lax Lane. On the left of this pathway is Gardners Meadow and at the entrance was a timber yard owned by Tommy Gardner who lived at Severnside. He owned several timber wagons and teams of horses and brought all the local timber he collected into Gardners Meadow to store for approximately 12 months to season prior to being cut on the saw bench in his yard. In the meadow alongside Lax Lane School playground he had an orchard and vegetable garden and also he was a coal merchant based at his home in Severnside South. The meadow was also used as a football field by Bewdley Comrades and Lax Lane School and when we lived at

Winterdyne we used to watch all the football matches from the walks around Winterdyne Estate, often from Rosehill, which provided a very good viewpoint as it was in an elevated position. I would do this with Dad most weekends in the winter.

Another major celebration in Bewdley in August was Carnival Day. There were at least a dozen jazz bands (mostly from the Black Country) who took part and each one dressed in lavish costume, marching around the town – different colours for different areas and they were judged on Gardners Meadow (which is now a car park and a small housing development). There were a large number of floats, mostly driven by horse, but some lorries were present and the procession started at the meadow and they would march around the town and then return. This was later moved to Stourport Road where the school playing field stands today and in the evenings there were about a dozen boats decorated on the river. Candles were placed in jam jars to light up the night and it was certainly an impressive sight when darkness fell! Most people turned out for the carnival and a good time was had by all. This event was very much looked forward to as local events were very well patronised in those days. It was a major source of entertainment for Bewdley residents.

Severnside South

Severnside was historically a very important inland port where goods were shipped to Bewdley and overseas. The first house on the corner of Severnside South was where the Purcell family lived in my youth and this is now known as The Arches. The fishing tackle shop situated next door, S. R. Lewis, was a domestic dwelling in my youth and No.3 belonged to Mr Mountford who ran a plumbing business from his home, now known as The Bridge (providing accommodation) and spans both sides of the passageway. Saracen House belonged to Mr and Mrs Stevenson, Mr Stevenson being Ribbesford Church Organist and Choirmaster. On Tuesday evenings we used to have Choir Practice at Mr Stevenson's house which was situated just a few doors away from the Midland Bank. I remember there being a serving hatch between their front room and dining room and Mrs Stevenson would periodically peer through the hatch to ensure everyone was behaving themselves and singing!

After Nos. 6 and 7 Severnside South we arrive at Mr. Perrin's home, who was the local bank manager of the Midland Bank. This is now Inces the Funeral Director and next to the archway was the Midland Bank (No.9) which was built in 1832 and was where I opened my first bank account. Dad used to take me here periodically to have my savings box emptied and

I would deposit them for my future. The buildings to the rear were also owned by the bank. On the opposite side of the road was the bandstand which was erected with money collected by the local people. This has since been removed and the appearance of the quay was changed dramatically during the flood alleviation works in 2004. At the time the bandstand (purchased by the local people) was dismantled it was said the local council would re-erect this elsewhere in Bewdley but sadly this has never been done, much to the disgust of many local people of my generation. Historically, in my Father's youth, there used to be two bands, one belonging to the E Company of the 1st Voluntary Battalion of the Worcestershire Regiment and the other, of which he was a member, was the Town Band and they often played on the banks of the river in Summertime.

We now arrive at No.10 Severnside South (currently called The Cottage) which was a 17th century river house and has a wrought iron balcony on the first floor. This was Bill Coldrick's family home, the local builder with whom I served my apprenticeship and I remember it had tanning pits for soaking the pelts at the rear of the house which previously belonged to the tanning industry. After the skins were soaked the hair was scraped off, leaving a clean leather and the hair and skin was dried and bagged. It was then sold to the local plasterers and builders where the skin and hair was beaten to remove the hair from the remaining skin and any dirt until it was fluffy. We would then mix this with a lime mortar to plaster ceilings in houses etc.

When I was an apprentice, there was an occasion when I was sent up a ladder to repair the roof on this property with two other men. This is a very high building, and when I reached the top I stepped off into the gutter and the wind blew the ladder down. One of the men, called Snig Davies (who was profoundly deaf) should have been footing the ladder but he must have stepped off it. This was the longest ladder in Bewdley and Jack Coldrick was fuming as it smashed to the floor and we missed this as we were never able to have it replaced. Mr Coldrick was nonetheless relieved I had not been hurt. I made my escape back to the safety of the ground by climbing through the attic window!

The owners of Styles the Chemist in Load Street lived at No.11 and later in life I recall the awful incident where Mr Styles took his own life a little further up Severnside South at the point in the river where Lax Lane ford is situated. This area has claimed several lives over the years. It was at this point where it was shallow and it has been said that before Bewdley Bridge was built the cowmen used to drive the cattle across to Wribbenhall. Also the owners of the pack horses carrying the wool from Wales used to take the wool across the river at this point to Wribbenhall and it was where people crossed the river prior to the wooden bridges being built.

The next house (No.12) has the initials T.R. Carved into the doorway surround but I do not remember who lived here. I know the adjoining cottage (No.13, now called Long Alley Cottage as it leads to Long Alley) was occupied by Granny Tailor who was the local midwife. Her Grand-daughter called Rose lived with her and later in life she married Les College who worked at the corner grocery shop in High Street.

There was an alleyway leading to two cottages in my early work life, and this would have been at the point of the right-hand window of No.16, now known as River Cottage. This, together with Kimberley House, was built at the end of the 17th century, and are fine examples of houses constructed on wealth accrued from Bewdley's prosperous river trade. The structural marks are still just about visible in the brickwork as this used to be two cottages. Since the 14th century people of Bewdley have traded on the River Severn and continued profitably until the construction of the Staffordshire and Worcestershire canal in 1772. Just past here was the old Brewery called Hopkins and Garlic where stout was made and this is the site of Riverside Vets today. They used to have horses and drays to deliver the stout to local businesses.

Calcutts the leatherworks was next-door, now No.18 The Quay. Years ago in this vicinity there was also a cap maker but I am not sure exactly where it was. In the time of the Tudors, Bewdley's cap making industry was very considerable when no less than 1,000 people were employed in this work. Protection of the working classes was one of Edward IV's characteristics and during his reign he prohibited the use of an ingenious machine which was capable of carrying out the work of 80 men as he "considered it very inconvenient to turn so many labouring men to idleness" and he decided no caps were to be imported from abroad. Soon after, the French Protestant refugees brought into England the use of hats, however, which caused this trade to decline, so that in the reign of Charles II it was reported that a great number of the ancient cap makers in Bewdley had fallen to almost nil. This is now a trade of the long, distant past.

We now arrive at Tannery House (No.20) which was owned by the proprietors of the local tannery but this was a timber merchant by the name of Williams' in my day and Bill Purcell was the manager there. There is a very large opening (now leading to Telford Court) which provided an extensive yard with ample space for delivering the large trees and there were open-fronted buildings on the right-hand side housing the wood-cutting machinery, together with Mr Purcell's office immediately on your right as you passed through the archway.

This now brings us to the area where a row of small cottages have been demolished. These were lived in by Alf Mole who worked at Coldrick's; Mr Moule and his family who worked at the Brass Foundry; Mr and Mrs Darkes and their daughter Vera and Mr Harrold Carter who owned the punt that collected the bodies of people who lost their lives in the river. He kept this vessel moored in front of his cottage, together with a hook and chain and the steps he descended to reach his punt are still visible.

This brings us to what was the Thurston Hotel which is still a grand building and has a portico style entrance at the top of a flight of steps. This is now Thurston Court, a series of flats but there are still a number of original features present, particularly the lead rainwater pipe in the corner. Next to this was the Pritchard family at No.27 (now called Acorn House) which was a very old black and white half timbered house. There is a passageway leading to the rear which is now domestic dwellings but this would have been outbuildings to the main house in my childhood. Mr and Mrs Pritchard adopted three children, two girls and a boy called Harry who became a Scoutmaster (and later in life a Fireman who married Flow Danby from The Hollow, Welsh Gate) and there is more to read about him under my chapter on Scouting. One of the adopted daughters was Gladys Lea who married and went to live in Stourbridge Road, Kidderminster. The other was Milly Ashford who became Cub Mistress for the 2nd Bewdley Cubs and also worked in the Picking Room at Brintons. The Pritchards were related to the Pritchard family living in Acacia Avenue and I will mention more about these later in my book under Scouting.

This brings us to Tommy Gardner at No.28, the local coal and timber merchant who had at the rear of his house stabling and a coal yard. This is now known as Pump Court and you may recall his name being mentioned under the chapter on Winterdyne as he used to cut the grass for Mrs Sturt. The last house on the corner belonged to Mr and Mrs Faulkner and family of three daughters with whom my wife was friendly.

Severnside North

Severnside North was previously known as Coles Quay in times past. We begin from the corner of Dog Lane, the first dwelling is No.17, called Quay Cottage, followed by Nos.16, 15 (which was half-timbered) and No.14, all of which were small private dwellings but some of these are holiday lets now. Next to these is a passageway with Court One overhead which currently leads to the garden of The Mug House Inn which was owned by the Gayle family in my youth after they moved from the Toll House on Bewdley Bridge. No.11 was the Page's family home and they sold weekend newspapers to both the local newsagents and direct to the public for those who called at their home.

The Quay Gallery used to be a builders' yard for Coldricks and opposite this was a flight of steps down to the river where there was a boathouse for hiring out pleasure boats and canoes. This was run by a Mr Dillon and I believe the boat business was owned by The Mug House in those days. At the weekends Mike Young and I used to fetch the boats back for Mr Dillon after they had been left by the courting couples! The ruling was that the boats had to be returned by 10 pm and if they had not been returned by 10.15 we would row up river to collect the empty boats and return them in a convoy tied to one another. It would take us a good hour to row from outside The Mug House to as far as Bridewell ford, situated half-way between Bewdley and Arley. Incidentally, The Mug House was named after the old system of sealing contracts with a mug of ale.

Passing No.7c known as The Quay Cottage, 8 called Chandler's Cottage, 7B called Kingfisher Cottage (now a holiday let) and Severn Cottage we arrive at the Riverside Cafe which was in fact two private dwellings in my youth. There was also a flight of steps opposite The Cock and Magpie public house leading to their boathouse used for the hire of pleasure boats. This was run by Mr Hurst and I believe he rented this from the owner of the Cock and Magpie. Lastly, at the end of Severside North is currently Merchants and this was two large private dwellings in times past but the Fish and Chip Shop just around the corner was in the same position as today. In those days the food was obviously fried in dripping which gave a totally different taste to those we eat now and Mike and I with a good many other friends would enjoy eating directly out of the newspaper wrapping – mostly chips as fish was a rare treat as it was beyond pocket money rates!

Dog Lane

Approaching from Dowles Road, on the left-hand side of the road is the car park which was previously a market on the site of the lorry/coach park section today. I well remember seeing the animal pens of cattle present but I have never actually witnessed a sale take place as this was later moved to Market Street in Kidderminster. The field around the market was the location of Bewdley Fair which was held on April 23rd each year and this was my Sister Florrie's birthday. It was also said that the cuckoo traditionally arrived on that day!

During the War the army had Nissen huts on the old fairground and the cooking was carried out in the cattle market sheds. I am not sure what the soldiers actually did because I was away in the army myself at this time.

Proceeding down Dog Lane, with the car park on your left, the first small house belonged to Frank Green, the Eel Catcher, whose wife would take the eels around Bewdley in baskets to sell. The next house (No.10) remains very much the same as it was when I was at school. This was originally occupied by the White family, but when they later moved to Catchems End the house was taken over by the local Postmaster. Next to this two cottages were knocked down and the remaining cottage (No.5) has changed little other than the fact that it was two dwellings at that time. We now arrive at Poppy Cottage and an adjoining cottage (which has no visible number) and both of these have the stable doors at the front which was a common feature at that time and the residents would lean over the bottom half of the door to watch the world go by and chat!

We now arrive at No.2 Dog Lane called Honey Pot Cottage and this has later had an extension on the side. No.2 was the Tolley family home and coal/timber yard as Mr Tolley was a local coal and timber merchant. On the site of the extension was previously a cottage and this was demolished in Wartime to enable an air raid shelter to be built. The house and yard was at the very bottom of Dog Lane and numbers 1 to 4 Tolley's Corner have since been built on the old coal yard. He kept a team of horses and wagons here and stored the coal before taking it around the houses in Bewdley. Mr Tollley had a wife, four sons called Jack, Bill, Harry and Jim and a daughter named Mary. Jim and Harry were in the Cubs and Scouts together and we became good friends. I was particularly friendly with Jim as he was my own age so Mike Young, Harry Purcell and Les Evans and I became a close group of friends. Mary was Cub Mistress of the 3rd Bewdley Cubs.

In the coal yard the family kept a range of pets. I particularly remember their large goat as I was interested in animals and it was very child-friendly and extremely placid! Mary married Ken Lewis who was in the Scouts also but has sadly since passed away. She now lives in Wheatcroft Avenue, very close to my home and I have been fortunate in speaking to her directly on the history of Bewdley and with particular regard to Dog Lane as her knowledge of this area is far greater than my own. With the yard being very close to the water, when the river was in flood they took the horses up to fields by Ticknell (off Park Lane) to graze.

I also recall my Father telling me how the horses used to be taken down a slope by the river (when they returned from working in the forest) to have their legs washed. On one occasion Dad told me about a tragedy which occurred here whereby one of the wagoners by the name of Chick Harrison was kicked during the process of cleaning the horses and was drowned in the river. A tremendous amount of importance was placed upon keeping the horses' legs and feet clean and this was carried out as a priority. Very early in the morning, before breakfast, the horses would be groomed before their days work as appearance was of utmost importance and they would always be turned out immaculately.

Standing at the rails by Tolleys' Corner, looking across the river is Bewdley Rowing Club but this was merely a patch of open ground when I was young and the Rowing Club was actually situated on the far side of the bridge on the riverbank where the flower-beds are now, opposite the old bandstand, with the river in-between. The boathouse was a flat bottomed boat with a changing room on top. Reverting back to the site of the current Rowing Club, to the left was several wooden bungalows and my friend Mike Young lived in the second one. To the right can be seen a concrete wall which was the area designated for swimming and a local person by the name of Tug Wilson taught people to swim there.

When I was at school, around the age of 12 or 13 years old, I recall the river freezing over from Blackstone to beyond Bewdley Bridge. There is a whirlpool at Blackstone Rock and the large blocks of ice in freezing weather became caught in the whirlpool and as this held them together in the spiral flow of the water, the blocks of ice froze together and this gradually built up across the river causing it to freeze solid. On February 21st, 1855 not far from the bridge a sheep was roasted on the river on one such occasion and people skated on its surface. Under one of the arches there is reference to this carved into one of stones and this can only be viewed from being on the river.

The houses to the right of the Rowing Club have changed little but The Chocolate Factory was situated between these houses and Bridge House (which was, of course, the Garden Cinema in those days). A friend of my late wife, Joan Purcell, worked at The Chocolate Factory in the 1960's making cake decorations such as sugar roses and other flowers. When I was 11 years of age one of the rooms was used for scout meetings and the leaders were Harry Williams, Norris Trout and Bill Gale. Sadly The Chocolate Factory burnt down in latter years and the land was built upon. Just past the cinema, at the end of the lane, on Bewdley Bridge was the old Toll House, which, as previously mentioned, was a sweet shop owned by the Gale family. Across from the Cinema, where the Bowling Green is now, were two fields owned by Mr Hurst until just after the War and when he sold this land the bungalows in Northwood Lane, then known as Rag Lane, were constructed.

Crossing the top of Dog Lane, on the corner of Severnside North are two cottages, Nos. 24, called Swan Cottage and 25 which I believe could have been four small cottages when I was young. Next to these is a gap providing access to Court One and other properties to the rear of Severside North plus a garage to the right belonging to Court Cottage. I believe a small cottage was probably knocked down to create the access. Reverting back to the doctors' car park, which was Dr Miles garden originally, can be seen a large copper beach tree in full splendour and is possibly all that remains of his garden. The school room was situated where the surgery currently stands and this wooden structure was where we had our metalwork and carpentry lessons and the girls had laundry and cooking tuition here.

The Fire Station was gardens when I was young and there was no access road through as this was housing in those days, joining the four terraced cottages built in 1826, which still remain, called Pleasant Place. Next to these private dwellings was access to the rear of the George Hotel and the Elim Church was built on the corner on land previously owned by the hotel but I believe this is now a WRVS luncheon club. During the War this was a factory.

Next to the passageway is the Bewdley Farm Shop which appears to have been stabling in times past, possibly belonging to the Tonks family who kept horses to pull the timber wagons for their forestry business. They lived in a house, since demolished, which was built on the triangular piece of open land opposite the Farm Shop. There was also another house next door which was called 'the coffin house' due to its shape but I never saw the people who lived there.

From the turning to No Road was an open yard with sheds at the rear used for keeping fish for Woods' shop and also for their delivery lorries. Harry Bishop from Load Street wool shop used to drive for Woods, collecting the fish from Birmingham Market very early in the morning. They used to stand outside in front of the sheds cleaning the fish and I recall witnessing this on my way to woodwork classes with the school.

Dowles Road, Patchetts Lane and Bark Hill

On the right hand side of where Woods Fishmongers shop was situated is the Horn and Trumpet public house which was the local drinking place my Grandfather and Uncle Cyril used when they played bagatelle. Next was an open yard belonging to the Coles family with their house at the rear. One of my school friends lived here by the name of Quacker Coles' and his Father was the local bookmaker, Unofficially, he used to take bets at the house and the local police were aware of this but turned a blind eye! The Coles family kept fowl and ducks which were left to roam freely and they would often wander into the road. To the right hand side of the yard is now the entrance of Mulberry House and this was built on part of what was previously Coles' land.

A little further on, covering part of the area where the bus stop is now situated, there used to be a Blacksmiths' shop owned by Ralph Jones who lived in Welsh Gate. Ralph used to shoe the horses for Winterdyne and Dad would deliver them to him, leaving them for me to collect when I finished school. Ralph would not be rushed and I often had to waste time waiting for him so I would help by pushing the handles of the bellows up and down to maintain the heat of the fire to enable him to get the iron shoes sufficiently hot to bend them into the right shape.

When the shoes were hot he would drive a chisel into one of the holes in the shoe in order to apply it directly onto the horses hoof to check the fit. If it did not fit he would heat the shoe again and get the right shape by hammering it on the anvil. He drove the nails into each hoof, twisted the end of each nail off with a claw hammer and using two hammers, one underneath the nail and the other he would use to hit the nail flat into the hoof. When this was complete the shoes were fitted with seven nails into each shoe and he would file the hoof and nails flat. This completed, I would ride the horses back to Winterdyne and during this time I absorbed a great deal of information on the process of shoeing horses.

The new Telephone Exchange lies back from the road and beyond this was a row of 5 terraced houses with a central path servicing them all and an outdoor toilet which still exists today. In the second cottage lived George Bishop who kept ferrets and each Summer I would take my ferret to him for breeding purposes. I had a Jill, the Hob being the male, and my first experience in trying to breed was a disaster. Being young and inquisitive I tried to take a look at the young ones which resulted in the Jill eating them. I learned very quickly that other than feeding there should be absolutely no disruption to their bedding when they have young.

There is currently a series of steps up to Venus Bank from this point and there are six recently constructed three-storey terraced cottages and a very old house to the right, set high upon the bank called Gibraltar. The next dwelling is now called Kendal Lodge and the land on which this was built I recall belonged to Bert Dalloway who was foreman bricklayer at Brintons. He constructed the sandstone garage at around the same time that I built The Glen (my current home) but the land was later sold undeveloped and the current house was later built. Beside this is a footpath leading to Patchetts Lane.

Crossing the road now to the opposite side of the Dowles Road is Sabrina Drive which was partly built on the site of the old Bewdley Tip where the local residents and businesses disposed of all their rubbish. Staying on the right-hand side of the road is Cherry Cottage which used to be occupied by the Ranson family and this has since been extended quite considerably from the original home. There is next a private road to the caravan park and to several houses in the region of the old Gas Works.

The land on the opposite side of Dowles Road was entirely farmland in my youth belonging to Patchetts Hill Farm and this is now Woodthorpe and Bark Hill housing estates. The large house to the right of the turning into Woodthorpe Drive belonged to the Pritchard family, the Mayor and Mayoress of Bewdley. A few years later Mrs Pritchard became Mayor in her own right after her husband passed away. A short distance past Pritchard's house, on the opposite side of the road was situated the Old Toll House which was occupied by the Poutney family and this is now the site of the Gas National Grid.

A little further along the Dowles Road, past several recently built properties, on the left-hand side is Highfield House which belonged to Mr and Mrs Terry Tolley and family, Managing Director of Brintons Limited. This house was built by Perrin the builder for himself but he never lived there as Terry Tolley purchased it from new. After he moved in I arranged for Brintons staff to carry out a considerable amount of work to the grounds in the form of creating ornamental fish pools with waterfalls, constructed with concrete and lined with fibreglass and resin. These were fed by a natural spring from the fields above. Eventually, we dammed the spring to form a large pool but it was a continual problem, not to mention the on-going battle with herons who were intent on devouring the fish!

Mr Tolley had a vegetable garden and when he retired and became infirm I carried out several alterations in the grounds, including building a footpath from the house to the vegetable plot to enable him to access this from his wheelchair. I constructed an exercise frame indoors to practice walking and generally spent a considerable amount of time with both him and his wife. I did this in appreciation of his kind help with the Scouts – in particular his donation of an old company van which enabled us to take the Scouts on trips to Scotland, Switzerland, Wales and many other places.

Mr Perrin sold an adjoining parcel of this land to William Birch who built a bungalow on there with his son. They were distant relations of mine and both worked for Hunts the builders. They later sold it on to people who became very friendly with Mr Tolley and I have not seen them since the home was being constructed and Mr Tolley's former home was sold.

Mr Tolley and his wife had two daughters named Janet and Elizabeth. Elizabeth married and Janet lived in a house on Meadow Rise and I helped on several occasions whenever Mr Tolley needed me. She spent more time living with her parents than at Meadow Rise, however, as she took care of her parents during their illness.

Next door lived Mr Tolley's brother who was an auctioneer for Phipps and Pritchard Estate Agents and there was a footpath running along the side of his property which led to Bark Hill. When Mr Tolley passed away I continued to visit Mrs Tolley to assist in any way I could. If she had any problems she would ring me and if I could not do the work myself I would arrange for someone who could. Sadly, Mrs Tolley contracted cancer and two days before she passed away she rang and asked me to visit her so she could thank me for everything I had done for her. She was a very nice person and I felt humbled by the thoughtful gesture. She also asked if I would continue to look after her daughter. This I did for a short time but sadly she too died soon afterwards.

Approximately one mile further down Dowles Road is a lane (I believe it was called Church Lane) and on the right-hand side is a gateway with ruins of what used to be the Berwick family home. It is hard to believe a group of five people lived here in this small detached cottage, four of which were fully grown men, two of whom were boxers! You may recall the Berwick family had a blacksmith's shop on the corner of Northwood Lane and were Churchwardens of Dowles. Their home was built in the clearing behind the church. The gravestones can still be seen but sadly there are no remains of Dowles Church today. I personally have never witnessed a church on this site.

In 1127, Wydo, son of Helgot, gave Dowles to Malvern Priory. Dowles was formerly in Shropshire but was transferred to Worcestershire for administrative purposes in 1895 and is divided into two parts by the Severn. Near to the former site of Dowles Church (the Church of St Andrew) is Dowles Brook which flows into the Severn and Skeys Wood lies to the west. The original church was of 10th century but was reconstructed in 1784 when the walls were partly demolished and encased with brick, destroying the mediaeval details in the process.

Dowles Manor, situated half a mile from the old church site, carried the date of 1560 above the main doorway but in reality it dated back to well before this time. It is interesting to note that on the suppression of the monasteries the Manor was sold in 1543 to Thomas Grey of Staffordshire, together with all the rights held previously by the monks for the sum of £320. Dowles was not mentioned in the Domesday Book, however, and at that time possibly formed part of the Wyre Forest. It was regarded as a lively country village in times past, boasting mills and a chemical works (which later became The Gas Works) as the following poem describes:

> *"Sweet was the sound, when oft, at evening's close,*
> *Up yonder hill the village murmur rose;*
> *There, as I passed with careless steps and slow,*
> *The mingling notes came soften'd from below;*
> *The swain responsive as the milk maid sung,*
> *The sober herd that low'd to meet their young;*
> *The noisy geese that gabbled o'er the pool,*
> *The playful children just let loose from school;*
> *The watch dog's voice, that bay'd the whispering wind,*
> *And the loud laugh that spoke the vacant mind;*
> *These all in sweet confusion sought the shade,*
> *And fill'd each pause the nightingale had made.*
> *But now the sounds of population fail,*
> *And only the sound of the waters fluctuate in the gale;*
> *While no busy steps the grass-grown footway tread,*
> *And all the busy flush of life is fled."*

History records state that in 1783 the Manor was conveyed by John Ottley to Samuel Skey of Spring Grove and upon his death was succeeded by his Son Samuel Skey. When he passed away in 1806, Dowles Manor passed to his daughters and co-heirs, Mary, Louisa and Caroline. Mary and Caroline later transferred their thirds to Louisa and her husband James Taylor. She died in 1822 and in 1856 the Manor was held by her son James Arthur Taylor.

Dowles Manor was later purchased in 1871 by Edward Pease of Darlington whose daughter and heir Beatrice Mary married Newton Viscount Lymington on 17th February, 1885, who succeeded his Father as 6th Earl of Portsmouth in 1891. In 1902 the Bewdley estate, including Dowles Manor, was sold in lots and the Manor House was purchased by Mr Jannion Steele Elliott. Since the War there was a serious fire there sadly which caused a great deal of damage.

Taking the exit through the gateway at the bottom right-hand corner of the churchyard, across the field until the riverside path is reached, turning right towards Bewdley, after a walk of approximately a quarter of a mile is a clearing of silver birch trees which marks the site of the old Bewdley Brickyard owned by Tommy Gardner. There was a stack in the yard and I helped to dismantle this when I was an apprentice at Coldricks at the age of

16 to 17 years. The clay for manufacturing these bricks was dug from the fields in this area and the four houses on the left-hand side of Spencer Avenue, numbered 5, 6, 7 and 9 were exclusively built with Bewdley bricks. These homes were owned by Tommy Gardner as the builder became bankrupt and he took over the houses in payment for the bricks. He completed their construction and the first house (No.5 in the block) was lived in by Elsie Postins and her son Stan. She was sister to Tommy Gardner and eventually became the owner of them all.

We now arrive at Gas Works House, Severnside which was built in 1840 to house the Manager of the Gas Works next door. Barges collecting the tar from the Gas Works used to call at high water just in front of the yard. When the coal was burnt off to produce tar the coke and breeze which remained was sold for burning domestically, in schools and larger houses for the central heating boilers – such as Winterdyne House. The coke was stacked in the yard and different local dealers would pick it up and deliver locally. Hubert Taylor, an extremely obliging man, worked for Coldricks and had a business of his own delivering coke and wood to the people of Bewdley. Sadly, while only in his 50's he had an accident while using a saw bench he kept in Tolleys yard whereby he fell on the blade and it killed him outright.

Beside the yard is a turning to the right (formerly into Gas Works Lane but now called Greenacres Lane). On the left-hand side is a large Georgian house which was the home of the Marlow family, owner of the Gas Works and the family grave can be found in Dowles Churchyard. Further up the lane, there is a new build in the Gas Works Yard on the right and next to this is Gas Works Cottage, currently still occupied by a member of the Bourne family.

Mr Bourne was the lamp lighter from High Street and immediately next door was a gentleman by the name of Jean Francois. He was a member of the Free French Army during the Second World War, staying at Ribbesford House and married a sister-in-law of Dick Keightly, called Renee. Dick has since passed away but used to occupy the bungalow on the corner of Greenacres Lane. He was an apprentice Painter and Decorator at Hancocks in High Street while I was serving my apprenticeship at Coldricks and when I purchased my first house in Lorne Street, Kidderminster Dick assisted me with the decoration. This leads us to the entrance of the Caravan Park and walking through here brings us back onto the Dowles Road.

Walking back towards Bewdley after approximately 50 yards, crossing over to the right-hand side of the Dowles Road (to the right of the driveway belonging to Kendal Lodge) is a pathway leading to Patchetts Lane. At the top of the lane on the right-hand side was the old entrance to Patchetts Farm upon which part of Bark Hill and Woodthorpe estates were built. This is now known as Patchetts Lane Conservation Area which in 1995-2000 there was a project in partnership with Worcester County Council Countryside Service and the local residents to create a natural wildlife habitat.

To the left is Patchetts Lane where a number of recently built dwellings exist but this was open fields in my day and part of the farm, with exception to the house in the left-hand corner, now known as No.109 'Jenton'. This was built for John Hamilton, a local Councillor and Son of the owners of Hamilton's shoe shop in Load Street in my childhood. This lane meets with The Hollow and on the left-hand side of the road there are two cottages on the bank above but these were three *small* cottages in my youth. The first one on the left was lived in by Hux Jones, a fellow member of the Bewdley Methodist Church where we were both Property Stewards and he was also the owner of the caravan site by the Hop Pole in Cleobury Road.

Welsh Gate, Sandy Bank and Wyre Hill

We now reach the bottom of the bank and to the right, where Venus Bank meets what was known as The Hollow (but is now called Bark Hill) there are several three storey houses on the left and on the side wall can be seen where the old houses of a similar style were demolished but there are recently built properties in their place now. These houses on the left go down as far as Gazelles the hairdressers and this used to be a pork butcher whom we nicknamed Porkie Bill Millward! Chris Poutney lived at 20A Welsh Gate (and his brother known as "Mann" who lived on Sandy Bank) worked as labourers in the Building Department at Brintons.

The large house on the right (No.37) was occupied by Sam Danby and his family. His daughter called Flow was a good friend of Mike Young and I. she also worked at Brintons in the Picking Room with her sister and later married Harry Williams who was a Scout Master and Fireman. It is interesting to note Welsh Gate was so called as it historically contained a toll gate on the road towards Wales. There are several around Bewdley which have been mentioned in the book under Dowles and Kidderminster Road in particular where criminals entered the town and could not be punished for their crimes once they had successfully reached this safe haven. This is the reason why Catchems End was so called as once those committing crimes reached this point they could not be arrested!

The beginning of Welsh Gate from Load Street end was The Star and Garter

Hotel (now the Welsh Diner) on the right-hand side and The Hole in the Wall on the opposite side (known as Granny's Tap currently). Next to The Star and Garter was James the butchers shop and in those days he had his own slaughter-house at the rear but this is an alleyway now leading to domestic dwellings. Beyond this was another greengrocers shop owned by Fred Harvott's family who originated from Far Forest.

We now arrive at another pub owned by Wilf Bishop called The Anchor which sadly suffered a dreadful fire in February, 2011 necessitating substantial repairs and beyond this was a sweet shop owned by the Poutney family. There was a private dwelling next door followed by a fish and chip shop owned by Mr and Mrs Nelson Darkes. I also attended school with their Son by the name of Jack and we were in the school football team together. When we won the cup at Aggborough I recall Nelson Darkes had the entire team to their family home for a fish and chip supper. Mrs Darkes was a lovely lady who helped in the family business serving fish and chips. This brings us back to the turning to Bark Hill and the entrance to The Hollow which I have covered at the beginning of this chapter.

Reverting back to the beginning of Welsh Gate, taking the left-hand side of the road now, the first of which used to be called The Hole in the Wall and is now Granny's Tap a Victorian Tea Room. All these properties were rented cottages in my childhood. A number of them have been used as shops since but when I was small they were all dwellings. Opposite the Anchor lived Cyril Poutney who moved from the opposite side of Welsh Gate after his parents passed away. A family also named Poutney lived in one of the cottages above. Another family by the name of Evans lived opposite the Woodcolliers Public House and I went to school with one of the daughter's by the name of Edna. Carrying on up the hill to what is known as Sandy Bank (which leads up to Wyre Hill) on the left-hand side was a cherrry orchard belonging to Jack Coldrick and this went through to Park Lane but a housing estate has since been built on this land.

Crossing the road now to the right-hand side, Hux Jones lived in No.37, across from which was Wyre Hill School but this was demolished after the War. It was a primary school when I was young which I believe my Father would have attended. From my memory, the families living in this area of Wyre Hill were: Birches, Blackfords, Whites, Darkes, Bishops, Shentons, Charlie Powell and the Dalloways. Charlie Powell had a speech impediment as my Father told me he fell and bit off the end of his tongue when he was a boy. He used to keep a donkey and cart in adulthood and went around the houses in Bewdley selling logs to the people and I recall the children used to taunt him due to the way he spoke.

Reverting to the left–hand side now and climbing to the top of the bank, Dad's family lived at No.14, in fact he was born here and my Uncle Chris and his family owned next door (No.15) together with the damson orchard at the rear which stretched as far as Park Lane, together with the land to the right–hand side of his property where several bungalows and houses have since been built up to Birch Tree Road which was named after the family. There is a commemorative plaque on the side of Uncle Chris' old house which reads "Bewdley Civic Society Award for Restoration 1994". A further sign advises these buildings were restored in 1992 by the County of Hereford and Worcester Building Preservation Trust Limited.

Cider Press

The yard at the rear of my Uncle Chris' home at No.15 is still visible and this was where the basket and besom making business was carried out. The Wyre Forest provided a ready supply of oak trees allowing an important local industry to develop. Uncle Chris employed some of the Bishop family in his business (who were related to his Wife, Aunt Emma) one of which was called Yarby and he helped my Aunt construct the besoms and baskets. This was big business in those days as besides the domestic market, Uncle Chris supplied baskets to all the carpet manufacturers in Kidderminster to carry the yarn.

The rim was made of hazel and the bowl of the basket was constructed from interwoven oak laths. A bill hook was used to shave the strips and

My cousin Alf weaving baskets

close-weave laths were used to make the baskets which carried the bobbins of yarn for the looms. He also made besoms from birch cuttings which came from the Devil Spadeful. The cuttings were made into bundles and stored for seasoning, then tied using strips of oak mostly, but hazel and willow was also used for this purpose. The end of the binding was tucked in using a bond poker and the pointed end of the handle was pushed into the broom-head and secured with a nail or peg. These were sold to all the large estates in the area. Some of the birch twigs from which the besoms were constructed and the oak for the baskets came from the Wyre Forest.

Uncle Chris' Wife made whisks which were small brooms constructed from silver birch twigs. They were made by stripping off the twigs using a cleft stick and the handful of trimmings were bound at one end with oak bands which formed the handle. Whisks were mainly intended for cleaning carpets and I well remember these being used at Winterdyne, including the use of besoms for sweeping the drive and stable yard. Some of the Bishop family also carried out charcoal burning in the Wyre Forest which was another of the local industries for which Bewdley was renowned.

Uncle Chris and Yarby Bishop making besoms

In the spring, when the sap was rising bark peeling was also carried out (mainly by women and children) as it was easier to remove at this time of year. Bark was an essential ingredient in the production of leather as it contained acid used during the tanning process.

Next came The Town Hall as I believe Wyre Hill was a separate village in those days and is actually one of the older areas, as was Wribbenhall, which developed before the town of Bewdley as we know it today. On the right-hand side of Wyre Hill, still ascending, there are a number of very old houses and Nelson Darkes lived in one of these and also a Mrs Shinton who it was stated had 22 children "twice over" as the saying goes. Child number 22 sadly died, but she had a subsequent child bringing the total to 22 once more, hence the saying she had 22 twice over! My Father told me that when they were children he used to play with Nelson Darkes such games as "Shoe the Donkey" where one lad, chosen as the donkey, was blind-folded and while he was being "shoed" and standing just in front of someone's front door, the person posing as the donkey would kick out at the door and the children would then run off leaving the "donkey" by the door to be caught! The Black Boy Public House (which was then known as The Blackie Boy) is next to this row of houses and Dad, Cyril and Joe Dalloway used to play dominoes here with some of their old school friends.

Eric Finch (who belonged to Bewdley Methodist Church) lived at the top of Wyre Hill opposite the Town Hall in a house with a long driveway, which was situated where the turning to Forest Close is now. This was demolished and Forest Close built on the ground. Eric was also a member of Bewdley Council for a number of years and was Mayor of Bewdley several times. He wanted to build a new Methodist Church and asked me to help him find a suitable site but unfortunately, despite many attempts, we never managed to achieve this. An ideal plot was suggested at Tickenhill but Eric was unable to gain permission as I imagine this was regarded as greenbelt land. After this he left Bewdley and went to live in Wales and I visited him there several times, together with his Wife, a retired school teacher. They had a son called David who did Morris Dancing and a daughter who lived in Bridgnorth. Sadly, Eric's Wife eventually ended up in a nursing home in Bridgnorth after he died. Gladys and I visited her there on several occasions until she too passed on.

Past Birch Tree Road, continuing along Wyre Hill, on the right-hand side is the site of the Old Granary which is now domestic dwellings, numbers 26 and 27. Beyond Saint Annes Primary School, on the right-hand side is a house by the name of Clovelly (No.22) which is a sizeable, architecturally interesting property with double bays and arched windows with a coach house to the left. This was possibly The Rectory and it is interesting to note this was the family home of Anneka Rice the famous action girl! She was a member of the Ranger Guides, under the direction of Diane Crane, who used to run this from her home and the Venture Scouts used to have joint meetings with them sometimes on Bark Hill, in which I was involved.

A little further on the left-hand side of the road was an area called The Pound. This was used to house stray cattle until they were claimed by their owners. When Bert Dalloway was Councillor, Bewdley Town Council tried to sell off the land on which The Pound was situated but Bert stopped the sale as he felt it was part of Bewdley heritage. Since then, however, part of this land has been used to create the layby near the school. Wyre Cottage is on the opposite side of the road and was possibly the original farmhouse as the farmland, owned by the Birch family, was situated immediately behind this and went down as far as the Cleobury Road. It consisted of grazing for the cattle and a cherry orchard and this is now Hales Park Estate.

Further up on the same side is No.132 Lavender Cottage and 134 is adjoining. These were the old cow sheds and milking parlour belonging to Mr and Mrs Birch and after they sold the farm they ran their milk round from here with their daughter, delivering to the houses in Bewdley until they later moved to rent the farm at Red Hill from the Whitcombe family who owned Kateshill, taking over from my Uncle Wilf Birch.

Opposite the farm are Tudor buildings dating back to 1165 and 100 yards further along on the left-hand side is Wyre Court, a black and white timbered building. All the land to the rear belonged to the Court and was owned by the Mayor of Bewdley (called Mr Frost) in my childhood but this, of course, has since been built on in the form of domestic housing. I have always considered it strange that there is no church in the immediate area of Wyre Hill, particularly as it dates back to the early 1600's and everyone attended church in those days, but thinking on it is possible the building further along the road which takes on the appearance of a church tower, possessing the same style of windows and bearing a similar weather vane, is the remains of an old church. At the very end of Wyre Hill is Summerdyne House and this was a private estate in my youth.

Reverting back to the site of Saint Annes School, to the left is a walkway from Wyre Hill which brings us to the school football field and provides access to Park Lane to the left, Wharton Farm (which used to be owned by the Wilkes family) is on the right-hand track and straight ahead leads to The Golden Valley. There are a number of footpaths covering both of Mr Wilkes' farms, so following the footpaths from the school playing field towards the Golden Valley; this was then a large wood of oak trees which have since been felled. At the bottom of the woods were two pools known as the Golden Valley Pools and these were surrounded by rhododendron bushes. In those days, this provided a Sunday afternoon walk for the local people, especially those from the Wyre Hill area.

At the top of the woods, after a very steep climb up to Light Lane, before the by-pass was built it was possible to walk along the top of the woods and across the fields to Park Farm and Haye Farm entrances. When you reached the stile there used to be a white stone-built barn beside an oak tree and my Father told me there had been a murder committed in this barn but this building has since been dismantled. The oak tree is still there to mark the area where the barn was situated and this must be in the region of two to three hundred years old.

Cleobury Road

Starting from the Woodcolliers Arms, this was owned by Mr and Mrs Holiday and their son John with whom I attended Lax Lane School. Next to the Woodcolliers was a coal yard run by Mr Moule a local coal merchant and their family home was adjoining, which is currently called Lilly Pad Cottage. We now arrive at No.74 Cleobury Road and this used to be occupied by Mr Ralph Jones, the local blacksmith who worked in Dog Lane. During the War Mr and Mrs Jack Alberts and their son moved in here from Winterdyne after Mrs Sturt passed away.

Crossing the road, the house on the corner of The Hollow and Cleobury Road (no.39) was lived in by Mr and Mrs Danby and I have covered this family in greater detail under the chapter on Welsh Gate. No.40 was occupied by Mr and Mrs Bert Bond, originally from Winterdyne but he later moved to work at the Sugar Beet Factory on the Stourport Road in Kidderminster. Bert married Jessie Parmenter from High Street and they lived in this house for a great number of years until they both passed away. The neighbouring row of houses, unfortunately, I cannot recall all the names of the occupants but Hubert Taylor the local haulage contractor lived in one of these. You may recall reading about Mr Taylor's tragic and fatal accident at Tolley's Yard in Dog Lane. Mr and Mrs Yapp lived at No.46 and this is now known as Daisy Cottage. As far as I am aware he was a labourer and I believe he worked for Coldricks on occasions and had connections with timberwork in the Forest.

Returning to the left-hand side of Cleobury Road now, No.71 was owned by Bert Dalloway and family and this is now known as Basils Cottage. Bert carried out his bricklaying apprenticeship with William Hunt and it was his employer who persuaded him to purchase this house. I remember Bert was as strong as a lion and on one occasion his workmates tied a large paving slab to his back and he rode his bicycle to deliver it to its destination! He was the person who obtained my job at Brintons and I well remember Bert was well known for his part in the tug-a-war team at the Company! Twelve months before I completed my apprenticeship with Coldricks he asked me to work with him at Brintons but I would not have been prepared to move at that time as I needed to obtain my papers but once I had finished he approached me again and that was how my career at Brintons began. I was happy working at Coldricks but they were paying a halfpenny under the union rate which was quite a lot of money at that time and that is another reason I moved. To the left of Dalloway's garage is a flight of steps called The Gob, which led onto Sandy Bank.

On the opposite side of the road are the steps leading to Bark Hill and this is called The Racks. A little further on brings us to the site where an old cottage has been demolished to make way for the large home which has been erected in the hillside. Many years ago I tried to buy the cottage that has since been taken down at auction. Although I bid up to £7,000 I was not successful as I could not afford to go any higher. Next to this was an orchard which stretched a considerable distance along Cleobury Road,

Returning to the left-hand side of the road now, a little further on from the Dalloway's cottage was a number of houses which have since been demolished. Next we arrive at a very large old house called Winbrook House where friends of Gladys lived and they had their own coach house to the right-hand side. Next to this was a large orchard owned by Joe Dalloway, a cousin of Bert who lived on Wyre Hill. In the orchard, close to the road was a pool in which watercress grew and people passing by often used to pick it.

We now arrive at Winbrook Cottage, built in 1782, which was occupied by Mr and Mrs Maynard. This holds special memories for me as Gladys and I spent our honeymoon here during the War. It has been extended on both sides (left and right) so it is much larger than when we stayed there. We stopped at Winbrook Cottage on another occasion after we were married and I recall there was a fire in the front room underneath the fireplace which set fire to the timbers. I spent the next two days replacing these and repairing the damage before returning to Kineton during my army days. I believe this could have been the toll house for Cleobury Road in times past. There was open land and an orchard from this point onwards and it was on this area Fort Mahon Place was built. This was so named to commemorate Bewdley's twinning with Fort Mahon, France and more details on this will follow under Scouting. This brings us to the turning to Merricks Lane, leading up to Wyre Hill.

Crossing to the other side of Cleobury Road again, just across the road from Joe Dalloway's orchard was another orchard continuing along the road until we reach Cherry Cottage. This house was built in 1899 and in my youth was owned by Jake Williamson and family. He had three daughters and I have talked about one of these by the name of Kitty under Lower Park. She married Reverend Hollis and lived in The Rectory for a short time before her husband retired and they moved away, taking his sister with them. I had a good working relationship with Jake and I eventually took over from him as Building Manager at Brintons after he sadly passed away suddenly while at choir practice in Wribbenhall Church. All his drawing equipment was passed onto me by his daughter, Kitty, which I was most grateful to receive. Past Cherry Cottage was a bungalow with another bungalow further along which was lived in by Mr and Mrs Hinton and their daughter. They owned the garage and petrol station which was situated next door but the garage has since been demolished and now has five houses (called numbers 1 to 5 West Court) built in its place.

Crossing to the right-hand side of Cleobury Road again, opposite the turning to Merricks Lane is a pathway up to Bark Hill with a cottage built in half brick and half stone to the side. There was an orchard next to this where several houses have since been constructed and the last house on the corner of the Lakes Road "Hill Side House" was built for Sid Exley from the brass foundry in Load Street. The entrance is approached by turning into Lakes Road and just beyond this is Yew Tree Lane on the right. At No.47 lived Bert Lancett, a Carpenter at Brintons and part-time Fireman in Bewdley and No.53 was the home of Neville Williams, a local Bewdley Policeman. He was well known by everyone, very popular and was great friends with Marjorie and Stan Woster and also my wife Gladys.

One occasion I had an accident in my Austin Princess car while returning with some of the Scouts from an outing. The Scouts stayed in the car until the Policeman arrived (which turned out to be Neville!) and then filed out one by one ...... about nine of them, to which Neville said "how many more have you got in there!" On another occasion Neville met my daughter Des in the street and asked her if she would like some sweets and she answered " no thank you. Dad says I am not allowed sweets from strangers." His response was "you know me. I was at your house yesterday!" to which Des replied "not in that uniform you weren't!" After he retired from the Police Force he and his family moved to Droitwich and while Gladys was alive we visited them on a number of occasions.

Reverting now to Lakes Road, the first house called The Lakes Bungalow was owned by Dr Lillie who practiced from Dog Lane Surgery. Returning back towards the direction of the Cleobury Road, the last existing bungalow on the Lakes Road (No.2) was lived in by the late Tony Goodwin, a local plumber and very well known character in Bewdley. Tony was involved with the Scouting all his life and he was friendly with fellow Scouts: Ken Beeston, Bill Cordle and Doug Aston, all of whom have now passed away. When they were too old for Scouts they started up a section called the Service Group and carried out any work required by the different Scout groups in Bewdley, ran competitions and helped at concerts to raise funds. Tony used to sing and Ken, Bill and Tony formed a band which was very successful in the local area. I recall one occasion where Tony sang a brilliant rendition of Al Jolson's "Mammy" at Callow Hill Church to raise funds for them.

Leaving the Lakes Road, we return to the Cleobury Road, and the housing estate now known as Hales Park which in my childhood was a large cherry orchard belonging to the Birch family at the farm on Wyre Hill. Keeping on the right-hand side of the road is a very large house at the top of Cleobury Road called High Bank and the following row of houses was another orchard in times past. This brings us to Hop Pole Lane with the Hop Pole Public House on the opposite corner. Further along the lane leads to Tanners Hill and what was known as The Bloody Hole. This I have been told was where a battle was fought in Charles 1st time and there is a small brook at the bottom with a bridge over which it is said was turned red from those injured in battle and this is how it gained its name.

Across the road from the Hop Pole is a row of Council houses which were built when I was at school. During the time I was an apprentice at Coldrick's I worked on several of these with Arthur Millward, a bricklayer and Bill Clark, a labourer, namely numbers 19, 34 (occupied by a Chemist by the name of Mr Master who worked in Load Street) and lastly 36 which was lived in by Miss Joiner, the teacher at Lax Lane School. There was another orchard alongside leading up to a house occupied by the late Ted Lloyd, a weaver at Brintons and very keen gardener, which has since been demolished. This brings us to Summerdyne House which is now a nursing home but was a private residence and part of a large estate in my childhood.

Returning back towards the Hop Pole Public House and continuing on the right-hand side there was an orchard, followed by a bungalow named Norley, which was constructed by Hux Jones who owned the Hillcroft Caravan Site in the 1960's. He later moved back to Wales with his wife Nora where I visited him several times until they both passed away. When Hux was leaving he asked me if I would like to buy the caravan site as I had carried out various jobs for him, including laying the concrete road up to his bungalow but Gladys did not want me to take this route and I was quite happy working at Brintons so I declined.

There used to be a post office and shop to the left-hand side but this is now a dwelling and past this is the road leading to the caravan site which is now filled with mobile homes and tarmac roads set amongst the beautiful countryside. Walking a little further along the Cleobury Road on the right-hand side is a semi detached stone cottage painted white (now called 1 Hawthorn Bush Cottage) which was lived in by Mr and Mrs Perks, a friend of the late Mary Marcus who lived a little further along at Summerdyne Cottage with her parents. Mrs Marcus was the daughter of Ben Bond who lived at 41 High Street and they had two daughters, Mary and Rosie and a son called Ben. When Mary left school she went to work at a grocer's shop called the International in High Street, Kidderminster.

When I went to Kidderminster with Mother we used to shop at the International so I got to know Mary very well and at times I would meet her from work and cycle home with her. She later married a person on the Scout committee at Bewdley by the surname of Clark and continued living at the family home to care for her parents. She often rang Gladys for a chat and the last time I saw them was while returning from a walk one Saturday and they told me they had been broken into several times and had paintings stolen. A few years ago she sadly passed away. I do not know much about Rosie other than the fact that Mike Young was very fond of her! I can remember Mary's brother, Ben, when he was very young standing at the garden gate. He was a friend of John Gardiner and myself and joined the RAF at the beginning of the War but unfortunately was killed just before the War ended in a plane crash. The incident did not happen during the course of active service but was a tragic accident.

Across the road from Summerdyne Cottage is a lane leading to the fields of Wharton Farm, together with a bungalow on the right. Back on the Cleobury Road, however, the next house used to be a private dwelling but this is now Jaycourt Kennels. Opposite the kennels, along a stretch of open land, we arrive at a large white house called The Hawthorn Bush which used to be owned by the Machiness family. The entire family worshipped at Ribbesford Church every Sunday while I was in the choir and Mr Machiness was the local Dentist. Hopleys Farm Shop and strawberry fields was simply open fields in my youth.

Opposite the gates to the farm shop is the entrance to Wharton Farm owned by Mr and Mrs Nellis Wilkes and their son and daughter. Mr Wilkes was the District Commissioner of the Bewdley Scouts in my youth. In those days he ran a large herd of dairy cattle but the farm has now been turned into a builders merchants and haulage business still owned by the Wilkes family. All the land up to where the by-pass is currently situated, together with the ground on which the golf course was built was owned by them.

On the left-hand side of the original farmhouse (which can be seen from the Cleobury Road) Mr Wilkes had two cottages built and these were originally lived in by the Butcher family. He also owned Park Farm which was where the Butcher family later moved to run the pig farm for Mr Wilkes. There were a large number of pigs kept here and all the sheds have now been converted into dwellings. The well in the field which supplied the water to Winterdyne has been repaired and is used by the Scouts when they visit the log cabin for their activities.

The entrance to Wharton Park Golf Course and clubhouse has been built on Wharton's Farm. At the right-hand side of the golf course is a small holding called Black Man's Titch. This was occupied by Mr and Mrs Dalloway, brother of Bert Dalloway and they turned this into a nursery and garden centre before moving to the flower shop in Load Street but they have since retired.

There are open fields until we arrive at the Running Horse and I worked on these premises while at Coldrick's when we re-roofed the public house. Next to the Running Horse is the reservoir belonging to Severn Trent Water, followed by a small holding called Rowan Oak which belonged to Mr and Mrs Millward who owned the greengrocers shop at the top of Dog Lane. This shop was later demolished to enable the Dowles Road to be widened. The family moved to Long Bank and continued to sell their vegetables by delivering them by lorry to the houses of Bewdley every Saturday morning and did extremely good trade until they retired. We now arrive at St Marys Church (which is currently a private dwelling) and I attended special services here while I was in Ribbesford Choir.

Returning to the by-pass island now, continuing up Long Bank, on the right-hand side there is a very large black and white house but I have absolutely no knowledge of the occupants past or present. A little further along, however, are two semi-detached cottages, and the first of these, called Hawthorn Cottage, was lived in by Mr and Mrs Cliff Lancett (son of Mr and Mrs Lancett of Park Alley in Bewdley). Cliff was a weaver at Brintons and I also attended Lax Lane School with him. This forms the beginning of Long Bank and I believe in times past these cottages were owned by Beau Castle Estate. The distinctive turret of Beau Castle can be seen on the horizon to the left of the cottages and what appears to be a maze is bordering the road. Next to this is the entrance to Beau Castle which was owned by the Butcher family in my childhood and I have talked about this family earlier in my book in the chapter on Winterdyne as Mr Butcher was Master of the Albrighton and Woodland Hounds.

Beau Castle was built in 1877 and dates from the Arts and Craft period, having been built in the Gothic style. George Baker, an industrialist and Mayor of Birmingham and Bewdley purchased the estate two years previously in 1875 and the castle was designed for a Quaker family by Baker, John Ruskin (Art Critic) and Richard Doubleday (Architect). It is said that the elaborate Alpine Oak balcony running across the rear of the property was inspired by Ruskin's travels through the Alps, the famous artist and Pre-Raphaelite. It is interesting to note Edward Byrne-Jones designed all of the stained glass windows throughout the castle.

The bungalow on the left of the driveway was where the gardener of Beau Castle lived; Mr and Mrs Williams and family. His son Rob was in 3rd Bewdley Scouts when he started and has been the DC of Bewdley Scouts but is now an instructor on a number of activities. The neighbouring house, called Orchard Cottage was built by the late George Tolley who was a bricklayer for Alf Hunt the builders in Stourport Road and he served his apprenticeship there at the same time as me at Coldricks. His parents lived on the site before he built his house and when it was completed he moved in with his wife (Ruth Gittins from High Street). After Ruth passed away, sadly George had an accident whereby he took a fall outside Teddy Gray's sweet shop and died.

The next property is Longbank House, and I well recall an incident with the owner of this property and Mike Young and myself when we fell off our tandem. Mike took his feet off the pedals and rested them on the handlebars which unbalanced us and we were unceremoniously thrown into the road. The owner of Longbank House just happened to be standing outside his home at the time and chastised Mike for behaving so irresponsibly.

The next property of interest is called Mussoorie. This is where the Busby family resided when they left Pleasant Place and next door to this was the old Post Office which was run by Connie Bray. This property has since been demolished, however, and on the right is the driveway to Spinney Wood. I attempted to purchase Connie's with 9 acres of land attached with the idea of building a bungalow but after bidding my maximum of £14,000 I was forced to drop out as it sold for slightly more. I was very disappointed.

This brings us to Pleasant Place, the previous home of the Busby family and my wife Gladys lived here with Betty Stanley when they first came from Birmingham. This property is now owned by Mike and Sue Durnie, Mike being a Lay Preacher and member of the Bewdley Methodist Church. This is followed by The Poplars which was owned by Mr and Mrs Jakes and family. Their son Bill was called up into the army on the same day as me, with Colin Harrison, Jack Bradley, Wokham Evans and also someone by the surname of Tyler from Kidderminster.

Next is a row of six semi-detached houses and the first one, called Runners End, belonged to the late Harry Bishop where he lived with his son Eric who now lives in Canada and I often receive calls from him from across the miles. I visited Harry frequently, especially when we were building the Scout headquarters, and he sometimes cooked me a dinner on Sundays before going back to work. The end semi, called St. John's Corner, just bordering St John's Lane was owned by Peter Johnson. Incidentally, the well known cookery presenter, Rustie Lee used to live in St John's Lane and Gladys has spoken to her on several occasions.

Opposite St John's Lane is a water tower followed by a house which has just been renovated. It was unoccupied for many years and I tried to find the owner (who lived somewhere in the Black Country) but unfortunately I was never able to locate them. I was interested in buying this type of property which needed renovation in those days. The next house was owned by Dr Malin's wife. She moved here after Dr Malin (one of the Bewdley Practitioners) was taken ill. She later moved to Pleasant Place, however, before selling it to Mike Durnie.

We now arrive at Lye Head Road which eventually leads to Bliss Gate and Heightington. Keeping on the Cleobury Road, the next property is a small holding which is owned by the Bray Family. Mr Bray's family came from Haye Farm in Light Lane and he now does a great deal of tractor work in the area. He has a steam exhibition some weekends and at other times he holds car-boot sales on his land. The next property of note is the Duke William Public House and the entrance to the Wyre Forest Visitor Centre is immediately opposite. This is used by walkers and horse-riders and also tuition in the education centre.

Wyre Forest is also the home of the famous Whitty Pear tree and the first record of this tree growing in Wyre Forest was placed by Edmund Pitts of Worcester in 1678. Much later, at a meeting of The Royal Society it was discussed and many interested people visited it. By 1862 it was dying and had begun rotting away and someone later set fire to it. The Woodward family living at Arley Castle across the river Severn had recognised the importance of this rare tree and fortunately had grown some from cuttings from the old tree before it was burnt down. These seeds do not germinate naturally so it is difficult to propagate them. At Worcester Naturalists' Club Field Meeting at Arley in May, 1898 it is documented that they admired two trees grown from cuttings from the old Wyre tree. One died and was felled in the early 1950's,

Very little has been written about these trees for some time but Mr Woodward possessed a young sapling he wanted to plant in the forest as near to the spot where the old tree grew. The date 30th March, 1916 was set for Mrs Woodward to plant this specimen and many influential people gathered from Naturalist Groups and friends from around the district. The sapling was about 6' tall and a plaque was laid to commemorate the event.

It is stated that this is the only tree of this type in the country until others were grown from its seeds or cuttings, so it was extremely rare indeed. The Whitty Pear has bunches of white flowers in May and June which produce small pear-shaped fruits in October. Its natural habitat is Asia Minor, eastern Europe and the Balklands but there are lots of trees, some quite old, in Western Europe; France, Austria, Germany, Italy, Switzerland Greece and Spain.

The next opening alongside the Forestry Centre is a lane off the Cleobury Road leading to approximately six houses owned by the Forestry Commission for people working in the forest. Dorothy Bowles lives in one of them as her late husband worked in forestry. She can also take the blame for me writing this book! Dorothy, an ex-teacher, is also a member of Callow Hill Methodist Church and started the luncheon club, taking place once every month, for pensioners to enjoy home cooked fare and friendship.

As you progress further along the road you will pass a cherry orchard and then a track which leads down into the forest, passing where a large amount of timber has been prepared for fencing and logs for burning. This path also leads to the old railway line towards either Button Oak straight ahead or left for Far Forest and right for Bewdley.

Returning to the Cleobury Road there are a number of houses on both sides of the road which I have no historical knowledge of as they are mainly recent constructions but on the right there is a turning called Chapel Lane which leads up to Callow Hill Methodist Church, or straight ahead leads to the Forest. In Glady's childhood, Callow Hill Sunday Schoolroom was attached to the church but it is no longer used for this purpose. It is a meeting room now which is rented out on occasions for weddings, funerals etc and is the home of the luncheon club which meets once each month. On the opposite side of the main road is The Foresters Pub and the turning to Bliss Gate Road on the left. About a quarter of a mile down this road is a turning to the right called Gorst Hill where my Uncle Jack Smith, Auntie Ethel and their daughter Jean lived.

When I was about 17 years old, Mike Young and myself used to cycle around the Far Forest Area and sometimes we would call and see Auntie Ethel, Uncle Jack and cousin Jean. They used to live at a small holding called Alton Cross which was owned by Uncle Jack's mother. She used to go to Kidderminster Produce Market on a Thursday and took vegetables, eggs and flowers or whatever she could sell. This enabled her to purchase a number of properties around the Far Forest area.

I always enjoyed going to see Uncle Jack as he was a very interesting person with his knowledge of the countryside. We used to take a walk around the lanes and he always carried a catapult, on one occasion he stopped and shot a rabbit in the hedgerow. I was fascinated by his knowledge of how to bud and graft roses and fruit trees, together with budding ordinary holly bushes with variegated holly and these can still be seen in this area today. Uncle Jack taught me how to do this and I certainly learnt a great deal from him. He also kept a pony which was about 12 hands (a hand is 4"). He kept this in the orchard but it was too small for me to ride.

Another of Uncle Jack's gifts was water divining. He used two hazel sticks which he carried in either hand and when walking over a spring the sticks would move inwards. I tried this but it never worked for me. When he found water, with the help of Mr Griffiths (Jean's father–in–law) he would dig down to the water and when he reached this he would begin to build a well with bricks. He would build up six to eight feet and then insert a piece of hardwood timber all the way round and continue building to the next six to eight feet until he reached ground level. All the brickwork was dry walling, which means no mortar was used, then from ground level he built a brick top to the well with mortar joints. This allowed people to construct a structure over the top with a winding mechanism so a bucket could be lowered to water level and raised again once full for household purposes.

Auntie Ethel always made Mike and myself welcome, was a very kind and homely person and as I was leaving she often gave me eggs to take home. She was just like my Granny Birch who moved nearby after my Grandfather retired from his coal business in High Street. My grandparents had a small–holding with cherry trees in Dark Lane and I enjoyed visiting them there. After Granny died my Grandfather moved to one of the Almshouses in Lower Park.

Wribbenhall

Starting from the Toll House by Bewdley Bridge which I have already explained used to be a sweet shop and was the home of the Gale family. The lane beside this (with Bridge House on the left) currently leads to the Rowing Club but this was the site of The Garden Cinema in my childhood and just beyond was the Chocolate Factory. There is a row of terraced houses where the Carter family lived in the very first one and the boat club next door used to be a large piece of open land with a footpath running across it leading to the wooden bungalows on the riverside. My friend Mike Young lived in the second one and I spent a great deal of time there in my youth. I recall in my younger days, during times of severe flooding the only way of accessing these homes was by donning a pair of wellington boots as they were always among the first to be under water. In fact their bungalows were totally surrounded by water until the floods subsided. The footpath makes its way along the riverside to Arley.

Returning in the direction of the bridge in Bewdley town, opposite the Chocolate Factory was a large piece of land going out towards Rag Lane (now known as Northwood Lane) owned by Mr Hurst. It was this gentleman who constructed the caravan site on this ground where the holidaymakers used to visit from Birmingham. Just past this is a footpath which leads onto Northwood Lane and next to this footpath was the gate to Pleasant Harbour House belonging to Arthur Goodwin and family. We are now back on the Kidderminster Road and we pass a number of houses on the left including the black and white semi-detached bungalow in Pewterers Alley which belonged to Miss Joiner, the teacher at Lax Lane School. Opposite this lived Miss Coldrick at The Nunneries, sister of Jack Coldrick the builder.

Immediately after Pewterers Alley, continuing on the Kidderminster Road is an old timber-framed house overlooking the river which has just undergone renovation, followed by a number of terraced cottages which have seen many hundred years of Bewdley life and have mainly remained unchanged throughout!

On Beales Corner is Severn House which was occupied by the Bainbridge family and I remember the daughter called Grace very well. She had a brother but I do not recall his name. Grace worked as a Secretary to Mr Rowe, the Bewdley Surveyor. Two large houses follow but the occupants of these were unknown to me. When we arrive at the other entrance of Pewterers Alley there used to be a large house which was demolished to accommodate the current Police Station. Just past the Station is the third entrance to Pewterers Alley and next to this is the garage which in my childhood was owned by Mr Jenks who lived in Park Lane, He had an assistant by the name of Bert Pye who carried out the mechanical repairs and lived in Severnside South with his parents where the local people visited to buy their weekly Sunday newspapers.

This brings us to the old Blacksmith's Shop which, as previously mentioned under Dowles, was owned by the Berwick family. Continuing along the

Kidderminster Road towards the railway bridge, just under the bridge on the left was a building where Palmers the butchers in Westbourne Street used to keep their animals. Sadly, the building no longer exists and this is just a patch of spare ground now. The next property of note is 33 Kidderminster Road which is a large house designed by Jake Williamson and was constructed by Hunts builders as their family home. Above this were fields belonging to the Binnions of Summerhill Estate.

The Binnions home was situated at the top of the hill and the French style homes have since been built upon their fields. The next property of note in Grey Green Lane is Yew Tree Cottage which used to be owned by Len Thomas and was lived in by Mr and Mrs Poutney and family. Len also owned the orchard next door on which he had a house built in 1938 for himself. This area is now called Gerlensta Court containing four detached houses and Len's family home called Gerlensta was demolished to make space for these. The original house was built by Coldrick's, the Architect was Godwin and the Bricklayer was George Bishop. I was the Apprentice Bricklayer at this time and George Davies (Snig) was the Labourer. The Carpenter was George Wallace and his assistant Bert Ince also worked on the house. The name Gerlensta came from a combination of the three family names of Gertrude (Len's Wife), Len and his son Stan.

A little further along Grey Green Lane now, on the left-hand side are a pair of sandstone piers marking where the main entrance to Summerhill estate was situated with Summer House Lodge on the corner. The main drive to the estate used to be through the sandstone piers, crossing over Grey Green Lane. It continued along the lane opposite until it reached Kidderminster Road and was bordered by Cherry Trees on either side. This section is now a lane servicing domestic dwellings on the left but in my youth there were no buildings along the route as it was just part of the beautiful driveway leading to Summerhill House. The lane then continued up towards Grey Green Farm owned by the Grangers.

There were allotments situated on the site of Damson Way, off Grey Green Lane, which was where the Smith family grew their vegetables for their shop in Westbourne Street. Carrying along this lane, past the footpath on the left leading to the railway lines (and beyond the pathway cutting across the field) was a bungalow opposite, belonging to Solomon Mann. This gentleman sold me a 4/10 shotgun when I was 17 which was very easily stripped down so it could be placed in a pocket. I still have this and have occasionally used it for shooting rabbits and pigeons. I worked with Solomon at Codricks as he was a part-time bricklayer. After he left the bungalow it was sold to a woman who regularly sold flowers from her home. If ever Gladys needed flowers we always purchased them from there.

Returning to the point where Grey Green Lane meets up with the Kidderminster Road, there is a black and white house and to the side of this was more fields belonging to the Binnion estate and further houses have been built on this land in recent times. Immediately after this is a driveway to 57 and 58 Kidderminster Road. On the right hand-side of the road was number 57 which was George Wallace's home and workshop. He was the local Carpenter and Undertaker and was assisted by Bert Ince. Number 58 was situated at the top of the drive and was a dwelling with an orchard occupied by George Wallis, his son and later his grandson Keith. Returning now to the Kidderminster Road, the next house was owned by a Mr Frank Green who was a gardener.

The next property of interest is No.69, called Cherry Cottage which was lived in by Mr Smith who farmed the fields next to the drive. This has sandstone piers which formed the main entrance to Summerhill in my childhood and I vividly remember the white gate leading to the house which was a continuation of the drive. The fields on which Mr Smith grazed his cattle are now Queensway, the council estate. There used to be a footpath passing through this land and I used to walk through here with Mike on a Sunday night after church.

Number 71 Kidderminster Road was built by Bishops, the builders of High Street, situated on the corner of Kidderminster Road and Queensway and the builders' son used to live here. Just past this were fields belonging to Jacksons' farm in my youth and a row of houses were built facing the Kidderminster Road, the last one being lived in by the late Fred Bishop who owned The Talbot in High Street at that time. This house was eventually passed down to Fred's daughter Sheila (now sadly deceased) and her husband Ken. Next to this there were more fields which is now a housing development, followed by The Old Wagon and Horses public house, owned by Simon Lloyd in my youth. He also owned some fields along the Habberley Road as he used to run the night soil cart business responsible for collecting all the waste from the houses around Bewdley as majority of homes did' not have water toilets in those days.

Stan Woster (who lived with his wife Marjorie at 99 Florentine Terrace, Catchems End) used to work for the council on the night–soil carts and after collection they would take the waste to Habberley Road and spread it on the fields. It was here where the vegetables were grown and sold directly to the public years after. The driveway marked No.87 Kidderminster Road was part of a farm owned by Mr Jackson and the entrance was on the corner of Habberley Road and Kidderminster Road. I worked on this farm while an Apprentice at Coldrick's.

Taking the turning into Habberley Road, just past the field where the night soil carts were emptied is Wassel Lodge on the left-hand side and adjacent to this was a drive a mile in length up to Wassel House. I recall many years ago, just before you approached the entrance to the main house, there used to be two whale jaw bones either side of the driveway! The Foster family who lived at Wassel House were wholesale merchants and they were related to the Woodward family. The Gordon-Smith family, that Gladys and I lived with in Parkfield, Chester Road, Kidderminster, also had family connections with Wassel House as Mrs Gordon-Smith was a Foster before marriage.

Just past the Lodge was a stile and a footpath going across the fields to Habberley Valley but this of course is now a golf course. The footpath led to Habberley Valley where in my youth Kidderminster held the Whitsun Parades. The children had their games in this area afterwards and of course Jennings Fair was also held here on a fairly regular basis. The Jennings family used to live in the house there and there was a small shop incorporated within the house selling sweets and treats.

Reverting back to the Habberley Road, opposite the golf course was a house lived in by the Mortimer-Smiths who bred spaniel dogs. Making our way back towards the Ramada Hotel, this was a family estate in my childhood owned by the Bache family. When in the Scouts we had our meetings in the barn here before I built the Scout headquarters. There are several open fields which lead up to some terraced houses aptly named Habberley Terrace and Gladys and I lodged here for a while shortly after we were married. Then there is the entrance to New Road and more terraced homes until arriving at The Rectory where the Reverend Hands lived with his family. There are several more terraced houses which brought us down to the old Police Station followed by two more houses, one was occupied by Don Williams while living with his parents and at 117 Kidderminster Road (the corner house) lived the Lawley family. Their son "Leo" was a School Teacher at Lea Street School, Kidderminster.

Keeping to the left-hand side of the Kidderminster Road we pass what is commonly known as the *smallest house in Wribbenhall*. This house is not numbered but is situated between 127 and 131 Kidderminster Road, close to the Rising Sun public house, where I used to collect the beer for the grooms at Spring Grove.

Crossing the Kidderminster Road, walking back towards Bewdley town, there are two similar detached houses numbered 142 and 144 which were built by Walter Cross (brother-in-law to the late Nancy and Ken Sollom). He constructed these after he had built two properties in Trimpley Lane, one of which was occupied by the Vicar of Wribbenhall and the other by Nancy and Ken. Walter later emigrated to New Zealand with his daughter where he lived until his death and I keep regular contact with his wife Phyllis by letter. Catchems End Fish Shop used to be Coopers, a Bakers Shop and Mr Cooper had a horse drawn vehicle he used to deliver the bread to the shops and homes around Wribbenhall.

Next we arrive at the lane on Lodge Banks, now called Abi Lane, where there are two cottages, number 124 was occupied by Jack Holford and his family (a groom at Spring Grove Stables) and 126 was the home of the Butler of Spring Grove. On the right-hand side were the gardens to the two cottages and these were later turned into allotments. The small Lodge estate was constructed on this land. On the left-hand side of the lane is a field with a small copse which used to be called The Rookery where a shoot was held at the end of May each year and afterwards the young birds were used to make Rook Pie. We now arrive at the Lodge for the farm at Spring Grove and opposite this was the drive down to Spring Grove Farm. On the right of the lane is the Cordle Marsh field with a footpath walk where parishioners from the Estate used to walk to church. The iron gate into the churchyard also leads into Wheatcroft and Spencer Avenue. This still exists to this day.

Returning to the Kidderminster Road at Catchems End we arrive at several terraced cottages followed by The Old Rectory occupied by the Harper family. This is now an Accountancy firm and at the rear of this property there used to be a stable and coachhouse, including a house for the groom but these have all been demolished. Continuing down the road passing the Cordle Marsh we arrive at Wribbenhall and All Saints Church where my parents were both married and buried, together with my Sister Florrie. The church was built in 1879 on a site given by W. C. Hemming Esquire, DL and JP of Spring Grove. It cost £6,000 to build, £3,000 of which was presented by Mrs Hemming. The large bell originates from Christchurch in Wribbenhall and dates back to 1841. Past the church is the entrance to the Parish Room and Clubhouse behind followed by the turning to Spencer Avenue which has been covered in detail under my chapter on Gladys.

The next building of note is the old Toll House at No.66 Kidderminster Road which was lived in by George Davis in my youth and I worked with this gentleman during my time at Coldrick's. This is beside an alleyway leading to Castle Lane and the house to the right of this was lived in by Mrs Bishop and family, a Seamstress in Wribbenhall. Her son was Harry Bishop who kept the wool shop in Load Street and I have gone into more detail about Harry under my chapter on Load Street. Passing another set of terraced cottages brings us to No.44 Kidderminster Road, which used to be a grocers shop called Pipers where all necessities were sold.

Next to this is the Great Western public house and crossing Castle Lane, passing under the railway bridge, to the left is a lane leading up to the Severn Valley Railway Station and on the right of the railway arches is a house (now called 1 Ropework Cottages) which bears the inscription Lowes Rope Works on the gable end. This used to be occupied by Dick Lowe, the owner of the rope factory and he was also Group Scoutmaster of 1st Bewdley Scouts. Lowes Ropeworks was situated behind what is now known as Stephenson Place and there is still evidence of the factory's existence today as many of the buildings have been retained and converted into domestic dwellings. Stretching the full length of the site was a shed where the ropes were produced which was called The Rope Walk and the man who worked here was called Mr Taylor, as did his daughter and they lived in Habberley Road.

The history of Lowes Ropeworks dates back to 1801 when it was established and in 1870 modernisation was brought to the ropery in the form of the construction of a steam house. Local carpet manufacturers were their main customers requiring twine, cord and thread for various tasks in the manufacturing process. The rope was constructed from natural fibres, mainly hemp and flax. In addition, Lowes supplied pit ropes to surrounding collieries and made bell ropes and timber felling ropes for local communities. The Company was selling their products worldwide by the late 1800's and of course their business was aided by Government Contract Work during the First World War, however, due to the fall in demand in the years that followed the business began to suffer and the ropery finally closed in 1972.

Walter Cross bought the premises from Lowes, who I recall was a friend of Sir Tatton Brinton. There was need for the construction of a proper road and during my time at Brintons Sir Tatton asked me to send several loads of ashes from the boiler house to construct the driveway. Walter rented the property to Ken Sollom as it became the premises for Bewdley Print, with an entrance leading onto the Stourport Road. The Ropeworks site was later sold to Ken. The Wives of both Walter and Ken (Phyllis and Nancy) were Sisters and they all belonged to Bewdley Methodist Church. As previously mentioned in my book, the Cross family later emigrated to New Zealand and Walter's Son moved to Australia. In addition, I regularly visit Lilly Bridgeman (another Sister of Phyllis and Nancy) who still lives locally on Wribbenhall Estate and is unable to leave the house now due to ill health. Nancy sadly passed away just before Gladys and we were very close friends.

Next to the Ropeworks is The Red Lion in Westbourne Street (formerly known as Whispering Street in my childhood). A little further down on the left-hand side was a butchers' shop (No.14) owned by Palmers and this used to have a bow window to display the meat. Palmers also had the area of ground underneath the railway arch on the Kidderminster Road where they kept their animals for slaughtering. The doorway to the slaughterhouse was between 14 and 16 Westbourne Street and the animals were taken one at a time on a rope to the area behind the shop where they would be slaughtered and butchered. I well remember the dreadful noise from the pigs as they were being killed.

What was in recent times Severnside Studio, in my childhood was a Grocers Shop but today I believe it is a domestic dwelling. I remember carrying out roof repairs during my Apprenticeship to Whispering Cottage (No.12) which is next door and the double doors between 9 Westbourne Street and Caudle Cottage used to be a coachouse.

Several houses down there was a vegetable shop in the front room of a house occupied by the Smith family and they used to grow their vegetables in the allotments in Grey Green Lane to sell to their customers. Their Son (known as "Wockam") joined the army at the same time as me and we travelled on the train together to Cleethorpes. I transferred from the Worcesters to South Staffs while Wockam remained in the Worcesters. He was sent to the Middle East but sadly was killed in action. The Smith's cottage, with another two besides, was demolished and The Malt House has since been built upon this ground.

On the opposite side of the road is Malt House Row and on the site of the car park was another row of black and white cottages but these were demolished and I was involved with this process during my time at Coldrick's. Crossing the road which led to the old Wribbenhall School are several terraced dwellings with a courtyard containing more cottages at the rear, accessed by a passageway between 238 and 239 Whispering Street. My Granny and Granddad lived in No.2 for a few years before they moved to Spencer Avenue. At the corner of where Whispering Street met with the Kidderminster Road was a small shop selling groceries and sweets and this is now Severn Valley Guest House. The local Post Office was just beyond the row of terraced houses at No.24 and I used to collect my parents' pension from here. I often see the old postmistress when I attend the Methodist Church in High Street.

Reverting back to Whispering Street now, there was a piece of land attached to the corner house owned by Ted Miles, the local painter and decorator and he kept his decorating materials in the shed on this land which bordered the Stourport Road. The old coachouse and double doors with sandstone piers (comprised of Bath stone) at the corner of Stourport Road was the entrance to the yard and his home was the cream painted building to the right of the gates. The passageway to the right of Woodbine Cottage was a driveway to a dairy business belonging to Johnny Thomas who later moved to Load Street. The milk was bottled here and then delivered to the people of Wribbenhall and Bewdley.

On the corner of Stourport Road and Station Road was a small cafe owned by Bill Cordle from the Scouts. He applied to the Council to have mobile refreshment wagons positioned at Blackstone but permission was refused. On the opposite corner was Alf Hunt's family home with Hunts Builders yard behind, with the exit placed a little further along the Stourport Road. Further along, No.92 was Harry Oaks home where I used to take violin lessons every Saturday morning.

Crossing the Stourport Road now opposite what used to be Cordle's Cafe is No.8, called "Braeside" which was Ted Bath's family home. Ted was responsible for the purchase of all commodities for Brintons Limited and his Father constructed and lived in the first large house on the right-hand side of Spencer Avenue. He and his wife brought their family up in this house and both Ted and his brother Cecil worked for Brintons. His Brother, known as Ciss joined the Police Force and was made a Detective. When he retired from the Force he took up the position of Security Officer at Brintons.

The next building of note was Styles offices with warehousing behind which is called Mill House today. Opposite Styles was an open piece of land containing a selection of horse chestnut trees which were planted on top of the site of the mass grave of the people who lost their lives to The Black Death. It was out of respect for the deceased plague victims that people passed through this area quietly and it was thus called Whispering Street. It was not until 1930's the name was changed to Westbourne Street. On the corner of this land is now a transformer belonging to the MEB. There is a walkway beside which leads to a park containing a memorial cross with a lych gate in front of the old school buildings. This area in times past was the churchyard and church for Wribbenhall known as Christchurch. This was built in 1701 at the expense of the local people on land owned by Lord Foley since 1728.

In 1750 he and the parishioners had a disagreement over who should retain the keys to the church and Lord Foley had one door padlocked and another bricked up claiming he was in his rights as it was private property. The church and its grounds were not conecrated until 1841 and following the dispute the people of Wribbenhall decided in 1879 to erect the new church we know as All Saints today.   There is an inscription on the lych gate at the old site of Christchurch which reads *"This old churchyard was restored and made into a garden of rest by public subscription – 1949."* In addition, if you look very carefully there is another inscription on the front of the old steps (below the lych gate) dating back to the original church which quotes Psalm 26 verse 8 *"Lord I have heard the habitation of thy house and the place where thine honour dwelleth."*   It is interesting to note when Christchurch was demolished in 1890 the bricks were used to construct Westbourne Place on the Stourport Road.

Opposite the lych gate was the old Wribbenhall School where my Mother and Des attended.   There were two schools, the National School which belonged to the church which opened in 1830 and the Boys School which by 1834 welcomed girls also. These both took children of a similar age but latterly became the infants and junior schools for Wribbenhall children when they amalgamated but sadly both of these closed in 1978 and are now domestic dwellings. Past the old school building was a small lock up shop at No. 232 Westbourne Street (currently owned by E. R. Clifford Limited) which was a fish and chip business owned by 'Fanny' in my younger days but has also been a glass engravers. Next to this was an open space and a barn which I believe was a coach house belonging to the Black Boy Hotel opposite.

Immediately before the Black Boy Hotel is an entrance to Ricketts Place. This is so named as it was the workplace of Tom Ricketts, the Wheelwright and Blacksmith and this road continued down onto the Stourport Road in times past. From the Stourport Road entrance, facing Ricketts yard, on the right-hand side was the blacksmith and wheelwrights shop. Tom Ricketts used to repair the cart and wagon wheels, including replacing the iron rims around the wheels and brake replacements for the wagons. The wagons for hauling timber from the forest and carts and drays used on the farms often needed maintenance and it was carried out here in his workshops. He had one helper and this person did majority of the shoeing of horses. I had to take the cart horses from Spring Grove Farm here to be re-shod. The buildings have now been converted into dwellings.

To the right of this junction, facing the river was a warehouse belonging to Styles the corn merchant. As I was making my way to violin practice on a Saturday morning I remember watching the drays stood in the road and there was a large hoist protruding from the Styles building containing a pulley wheel to lift the sacks of corn from the drays onto the different floors. These doorways are still visible.

Adjoining Styles was a house belonging to the Whitmore family, Mr

Whitmore being a local Dentist. This is now called Victoria House and has been converted into individual flats. I recall Mr Whitmore had a son who was a painter and decorator called Viv and I worked with both him and Dick Keightley during my time at Coldrick's. The house on the corner of Stourport/Kidderminster Road (No.2) was lived in by a Mr Bill Davies and his family and he was a bricklayer, Just a short distance from this is The Dog Wheel at No.6 (formerly known as The Homestead) which was the family home of Tony Blackstock who worked in the offices at Brintons Limited. Records state that this property was extended in 1733 and I am sure many more alterations have been added since but this house contains an abundance of period features! The original dog wheel has been preserved in the kitchen as the spit used to be driven by dog power but the machinery to drive the spit I believe has since been removed.

The next property of note on this side of the Kidderminster Road was No.12 where Dr. Lawrence lived and ran his practice from 1929 to 1971. Gladys worked here with Marjorie Woster and I have talked in detail about this under my chapter on Gladys' life. A plaque has been erected on the house wall by the Bewdley Civic Society to commemorate this, which reads "*Dr. George Lawrence, Founder Member and Chairman 1947–65.*" Crossing the road from Dr. Lawrence's practice was a large house in my time which stretched a good distance into the road as the Kidderminster Road was very narrow in those days. This house was demolished to enable the road to be widened and the current Police Station was built upon this land.

This brings us to The Black Boy Hotel which holds a great deal of history. Bewdley was deemed a Royal Borough in 1472 and at that time was owned by the Crown. At the commencement of the English Civil War (1642 to 1651) Bewdley was a Royalist borough and an avid supporter of the King. After Charles I was beheaded in 1649 he was succeeded by his son Charles II. He returned to Scotland from France in 1650 to recover his throne but in the Battle of Worcester was defeated by Cromwell. This battle finally ended at "The Bloody Hole" in Bewdley which is situated in an area off Hop Pole Lane. While the Roundheads searched for The King he hid in an oak tree in Boscobel close to Wolverhampton and took exile on the continent until restoration in 1660. During this period the Royal Toast was forbidden and as Charles was of dark complexion they would toast to the health of "*The Black Boy Across the Water*" and this is how the Black Boy Hotel earned its name.

SCOUTING

Scouting in Bewdley was made up of three groups: 1st Bewdley Scouts was attached to the Baptist Church and was run by Mr Quayle and Dick Lambert, 2nd Bewdley Scouts was attached to St Annes Church and was led by Harry Williams and lastly 3rd Bewdley Scouts, Wribbenhall, was run by Dick Lowe.

Major Webb opening Scout Headquarters

I have been involved in scouting most of my life and have had only a few breaks from it for reasons beyond my control, such as when I was in the army and during various building projects. I joined the Cubs when I was 7 years old and the headquarters of the Cubs was in the School Room in Park Lane at that time but this was demolished many years ago to widen the road. The room belonged to St Annes Church and we were called 2nd Bewdley Troop, St Annes.

We met on a Thursday evening from 7 pm to 8 pm and our Cub Mistress at the time was Milly Ashford from Severnside South who lived with the Pritchard family. Milly had a helper called Peggy Wall and some of the boys who attended were: my friend John Gardiner, Neville Pritchard and his brother Gerald Clee, Jim and Harry Tolley. We were taught old–fashioned Scouting such as knot–tying the reef knot, bow–line and sheep–shank. We were also issued with a Tenderfoot Card which shows the flags of the British Isles: the Union Jack, St Georges, St Andrews and St Patricks. It also illustrated all the knots we were taught to tie, together with first aid. The first example of first aid I remember was fitting a triangular bandage as an arm sling and during my life it is fair to say I have found the knowledge I gained all those years ago have remained firmly with me and I have called upon the teachings often.

Some evenings in the summer we used to go up Park Lane to a field now used by the St Annes School which was part of Wharton Farm owned by Mr Wilkes the District Commissioner. He was a good friend of Baden Powell as they were in the Boer War together. We used to play cricket or rounders and other times on a Saturday we went to Habberley Valley to play. We also had two camps in the grounds of Wharton Farm and used to fetch the milk and drinking water from the farmhouse each day for the camp. I recall one day one of the farm dogs attacked Mr Wilkes' daughter and I shall never forget this. It knocked her over and I can still see her mother dragging the animal off her and I believe the dog was destroyed afterwards. Apart from that unfortunate incident, I enjoyed my first camp but I shall always remember the poor girl's suffering. I do not recall anything about putting tents up on my first cub camp as I expect the Scouts erected these for us but I do remember singing around the camp fire in the evening and I do not know how long we stayed but it would not have been more than a week.

At the age of 11 I went on to join the Scouts. In those days they used to meet at the old Chocolate Factory by the river, just past the Picture House. Harry Williams was the Scoutmaster and some of the older Scouts were Norris Trout, Norman Gardiner, Tom Wall, Bill Gayle and there were several others whose names escape me. They, of course, were much older than us and their interests were different. I did not find it very interesting at first as I found Milly's teaching style was more geared to my age group.

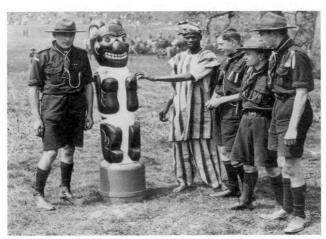

Eastnor Park Jamboree

Our first camp was at Aberystwyth about a mile or so from the sea. The site was on a farm by a river so most of the boys spent their time swimming. Dad had given instructions to Harry that I was not to go swimming so I had to watch which did not really please me and really spoilt my camp. We went down to the sea, however, where we went on a fishing boat and caught mackerel. Most of us were successful in catching something and I can remember the bait was strips of skin cut from the fish and was suspended on the hooks, attached to a line which had to be dropped into the sea from the side of the boat. We were allowed to keep the fish to take back to camp and cook for our tea. When the camp was over I do not remember how we returned to Bewdley but it was possibly by lorry. Another time I remember playing cricket with the boys at the Smethwick School Camp when they came down for their two-week summer holiday.

When I left school and started work at Spring Grove Stables I did not have time to go to Scouts as I had to work many evenings when the Webbs family had been hunting. When they returned at the end of the day we would have our work cut out in grooming the horses after the day's hunting but when I started my apprenticeship at Coldrick's I went back to scouting as I had more time on my hands during evenings and weekends. Dr Bob Miles was the Scoutmaster and we met at the Old Grammar School in High Street. The Scouts were Harry Purcell, Les Evans and Harry Tolley who were all in the 2nd Bewdley and Mike Young was in the 1st Bewdley Scouts.

When I was about 13 or 14 I went to a jamboree at Eastnor Park and we had to build heather huts for shelter. These were constructed by a series of panels 4 feet in width with sapling uprights and cross-bearers spread at approximately 4 inches apart, back and front, for the heather to be woven into. The heather and timber came from the forest and Devils Spadeful. The

The Gang Show, "Maypole Madness"

1st Bewdley huts were shaped like bell tents and the ones we constructed took on the shape of ridge tents. Dick Lambert was the Scoutmaster for 1st Bewdley Scouts at this time. Once again, I do not remember how we got to

Eastnor Park but the most important event was when Baden Powell rode around the camp on horseback and this is the only time I have seen him in person.

Things went very quiet in Scouting for a while. Although we still met some evenings until the War started I assume most had joined the TA in Kidderminster, which was called the REME (Royal Electrical Mechanical Engineers). I joined the St John's Ambulance when the War started and did my evenings on duty at the Parish Room in Wribbenhall with Harry Bishop. We were on duty from 9 pm until 6 am after which we returned to work. I also joined the Mounted Home Guard with Dad and used to meet at the Dick Whittington Public House on the Wolverhampton Road. The main member of this organisation was Mr Engleheart of Kinlet Hall and there were several other members of local gentry from around the District. I did not go into the army until I was called up in 1941 as I had to finish my apprenticeship first.

After the War, when I returned home I remained friends with Harry Bishop and it was at this point he approached me to draw the plans for the new Scout Room in Wribbenhall as he was chairman of the 3rd Bewdley and his son called Eric attended. He told me Major Webb had offered a piece of land to rent for the Scout Room at the top of Spencer Avenue in the area which formed part of the Maypole and the entrance could be made from Spencer Avenue. I agreed to do the drawings for him and surveyed the land. It was not an easy site for building on as it was far from level and on the side of a bank. In 1948 I had the plans passed by Mr Rowe, the Surveyor of Bewdley but at this time I had committed myself to building a house in St John's Avenue for Mr Jack Morris so I had a very full schedule of work!

Opening of Scout Headquarters by Major Webb

Harry Bishop asked me if I would build the Scout Room with the help of others, including Bert Dalloway whom I worked with at Brintons as he was Building Foreman at the time. Harry obviously helped, together with Charlie Ferris (as Group Scoutmaster he was referred to as Skip), his Father Mr Harry Ferris (who worked for Vales, the Building Engineers) and not forgetting the essential help we received from Mrs Sarah Ferris who kept us plied with regular cups of cocoa and on Sunday's she cooked Sunday lunch for me! Assistance was given by Bill Purcell (Mayor of Bewdley, also a manager at the timber yard in Severnside South), Arthur Goodwin (a local plumber), William Cordle (Gardener/Chauffeur in Wribbenhall) who had a son called Bill in Scouting and Mr Spencer also from Wribbenhall. Don Williams (who worked for the MEB at that time) did the electrics and the Scouts themselves helped with wheeling bricks and digging soil from the bank. Charlie used to try and keep these in order which was not an easy task with some of them! The Scouts used to meet in the loft over the stables at The Heath in those days which was owned by Mrs Bache. This, of course, is now known as the Mercure Hotel.

Building work commenced and as the site was on such a steep slope Bert and I decided to get the foundations out on the north-side of the building. We used the stonework and bricks from an old chimney stack previously situated at Slingfield, Brintons for the foundations as it had been decided to take 40' off the top of the chimney for safety reasons. The pieces of stone weighed approximately 1cwt each and the bricks were cleaned by Charlie and the Scouts. When we had built the north-side and half of the front and back to a height of approximately 6' this brought the foundations up to the existing ground level so we could level out the site. For the next few weeks, Charlie and the Scouts began moving the soil (which mainly consisted of sand) and this had to be rammed to compact it. The sand from the site was also used for building but it had to be riddled to remove the stones and Harry and his Father did the majority of the mortar mixing.

Once level, we removed the ground for the remainder of the foundations. With the help of Bert we soon built everything up to damp course level but then he seemed to lose interest as he was a very keen fisherman but came back on rare occasions after this time. I still continued with the help of Charlie, Harry Ferris and Harry Bishop, plus some Scouts who carried out the labouring duties. One of these which readily springs to mind was Lionel Poutney who was good company and very useful – in fact he also helped me with The Glen. On a Saturday night I was always on my own as everyone else had a night off. Harry Bishop was at the shop in Load Street until late and after this he used to run a Whist Drive at Wribbenhall Parish Rooms with the help of Nancy Lester to raise money to help to pay for the Scout Room. After I finished working at around 9 pm I used to go down to the Parish

Rooms and present the prizes. For the record, the total building costs for materials was £700 and, of course, all the labour was voluntary. In wintertime during darkness we loaned lighting from Brintons and the MEB kindly tapped into the mains for our supply so it cost us nothing. Ralph Osbourne, Works Engineer of Brintons supported us in many ways, for instance supplying a concrete mixer and numerous other tools. Jimmy Douglas (a Haulage Contractor) delivered the bricks to us and without this support the project would not have been so easy to organise.

When majority of the brickwork was complete we laid a concrete floor over the kitchen and Rover Room (the oldest Scouts at that time were called Rovers) for a storage area housing the tents etc. To do this we had to make a mixing area on the bank above the Scout Room so used timbers on which to wheel the concrete across from the mixer. The mixer was loaned from Brintons and had to be brought across the Maypole from the Lodge Banks via lorry together with the sand, gravel and cement (supplied by Thomson and Parkes including the bricks and cast iron gutter which they let us have at cost price). The brackets for the guttering were made at Brintons by the Blacksmith and Bert arranged for this. The windows came from Hopes of Birmingham and were supplied by Harry Busby, Gladys' brother who worked for them and these were also at cost price. On the day we concreted it was a very cold night so we had to cover it well to prevent it from freezing and spoiling the concrete. I do not remember all the helpers but there was a very good turn-out and that was the major part of the work complete.

Bill Purcell supplied the roof trusses and angle iron for purlins, covered with asbestos 'big six sheets' and also the wooden doors and frames. When it was completed Major and Mrs Webb came to open it and Major Webb said he never expected to see the building complete. He agreed to donate the land to the 3rd Bewdley Scouts and fence it in for us. When the fence was erected he extended the area of the boundary to the top of the Maypole. He also said we could have anything we would like so Mrs Webb donated a new wheelbarrow. Now the land was ours we decided to make a proper entrance at the top of Spencer Avenue so the Cubs raised the money for the gates and it was made official by Len Thomas who was a Solicitor at Hemmingways of Bewdley. After we completed the brickwork and hung the gates for the entrance, with the building complete I started back with Bewdley Scouts with Don Williams as Scoutmaster. I spent one night a week helping Scouts and had to cycle over from Kidderminster as Gladys, Des and I lived in Lorne Street at the time, which could be very cold in wintertime as Scouts wore shorts in those days!

Harry Bishop was chairman of the parents' committee and the members of this as I remember was Don's mother, Mrs Williams, Gladys (my wife), Mrs

Grainger (who had a son in the scouts), Nancy Sollom, Nancy Baker (a friend of Harry's who helped in his shop), Mrs Christie (who was in the choir with Gladys at Bewdley Methodist) and Bill Cordle (Senior). This was the committee responsible for raising funds for the group and at that time we had several hundreds of pounds invested which brought in an income. We were a very rich group in scouting in those days

I did not attend many annual camps as I had to work at Brintons at holiday times and after three or four years we started Senior Scouts for when the boys reached the age of 13 or 14. Don Williams and I ran this group. Eric Bishop was made Scout Master for the Junior Scouts, assisted by Eric Bradley and the boys ages ranged from 11 to 13 years in this group. Don and I always worked well together and Don always got the best out of the boys. The scouts were David Thomas, Pip and Neil Coles, Peter Johnson, Frank Owen, Graham Bickley, Grant Balmer, Paul Chambers and Peter Paige.

We all stayed on after 9 pm when the junior scouts finished for the evening. At our meeting we decided upon our hikes and annual camps, plus solved any problems which occurred. The first item I remember being raised was to go to Kanderstag in Switzerland which is an international camp site but as we had never done any mountaineering other than in Wales at our annual camp it was decided we would do two camps in Scotland before venturing to Kanderstag. To gain physical fitness after I finished a day's work I would run along Bewdley river side to Arley and return along the opposite side of the river.

One camp I particularly remember was a weekend spent at Gilwell Park. This began in 1919 as a Scout Activity Centre with training and conference facilities for Scout Leaders and was set in 108 acres of beautiful woodland on the edge of Epping Forest, north east of London. Scouts trained here when taking their Woodman's' Badge. I arranged for a van from Brintons to take us to Gilwell on a Friday evening after the van driver had finished work. The driver would be Fred Oaks and I arranged all the details with him so that he would collect us on the Sunday evening and bring us home.

I would like to acknowledge at this stage how helpful Brintons always were with scouting activities. I do not remember the date, but we prepared ourselves for Gilwell by erecting tents in the dark and being as quiet as possible to prevent disturbing other scouts camping there. So when we arrived we pitched our tents as practiced and the exercise proved very successful as the scouts next to us said they had not heard us at all! After pitching the tents we decided to go for a swim to freshen ourselves up but next morning we discovered swimming was banned after dark, certainly from 9 pm. No one else had seen us fortunately! There were different activities we had to do in the camp, one of which was attending the church service on the Sunday morning and all in all I think everyone enjoyed their weekend. On the Sunday evening Fred arrived to collect us and we packed everything on the van ready for our return home.

Another of our annual camps was at Callander in Scotland in August, 1961. We departed from Spencer Avenue at 6.40 pm after loading the van and collected Peter Page from Greatfield Road in Kidderminster about 10 minutes later as Don began to get used to driving the van. After leaving Kidderminster we made our way to Bridgnorth and everything seemed to be going well. Next we passed through Wellington, Warrington, Whitchurch and Preston when our first problem occurred whereby the pipe blew off the radiator. We had to wait for this to cool down before putting water in and to our surprise, in the bottom of the bucket was a fish! We took mercy on him and placed him back in the river then we were on our way but I did not feel we could really trust the van. It was not long before we were in trouble again but this time we were not so lucky with water and had to fetch it, about a pint at a time, from a pool in the field!

Once more we were on our way and began climbing up Shap which was very steep. The van began to rattle and my hope of progressing further began to wane but we did manage to get to the top and as soon as we started to descend again the noise abated. It was beginning to get light so we stopped to check on the water level in the van and to our surprise it was alright so we were on our way again … but not much further before the rattle deteriorated and the water level had dropped to nil. After filling it from a stream we now found it was running out of the radiator quite rapidly which Don felt was due to the pump. The only course of action now was to find a garage as soon as possible and how far we went I do not know but the van rattled on steadily to Lanark. We found a garage and the mechanic confirmed it was the pump as Don had forecast and he said it would take approximately three hours to fix. He advised us to take it to a nearby garage specialising in Bedford repairs by the name of Daniel Ross (Engineers) Limited, St. Leonard Street, Lanark. This we did and were fortunate enough to find they had a pump in stock. We were told to return at 10.30 am so we went to get a drink and Don bought some film for the camera while I rang Gladys. The work was duly completed and I still have the receipt for this. It is interesting to note it cost £5-0-8.

We eventually arrived at Callander to find the ADC and GSM waiting for us and they gave us some useful advice on the surrounding area. We progressed to the farm where we set up base camp and it was not long before we had our first meal ready. We decided to begin our hiking journey straight away, passing through Callander into the hills. It was a very clean place and the boys bought postcards to send home. That evening we began our first climb which we found rather stiff after being up all night. We set up camp, ate and decided to turn in early in preparation for the following day's climb which would consist of a three-day hike but some of the boys chose to go for a climb up the hills before turning in. They were not away long before returning to camp and I was woken by Pip's radio but decided not to tell him to turn it off as I felt he may be struggling to sleep but I was wrong. Next morning I found he had gone to sleep and left it on so his battery was run down by morning!

That morning we rose at 6 am so as to have an early start but it was raining and the progress was very slow as we did not get away until 8 am. We had not travelled far when we had to put our capes and leggings on as the rain was very heavy but we were still hopeful the weather would improve! We carried along the reservoir where we came across a fisherman who had been camping all night and started our first long climb up into the mist and rain. After climbing approximately 1000 feet we met other climbers and began talking to two young people out on their first climb. They confirmed we were on course for the direction in which we needed to travel to reach Loch Earn. We stopped a short time after to eat sandwiches and began to find the going rather tough with the boggy ground. The weather began to pick up a little and the sun shone through the clouds so we started our last climb of the day but for me this was the toughest. Once on the top, between the hills, Ben Vorlick was on one side at 3,224 feet and the opposite mountain range was 2,500 feet. The valley we walked between was approximately 2,000 feet above sea level.

We removed our kits and took a well deserved rest, while Grant, with all his energy, ran up the one side of the mountain until he could get the first glimpse of Loch Earn. Once again we continued our journey downward which was much easier now the sun was shining! About half way down we decided to have our ration of chocolate and Don also took the opportunity of taking photographs as we moved off once more. About a mile from the bottom I thought we might camp as it was very nice and quiet but the boys decided they would prefer to camp beside Loch Earn for the night.

Again we moved on and just before we reached the bottom Don and I decided to go forward and find a camp site while the lads rested. We searched around and decided to have a word with Major Stewart who gave us permission to camp anywhere near the loch. We wanted to walk about 2.5 miles along the road where he always gave the scouts permission to camp but returned with the good news they could camp by the Loch. We retraced our steps, this time with the scouts following and walked around the side of the Loch in search of a suitable site. There was little choice and we decided, against my better judgement, to make the best of it as the base was a mass of pebbles which did not provide very comfortable sleeping quarters!

Once we had selected our position the next important job was a hearty meal of potatoes, corned beef, rice and custard. It sounds awful but we were so hungry is tasted wonderful. The meal was followed by Ryvita biscuits and after a short talk with the lads it was decided after a night's rest we would aim to rise at 8 am. The hour was decided for me but I have to say I would have preferred an earlier start! We turned into bed but next morning it started to rain and before 8 am I heard movement in the camp and found some of the lads had wet bedding from the rain as they had moved during their night's sleep and ended up outside their tents! We decided to have our breakfast before starting a fire to dry the wet bedding and clothing. This consisted of porridge, sausage, Ryvita biscuits and jam, washed down with a cup of tea! We now gathered wood together for a real good fire which we soon had roaring away and the clothes quickly dried ready for our next expedition approximately 9 miles further on.

Going along the road soon began to take effect on my foot as I had only just invested in new boots and they had not been properly broken in. The going was tough and Don was having trouble with his feet also. We stopped at a small shop while Don carried on and we refreshed ourselves with an ice-cream. Grant ran to see if there was a train but without luck and we were soon on the road again. It really started to rain heavily and it was approximately 5 more miles to reach our destination. We caught Don up at the Post Office and he decided he would wash his feet in the stream. I continued to the next village to ring Gladys to let her know how things were going. Pip and Grant decided to come along as Grant was proving himself to be one of the fittest!

When we arrived at the village the local shop was raided for postcards and I believe everyone sent word home at this point to let their parents know they were well. Grant, as usual, was dashing around and managed to locate the grave of Rob Roy MacGregor in St. Angus Church, Balquhidder who died 28th December, 1734. The famous folk hero was known as the Scottish Robin Hood or simply as "Rob Roy" or "Red" (due to the colour of his hair) and was regarded by the nobles as an outlaw of the early 18th century as he stole from the rich to give to the poor.

We all decided to look around the churchyard and then moved onto our campsite, arriving at about 6 pm. It was a farm by the side of Loch Voil belonging to Mr Ferguson and we were certainly made very welcome. We sheltered in the tractor shed while a heavy storm passed over before climbing up to our campsite and pitching tents. We arranged our meal which consisted of cold food – sardines, jam, Ryvita biscuits, buttered biscuits and a cup of tea to follow. We discussed our plans for the following day, which proved to be the toughest yet! An early start was decided but during the night the wind became very rough and I rose at 5 am, much to the disgust of everyone. I think it proved to be a wise move as was discovered before the day was over! Breakfast consisted of meat loaf, Ryvita biscuits, jam and margarine, followed by a cup of tea. After clearing away I visited the farmer to thank him for his hospitality but unfortunately there was no response at the farmhouse.

At around 8 am it was decided at the last minute we should climb the hill Craig Muir (which was 2,156 feet high) instead of going round the mountain, as it was a beautiful morning. We were on our way once more to the summit but Peter Page found the going quite tough and when we reached the top we had to wait around 20 minutes for him. This gave us chance to take a little rest and we used this opportunity to have a good look around the countryside from such a brilliant vantage point before descending down the other side of the mountain. This looked absolutely beautiful on such a lovely day and Don was busy with his camera. When we reached the base we had to remove our boots to wade across the river Balrag. After we crossed the water we had lunch which consisted of cheese and biscuits and Ryvita and took advantage of the lovely sunshine and rested. I decided to carry on walking slowly as my foot was still giving me a great deal of trouble and at the time we were passing through boggy terrain which made the walk less pleasurable.

When we reached a farm we had hoped to seek permission to set up camp but surprisingly were refused by the farmer. I decided to send Don back for the van so we could return to base–camp for the night and while we waited for him to return with the transport we visited a local cafe for refreshments. On return to base we cooked our meal of potatoes, peas and luncheon meat and, of course, the usual Ryvita biscuits! We later agreed upon the time of 7 am to rise next day when we would make our way back to Brig O'Turk to complete our expedition. To do this we caught a bus at 10.15 am which took us to Brig O'Turk and we retraced our original route back to base–camp but alas the weather was inclement and we were not able to take any photographs. Brig O'Turk is derived from the Gaelic *TURIC* meaning wild boar. We had a very pleasant day around Loch Venachar, through the forest and hills and this I would not have missed for anything! At 1 pm we stayed on the side of the Loch for lunch and had cheese, jam, dates and not forgetting our old faithful 'Ryvita'! At about 5 pm we arrived back at base to cook our meal of potatoes, peas and corned beef, followed by prunes and custard and tea to drink.

This brought us to the end of the expedition and the lads decided to go to the pictures at Callander at 7.40 pm, returning to camp at 11 pm before prayers. We decided to rise at 7 am the next day and begin another journey into the Trossachs to the Lake Menteith, with the afternoon reserved for shopping. For breakfast we had bacon, biscuits, porridge and jam, plus Ryvita, followed by a cup of tea. We then began another beautiful day to Loch Katrine from where Glasgow's water supply originates.

After Don had done some filming, we made our way to Abberville where I bought meat pies for lunch, followed by a cup of tea before progressing towards Lake Menteith, the only lake in Scotland We went across to Castle Island in Lochleven by boat to visit Lochleven Castle where a guide informed us it was best remembered as Mary Queen of Scots' prison from June 1567 to May 1568. It was also the place she was forced to abdicate in favour of her infant son, James VI, on 24th July, 1567.

When we returned to base-camp we decided to go straight to Callander to buy presents for taking home. During the evening we advised the ADC we were leaving early the following morning and I again visited the farmer to thank him for the use of his land. At around 8 pm, in the pouring rain, we stopped to see the Forth Bridge but the weather was not good enough to loiter long so we made our way towards Edinburgh to pass down Princess Street. This we did and returned straight home afterwards as the weather was diabolical! We finally arrived home at 11 pm and I believe this was one of the best camps we have ever been on. For our first senior camp, we could not have had a better group of scouts for the task!

We next started making plans for the following year and decided upon Kandersteg International Scout Centre in Switzerland. The centre began in 1923 with Lord Baden-Powell, who, after the first World Scout Jamboree, had a dream about a place where all scouts from every part of the World could meet. I made all the arrangements for travel and it was agreed both Don and I would use our own cars for the scouts' transport.

The RAC provided us with maps of the route and also booked our crossing by boat from Dover to Calais. We travelled overnight and had one stop in France where we camped in a field by the side of the road. Next morning we moved on early as we wanted to get to Switzerland as soon as possible but it was still dark for the latter part of the journey. I rang Gladys to let her know I had arrived safely and we had to report to the scout headquarters at Kandersteg to give details of the party.

Afterwards we made our own arrangements for our stay, initially deciding to go for a short hike to get our bearings. On our second day our plan was to reach the glaciers where there was a wooden hut for us to stay the night. Soon after we started off we stopped at a cafe for the boys to obtain refreshments as this would be the last place they could buy anything before we returned to base. To our surprise there was a troop of girl guides from Kidderminster and the leader was a friend of Ralph Osbourne, the Works Engineer from Brintons Limited at the time! When I arrived back home, therefore, he knew all about our trip.

During the first evening on the glaciers, watching the clouds moving below us as the sun was setting, together with the snow on the mountains which reflected all the colours of the rainbow was a glorious sight I shall never forget. After a night's rest we descended back down to base camp and the following day we went by train to Berne to enable the boys to buy gifts to take back home. We had enjoyed our stay but it was over far too soon as it took us two days to return home because we camped one night at a farm in France to break the journey. After breakfast we were soon on our way again and made the journey back home.

We then began planning for the next summer camp and it was decided we would go to the Cairngorms in Scotland. It was in 1962 and as Hilda, Don Williams' wife was expecting their son Alan, he would not be able to make summer camp scheduled for August. At the same time Gladys was not well and was recovering from an operation. I really did not want to leave her but Dr Bob Miles felt it was important to not let the boys down and persuaded me to go with the assurance he would attend to Gladys while I was away. I drove up in the van but do not remember much about the journey or the hike as I was preoccupied with thoughts of Gladys, although I do recall we saw the workmen constructing the ski slopes that were not marked on the map.

We completed our days hike in the area and made our way back to camp. The farm we stayed at was owned by an old lady who seemed to be very lonely when I visited her and would have kept me there talking about the area all night if she could! The following day we made our way to Fort William and I contacted the District Commissioner of Scouts to find us a camp site. This he did and the day after we climbed Ben Nevis. When we reached the summit it was snowing, despite being the middle of August and the boys began snowballing each other in celebration! We made our descent and the following day visited Edinburgh and drove down Princess Street before returning home.

When the camp was finally over I cannot honestly say I was sorry as I was so worried about Gladys all the time I was away and it was a relief to return home. I am sure the boys must have been disappointed as it did not reach the usual standard Don and I had maintained at all other times which was due to our unfortunate circumstances. I believe it was the worst camp I have

3rd Bewdley on our way to Switzerland

ever been on but soon after we were arranging our next adventure where we planned to return to Kandersteg in Switzerland which was a great success!

The next trip was pony trekking in the Black Mountains in Wales. I contacted the farmer who had ponies to hire and made all the arrangements for a weekend expedition. When we arrived the farmer agreed to come with us and show us the way. About half-way around he stopped at a pub to enable everyone to take refreshments and Don has told me since that he fell off the pony and did not manage to remount very easily! Apparently, in an effort to mount the pony he was a little too energetic and managed to jump straight over the top and ended up on the floor the other side. He has told me recently he had not been pony trekking since and he never *wanted* to do this again. I was certainly not aware of his difficulties at the time!

As the boys were getting older, going to work and starting college, I decided to finish scouting as my work schedule at Brintons was very full and included many weekends. I was also constructing a bungalow for my parents and felt I could not manage it all. I missed scouting but had no choice but to give it up for a while. I had a break for two to three years and was then approached by Eric Bradley who asked if I would be prepared to return and run Venture Scouts. We met at Bark Hill at the old Air Scout Headquarters as they were not doing many activities with the boys at the time. I did not know how it would go as I had not met any of the scouts before but it soon settled down well.

I encouraged the Venture Scouts to arrange different outings and one of these was Mike Crane who was always interested in birds, so we went to Slimbridge Wildfowl and Wetlands Trust which was founded by the naturalist and artist Sir Peter Scott in 1946. It is situated on the banks of the River

St. Georges Day parade around 1956

Severn in rural Gloucestershire and was formerly part of the Gatcombe Park Estate. It is interesting to note Sir Peter Scott was the person responsible for bringing Canada Geese into the UK many years ago.

Another of the Venture Scouts was Nigel Fletcher who was interested in theatre so I arranged a trip to the Swan Theatre, Worcester which was enjoyed by all. We arranged several night hikes in the Wyre Forest and Rob Williams was very keen on this sort of pastime. Invariably, these took place during the winter and we used to build a fire and have our supper around it.

As Mike's Mother 'Diane' was District Commissioner of the Guides in Bewdley, we had several meetings with the Rangers and Venture Scouts at her home. We talked to the Scouts and Guides about going to either Switzerland or Fort Mahon. I explained to them the hikes in France would not be very good as it is all flat countryside but it was decided France would be the chosen venue. This meant we would need to visit the area before taking them to camp and January was decided for this to take place. As previously explained, Diane Crane was DC for the guides and I was acting DC for the Scouts. Eric Bradley was Group Scout Master for 3rd Bewdley Scouts and Vick Morgan was GSM for 1st Bewdley Scouts.

We travelled through the night in my car and were stopped by the Police for speeding but after a chat with the Officer he sent us on our way! After that everything went very smoothly and we arrived at the hotel I had booked through the RAC in Fort Mahon. We were welcomed by everyone and it was arranged we would camp at the School for the stay in August. We went down to the beach which would be used for some of the activities, including the camp fire and visited different shops to make arrangements about food and assess prices to see what we would need to buy or bring with us. With a busy weekend behind us, we travelled back on the Sunday, passing through London in the dark as the miners were on strike and there was no street lighting at the time.

For the next few months we prepared for our trip and it was decided the Venture Scouts and I would travel down before the main party. Diane and Eric would leave the following day with the Scouts and Guides. When we arrived we pitched our tents in what would have been the school playing fields and prepared for the arrival of the main party the following day. We cooked the meal for their arrival at noon and made the arrangements for each day's activities. I arranged to take them to the marshes where the ducks used to come to roost at night and also the locals would have hides for shooting the ducks when they arrive to roost. Unfortunately, no ducks came, the reason being we possibly made too much noise, so it was not a very successful expedition!

It was also arranged with local people for a parade to process around Fort Mahon and we were asked to lead with the band. This seemed to go down very well with a large number of people around the streets and was appreciated by the committee. We then did the campfire on the beach and quite a number of local people attended but unfortunately being by the seafront the acoustics were not very successful. The Guides and Scouts were allowed out during the evenings to do whatever they wanted and a good time was had by all. Each morning we used to collect French sticks for breakfast and any food which was needed. I recall we ate a large quantity of tomatoes at that time, which were cheap and very plentiful.

The main event was a trip to Paris and the Venture Scouts stayed behind to cook the meal. The coach and driver were our own from Bewdley and when they went to Paris they visited Le Louvre where they saw the Mona Lisa and completed the day with a boat trip on the Seine. They then returned to camp where a meal was waiting for them of chicken, potatoes and vegetables. The following day the Ventures travelled to Paris to visit the Louvre and the trip on the Seine and I remember struggling to stay awake and missed most of the boat trip as a result of the noisy duck shoot the night before which had disturbed my sleep! The main party returned the following day but we stayed behind to tidy up the camp site before our journey back to Bewdley.

MY FIRST JOB AT SPRING GROVE STABLES & FARM

I left school two weeks before I should have because Dad had arranged a job for me in the stables at Spring Grove. They asked for me to start before Christmas as it was busy at that time with Major Webb's children returning home due to the school holiday and also as it was the middle of the hunting season. I found it very hard as the grooms were older men. Head groom was Burt Evans and he became very friendly with the Ladies Maid to Mrs Webb. They had to get married and I remember Mrs Webb was not at all pleased about this but they were given a house at the farm where they lived for a number of years.

The other grooms under Burt Evans' direction were George Rogers and Jim Halford (who I particularly liked working with and he had a son around the same age as me). His job was cleaning all the riding boots and as Major Webb was ex-military, he was extremely particular about their cleanliness. Jim Halford lived in the second of the two cottages on the left hand side of Lodge Banks Lane at Catchems End. The Butler at Spring Grove House lived in the first cottage and the land opposite was allotments at that time but these have since been built upon.

Spring Grove was originally built between 1787 and 1790 by Samuel Skey. Samuel was born in 1726 and he lived to the age of 74. He began his business life as an apprentice grocer in Bewdley and amassed a considerable fortune manufacturing dye stuffs – Vitriol and Sulphuric Acid. In 1775 he used some of his fortune to buy 270 acres of land from Lord Foley on which Spring Grove House was built upon. This was completed in 1790 and the grounds were landscaped by Capability Brown. Its name is gained from the ground springs which bubble up through the underlying sandstone.

It is interesting to note John Constable visited Spring Grove many times from the year 1811 to 1835 to see Maria Bicknell, a relative of Samuel Skey, who became his future wife and created several sketches of the estate during his visits. The house remained in the Skey family until 1871 and continued in private ownership until 1970. The last private owner was Major Harcourt Webb for whom I worked when I left school, founder of the famous company of Webbs the seed merchants. Major Webb was a friend of Baden Powell, the founder of the Scout Movement, as they both served in the Boer War together which took place from 1899 to 1902. Major Webb was very involved with scouting in the local area and I have already covered this subject in more detail in my book under Scouting.

Mrs. Webb was a terror to the staff and was a stickler for detail. She used to come down to the stable yard each morning, sometimes with the Major if he was not at work and would go around all the horses with a basket of carrots and each one had to be washed thoroughly and cut straight in half for her to feed to the horses. There were about eight to ten hunters in the stables and she would inspect each of these in turn. One was called Gay Lassie, a dark bay coloured 'brood mare' who was extremely well behaved. She was famous having won top prize in several shows and featured in the Players cigarette packet photograph collection on horses which gave her history on the reverse of the card.

Another of the horses was called Golden Sands, a chestnut horse which ran in the point-to-point races at Chaddesley Corbett and Worcester and he won most of those he entered. Sometimes he was beaten by a horse named Odell so there was great rivalry between them both but I do not know who the owner of the latter was. I remember Golden Sands was a terror in the stable. He would come towards you open-mouthed as you entered the stable and continually kicked at the boards which shattered around him. He took some considerable strength in handling him but he was better behaved when being ridden.

One day when the Webbs were on holiday, one of Mrs Webb's horses had colic and died. This consists of a twisted gut, which is extremely painful to a horse, causing them to roll around the floor in agony. The first course of action in such cases is to make the horse stand. At the time it was our lunch hour and the other grooms were upstairs having their meal but I remained in the Saddle room to take my lunch. Soon afterwards, while walking in the stable yard, I noticed the horse lay on the floor (which is unusual) but it was too late. I had never witnessed a horse suffering from colic before and have never seen one since but this left a lasting impression on me. Understandably, when Mrs Webb returned from holiday she was none too pleased as he was one of her personal favourites.

When the hunting season was finished we were given other jobs to do as some of the horses were turned-out into the parks to graze. One of my tasks was to clean the clock tower in the stables which was full of flies so I had to spray them with fly spray which made me feel very nauseous. I can honestly say I have never seen so many flies with exception to when I was in Egypt!

The Chauffeur for Spring Grove House was Mr Howard Duce. Mr Webb used to drive his own car while Mr Duce was Chauffeur to Mrs Webb and it was a known fact by the remainder of the staff that Mr Duce had a drink problem. He was also the son of one of the Gardeners who lived in the Lodge on Kidderminster Road. His job was to see the gates were closed at night and at that time the living quarters were one side of the drive and the sleeping quarters were on the other. When they retired for the night the gates were locked but I am not sure whether Howard actually lived there.

I was later sent to work on Spring Grove Farm which I quite enjoyed. Mr Huckson was the bailiff and his son Raymond was the head cowman. His other son by the name of Geoff was an odd–job man and Arthur Philpotts was the Wagoner who lived in the cottage next to the Cordle Marsh and Maypole Piece in Lodge Bank Lane. Mr Burt worked in the fields including carrying out hedge cutting duties and he lived in one of the pair of Salantarn Cottages, while the Groom lived in the other. This name came from the public house which dated back to 1777 called the Salantarn Arms which was situated along a footpath used by the railway workers and eventually led to Kidderminster. The Gamekeeper on the estate was Captain Atkinson and he also used to carry out any building work required on the farm. Captain Atkinson served in the Boer War as did Major Webb during which time he was wounded by a shot to the head which left a raised mark where the bullet had struck. Major Webb found him work on the estate and he lived in a cottage at Rhydd Covert with his family. This is now the site of Kidderminster Scout Camp.

I used to have a horse and trap to travel around the estate to carry out some of my tasks. The horse was jet black and called Nigger. I would visit all the fowl runs most days which consisted of a wire netting enclosure to keep them secure. One day, when I was returning from lunch a fox had climbed the wire netting and set about killing the poultry. I do not remember how many were killed but he certainly managed to destroy a considerable number of them. I was also responsible for cleaning out the poultry houses and there were approximately 60 to 80 hens in each enclosure, totalling around 200 birds. There was one pen of Plymouth Rocks which were golden in colour; the other was Rhode Island Reds and both of the breeds were bred to provide good table birds for use at Spring Grove House. Some days I would have to collect the eggs when Mary Williams, the Dairy Maid, was busy.

The other task I had to carry out was to look after the calves and these were housed in wooden cowsheds which looked over Sandbourne Pool. There were approximately 5 or 6 sheds with one section belonging to Mr Morgan, the estate Carpenter, who was solely responsible for any repairs required on the estate and as I looked after the suckling cattle our paths often crossed throughout our work and we became very friendly. The cowshed housed a number of Shorthorn cattle which were used for suckling the calves and one Shorthorn Bull. When the calves had finished feeding for that day I would complete milking them (by hand!) and take the milk to Raymond Hudson the Cowman who was responsible for the Jersey herd which produced a lot of milk. This was later churned and sold.

There was a brick building used to house the pigs, some of which were to provide bacon for Spring Grove House. One other job I was expected to do was boil the pig potatoes in the furnace situated in the farmyard. These potatoes were used to feed the pigs mixed with Sharpes Mash and there were about 8 pigs kept in the park for fattening, although they also had a farm shed in which they could lie inside. When they were killed, Mr Tommy Timmis the local butcher from Bewdley would visit to do this. They were stunned with a pole-axe to the head, the throat was then cut and the blood collected in buckets for Mrs Huckson to make into black pudding. The pig was then hung for about a week before Mr Timmis returned to cut it up for making bacon and hams. Mr Huckson then had to salt it down to make bacon and rub salt peter into the bone area to preserve it. It was then placed on tiled slabs in the dairy and salted again several times. It was now ready to be hung from hooks set into the beams in the kitchen ceiling to dry out for anything up to 12 months.

Mary Williams the Dairy Maid was responsible for collecting the eggs, making butter and all dairy duties including separating the milk to make butter. After the cream had been skimmed off the remaining milk was known as buttermilk and some of this was used on a daily basis for Mrs Webb to wash herself in as it was considered to be very good for the skin. Mrs Huckson, the Bailiff's wife would help around the dairy when needed.

The sheep from Spring Grove Farm were driven on foot (with the help of the sheep dogs) for dipping to Blackstone Farm which was owned by Mr Richie and his brother as they were the only Farm that had sheep dipping facilities in the area. The animals were dipped once each year after shearing (to prevent maggots developing in the fleece) by being totally submerged in the solution and I well remember the dreadful smell of this exercise!

In the summertime various shows took place, namely the Bath and West and the Royal Show. Mr Huckson would select various sheep suitable to be exhibited, Ray would take care of the cattle and they would both choose one of each to be shown. This process involved a great deal of work as they had to be washed thoroughly. In the case of the sheep the wool would have to be trimmed square and a powder was patted into the wool with what appeared to be similar to a butter pat to improve the colour of the coat.

The cattle were brushed, their hair at the end of the tail was washed and combed and horns and hooves would be cleaned and oiled to make them appear shiny. Ray, clad in a white coat, would lead them around the arena with the judges watching closely from the centre of the ring before choosing the best beast. Major Webb was frequently the winner of the rosettes. The sheep would be placed in the ring and held in lines while the judges walked up and down to select which animal they considered to be the best turned out. Mr Huckson invited me to attend these shows on several occasions and this gave me an insight into exactly what happened at these different events.

I sometimes had to help Mr Harry Burt in the field with weeding between the mangles which were used for feeding the cattle in the wintertime. This was a back–breaking job and I have to admit not one I enjoyed but it had to be done! I was also involved with haymaking which I did not mind as I had seen this done at Winterdyne. I was given the job of horse–raking with Nigger but I really made him work too hard and after I completed the task when Mr Huckson returned from his tea break I was severely reprimanded for the state the horse was in. I remember being a little shocked at the time as I felt I had done a good job in very little time and this was the only occasion I was ever chastised by him but I learnt my lesson.

One time I went fishing in one of the pools at Spring Grove with Freda, daughter of the Bailiff, Mr Huckson. We only caught one fish, which was a good sized Roach and on my way home I met Gerald Clee, one of my school friends who was a keen fisherman. He saw the fish and was not overly impressed but still I took it home and cooked it for supper. I recall it was not the best tasting fish I have ever had as it had quite a muddy taste but I was quite pleased with my achievement. Fishing has never really been my sport and it is true to say I have not fished since!

The farm horses were looked after by Mr Arthur Philpotts and these were four chestnut coloured Suffolks and he tended them very well. One problem with these working horses, however, is their bodies are too heavy for their legs and this usually results in them suffering joint problems. One day Arthur had to take two horses to the blacksmiths for shoeing. On his return he called for a drink at the Wagon and Horses and the Major passed by and noticed the horses outside the pub. The Major was very angry and this resulted in Arthur getting the sack which must have caused him problems as he had a very large family and had to move to Habberley Road to live as he lost his tied house on the estate. At the end of the summer season I believed I would return to the stables to work for the winter but I was told they did not want me and I have to admit I was not really surprised as I did not like most of the staff there. I was given the sack and this is the only time this has ever happened to me in my entire working life!

WORKLIFE AT SANDBOURNE ESTATE AND STABLES

I was not out of work for very long as Dad arranged a job for me at Sandbourne Racing Stables which kept five racehorses. I was made Apprentice Steeplechase Jockey, which on the surface seemed very promising. Mr Chandler was the Trainer, his son was a jockey. The owner of two of the horses was Mr Chandler's brother and these were called Belky Bells (a two year old bay) and Alice Louise (a grey). Two further horses were owned by Mr Tommy Webster, a Bookmaker from Kidderminster and one of these named Otherial (another bay) was a particularly good racehorse, in fact the best in the stables. The remaining horse which was a grey called Sound Asleep was in shocking condition as it had previously been starved. I can honestly say I have never seen a horse in such a bad state of health in the whole of my life. He never picked up although they did race him but he was not successful and I do not recall the name of the owner.

The training ground we had was Dropping Wells Farm, near to Devils Spadeful. It consisted of three hurdles alongside the hedge in Sandy Lane and at the side of the farm, up the bank was a piece of common ground owned by Kidderminster Corporation which we used for flat racing. The horses used for this purpose were normally Belky Bells and Otherial who were flat racers. Alf Chandler, the jockey, became friendly with the daughter of the farmer of Dropping Wells Farm and he used to go around with her on the float delivering milk having fallen out with his father who ran the racing stables.

One day Alf Chandler came along the Stourport Road delivering milk and began shouting loudly, waving a stick with the intention of frightening the horse I was riding, Alice Louise. This caused her to rear up and I slid from the back of the horse but kept hold of the reins. I then attempted to remount but before I could place my feet in the stirrups the horse bolted along the Stourport Road towards Bewdley town. Due to the fact my feet were not placed in the stirrups I did not have sufficient control. Jim Reynolds who was also delivering milk along Stourport Road at the time commented afterwards "*I thought you were racing!*"

At the bottom of Westbourne Street where the road bends to lead towards the river the horse lost its legs and we both landed on the road with my left leg underneath the horse. Alice Louise was grazed quite badly as a result of the accident but in time she healed. I personally damaged my leg and struggled to walk but I was helped by Ted Miles (a decorator who lived in a cottage with outbuildings and a yard extending to the corner of Stourport Road where it leads into Westbourne Street). He took me back to his house and got a message to Dad who came and collected me and took me home where a Doctor was called to attend to my injury. It was a struggle to walk for a week but it was not long after this that the stables were closed. In the meantime, Mr Chandler asked Molly Knock and Nora Powis to help exercise the horses until I recovered. When I finished at Sandbourne I went to Coldricks to begin my bricklaying apprenticeship.

MY APPRENTICESHIP AT COLDRICKS

When I started at Coldricks, the Builders at Bewdley, I was an apprentice Bricklayer and this was arranged at the office of Hemmingway's Solicitors in the town. At the initial meeting those present were Dad, Len Thomas (the Solicitors' Clerk) Mr Jack Coldrick (the senior partner in the business) and I. Also in the firm was Bill Coldrick who did the estimating and wages, working from an office in Load Street called The Swan Yard where their Aunt lived in the living quarters at the rear. We all had to call at the office at 5 pm on a Friday night to collect our wages.

The staff I remember who worked for Coldricks was George Bishop, Bricklayer; Arthur Millward, Bricklayer and if needed Solomon Mann who was a part-time Bricklayer; Jack Stokes, Labourer; George Davies, Labourer (who was profoundly deaf) and Bill Clarke, Labourer (ex-Gamekeeper). My first job, with Arthur and Bill was at Mortimer-Smiths at Habberley Road (now a Plant Nursery) and I recall Mr Mortimer-Smith used to breed spaniels in those days. The work we carried out on this estate was sandstone wall repairs. The mortar consisted of lime and sand and at night we used to put the lumps of lime together in a heap and throw several buckets of water over it and cover it over with sand to keep in the heat, which slacked the lime down to make it soft ready for making lime mortar the next morning. The lumps then had to be broken down and mixed with the sand and riddled to take out the stone and lumps. If it was not riddled it was thrown through what was known as a timber 'gate' which was a piece of mesh fixed in a timber frame, propped up at angle so when the mortar was thrown onto it the stones would fall to the bottom and the sand would pass through onto the ground ready for mixing.

We then had to sort out the stones for the rebuilding of the walls according to size. The wall was double thickness and the centre was filled with small lumps of stone from the riddlings etc. The top was bridged with larger pieces of stone bedding in lime mortar to keep the rain out. Some of the stone needed dressing into shape with a chisel before bedding them onto the top of the wall where they would be pushed in tightly so they remained water-tight.

Other work we had to do was re-roofing houses. This consisted of erecting scaffolding which was wooden poles placed in drums filled with sand. These were spaced out at approximately 6 to 8 feet apart and then a ledger was tied to the upright poles with ropes. This was where my scouting skills came into good use. We had to tie rope to the uprights with a clove-hitch both on the upright and then around the ledger, finishing with a clove-hitch on the upright for security. As it was difficult to make the knots absolutely tight we used to drive a piece of wedge-shaped lath about a foot in length through the ropes to tighten each knot up fully. The putlocks were inserted into the wall by removing a brick and the end was tied to the ledger in the usual way, starting and finishing with a clove-hitch. The putlocks would be fixed tight into the wall with wedges of lath to prevent them from pulling out.

The next stage would be to fit planks in four widths for walking on and storing material. After the roof was stripped, a section at a time, it would be relathed and no felt was used in those days as all tiles had to be bedded on in lime mortar. The tiles would be carried up the roof and stacked ready for use and the bottom would be fixed off the scaffold. As soon as that was complete a ledger had to be inserted, consisting of a rope fixed to a piece of lath under the bottom side of the roofing lath to prevent the rope from pulling out. It was then tied to the ledger and this now provided a safe surface to stand upon to re-tile the roof.

At the very top of the roof, crest tiles would be fixed, bedded on mortar and pointed up with lime-cement to make it water-tight. All the tiles in those days were bedded on lime-mortar and as they were handmade they had no nail holes and one nib for them to be hooked on the lath. The rafters (to which the lath was attached for supporting the tiles) in many cases were timber saplings approximately 4" square and dressed straight out of the forest. These were mostly oak timbers. In later years the laths were replaced in soft wood (approximately 2" x 3/4" in various lengths, up to around 12' in length). The old rafters very often had to be levelled up with pieces of timber when they were repaired as when they were originally fixed they were constructed from green timber. These would bend with the weight when the tiles were placed on them after a period of time as can often be seen with old roofs where the smooth lines have been distorted by bowing.

Roofing work was best carried out when the weather was fine, although this was not always possible. During bad weather, as apprentice, I would have to return to the yard to be given other work such as making dry lime mortar mix, any odd jobs such as cleaning and painting old cast iron guttering to be reused – in fact anything to fill the time in. The workmen, however, were laid off when the weather was bad which meant they would lose income. Some days, when it was raining the Bricklayer and I would be sent to carry out inside repairs such a replacing a washing boiler or in some cases plastering ceilings etc.

MY CAREER AT BRINTONS LIMITED

In 1939 I was asked by Bert Dalloway if I would like to go and work as a Bricklayer at Brintons but as I had to finish my apprenticeship this was delayed for one year. The appeal with moving to Brintons was the remuneration was better as it was union rate which was one and tuppence an hour and Coldricks would only pay me one and a penny which in those days this was a big difference. Additionally, there was always a chance of overtime at Brintons as the War was still on and the carpet works was changing over to munitions. Of course, Gladys and I were saving to get married at that time. In 1940, therefore, when I finished my apprenticeship at Coldricks I went to work for Brintons. Bert Dalloway was in charge of the bricklayers' gang and there were approximately 20 of us. Bert and I were the only two skilled bricklayers and the reason there were so many labourers was because as it was Wartime, Brintons was turning the factory over to other types of industry. Bert was made Foreman of the Millwrights and I worked most days from 7 am until 9 or 10 o'clock at night but I did not mind this as it provided me with a good income.

I do not remember my first job but I do recall finding it very strange working inside after my previous job of working on old houses and farm buildings. The Works Engineer at the time was Mr Ralph Osbourne who was in charge. The Maintenance Engineer was Mr Harry Cooper and he was responsible for maintenance of any works engineering machinery. Mr Harry Starr was Production Engineer in charge of the Machine Shop and all the fitters and tuners on the carpet looms, including the engineers store. Mr Jack Lemon was Works Manager at that time, Mr Cecil Brinton was Chairman of the Company and John Brinton assisted him together with other members of the Brinton family. Tatton Brinton was serving in the forces as was Derek and Roy Woodward.

During Wartime we had to be prepared to do any type of work we were asked to do. We had to install new machines at Green Street and in the Andrews Building in Corporation Street, often necessitating me working from 7 am until 8 or 9 pm 7 days per week, which provided me with the much needed funds to save for our future. Most of the time that I worked at Green Street before the War it was where the carding and spinning was carried out so most of the carpet machinery was put into storage once they changed to munitions. There was a great deal of alterations and buildings to construct at Green Street at this time. Guests (the building contractors) were called in and they built the Canteen there. I constructed the Gas Works with the help of two labourers and it was a standby in case the main Gas Works was bombed as gas was required for the hardening of the tools in the tool shop.

Hunts the builders built air raid shelters at the side of the River Stour and Jake Williamson was their foreman at that time. I worked for Brintons until January 1941 when I was called up into the Army. I returned to Brintons in 1946 and Mr Osbourne was still the Works Engineer and Bert Dalloway was the foreman bricklayer. My work varied from maintenance to building and boiler repairs. Other people had been employed while I was away – Fred Hunt a Bricklayer from Bewdley, Harry Postins from Hagley as Labourer, Joe Binnersley from Kidderminster as Bricklayer and Jack MacDonagh was my labourer and we always got on very well together.

There were several very important items which I feel are worthy of mention as they contributed heavily to the smooth running of the Company during the period of my employment from 1941 to 1986. The first of these was the well in C Shed which supplied water for the cooling of the turbine and water for the dye house. A number of times I had to go down into the well to carry out repairs to the borehole which leaked on several occasions. The second was the tank situated on the roof of D Shed which supplied cooling water to the turbine and the third item was another tank on the four-storey building which supplied the dye house with water for dyeing the yarn. Moving on to B Shed now, there was a water softening plant for the dying process which is equally worthy of note (maintained by John Davis who was responsible for adding the salt to the softener tank).

Lastly, was the turbine on the first floor of the turbine house which was a two-storey building situated between B and C Sheds. On the ground floor was all the main switchgear which supplied the total electrical needs of the main factory and Green Street. To maintain this, three electricians were employed on a shift-work basis to cover 24 hours each day, seven days per week. On the ground floor there was an additional section which was a compressor house accommodating two compressors which supplied all the air requirements to the equipment in the factory. On the first floor was the turbine itself which was Mr Cecil's pride and joy and Ralph Osbourne (previously an electrical engineer at the tram station in Tram Street) was a stickler for the turbine being kept in pristine condition.

Each year an engineer visited to test the turbine, during the process of which he put a penny on its edge and if it stood stationary it was deemed to be functioning correctly but if the coin fell over it indicated a fault! The brickwork of the building was immaculate and was the work of Jake Williamson, a brilliant tradesman who later became Building Manager of Brintons. The person whose sole responsibility for keeping the turbine clean was Charlie Davies. He was certainly a colourful character with a good sense of humour. Ralph Osbourne was Double Base player and lived in Sutton Park Road. Charlie Davies with his friend George, were often sent to collect the Double Base carrying from Ralph's home in Sutton Park Road when there was a performance at the Town Hall. Charlie would take the spike end and George the stem and they would march and lark around like a pair of comedians! It was kept in the Power House during the daytime and they would both take it to the Town Hall at the end of the day in time for the concert. Ralph was a very good musician and wrote music himself but sadly I never attended the concerts.

In around 1947 new boilers were installed in the main factory by William Cooper which was a major job as production had to be maintained whilst this work was carried out. I was not involved personally but Ralph Osbourne, Works Engineer and Harry Cooper, Maintenance Engineer were responsible for the building work. Horace Cooper was in charge of the contractors and the entire project was very time consuming as only one boiler could be commissioned at a time before work could begin on another. Originally, the factory had a total of 7 boilers but after the refurbishment 5 boilers did the work which was previously serviced by 7.

In times past the slack for the boilers was delivered by barge on the canal into the works and it was then unloaded and wheeled straight up to the boiler house and the coal had to be fed by hand into the boilers. While the new boilers were being installed, however, a pit was put in at the bottom of the chimney stack to hold a slack elevator which would carry the slack or coal over to the hoppers above the boilers at the front end where they would automatically feed the boilers when required. The slack was brought in by Bradleys Haulage Contractors, Kidderminster and tipped straight onto the grid of the conveyor. Brintons also had storage areas for the slack in Worcester Road and Green Street and in the area where F Shed was built next to the Castle Road building. This was for any time when it was difficult to obtain supplies such as during bad weather or periods of industrial strikes at the pits and railways.

I had another Labourer with me by the surname of Wilkinson as we often needed extra help such as when we renewed the floors in A and B sheds which accommodated the Wilton narrow looms. To achieve this, a loom had to be stopped for one week to allow us to raise it off the floor to lay the concrete for a new floor after removing the old blue paving bricks. The floor was laid on a Saturday and on the Monday we would lay the loom down on the new floor after it had been dust-proofed with Watco, a liquid which stopped the concrete dusting. The tuners would then re-commission that loom while we moved to the next which needed a new base. As orders for new carpets were plentiful at this time we could not waste any time in carrying out this work.

In the early 1950's Brintons bought Slingfield Mill from Carpet Trades and contractors were needed to help carry out some of the building modifications to convert it specifically for mill work in the form of spinning and carding of the wool. Coopers of Blackheath were the chosen contractors and Horace Cooper, the Proprietor, was a good friend of Cecil Brinton, Chairman of the Company at that time. While Coopers were working at the Slingfield Mill Fred Hunt and myself had to put in new gates to both the main factory and Slingfield entrance. We also had to build a new gatehouse for the gatekeeper there to allow goods to be brought from Slingfield to the main factory. The Sling was the main thoroughfare from Mill Street to Castle Road at that time.

After construction of the gatehouse we had to build a new lift shaft in what is still called "The Piano Building" which was then used for storing wool. This building now houses the Carpet Museum in Kidderminster. In those days Mr Derek Woodward carried out the wool buying. A doorway was inserted on two floors with a hoist to take the bales of wool straight up from the drays (and later lorries) to the different floors for storage before being brought back down for dyeing. The basement of this building was part of the canal where the barges came in loaded with slack.

After the alterations to the boiler house an entrance was made at the back of the boilers to the basement. The one barge left in the basement was filled with rubble and sunk then the area was concreted over and converted into a storage area for the Bricklayers gang. This was where we used to keep our tools and lockers for our working clothes. We had a small table at one end of the room where we took our lunch and a gas stove to enable us to cook bacon and eggs or liver for our sandwiches. Only about four or five of us stayed for lunch; usually Bert, Fred, Harry and myself. After lunch we usually played darts and it was generally Fred who won the game!

In the building alongside the Sling were two trap-doors for the sand and gravel. This was brought down the Sling by Jimmy Douglas (Haulage Contractor in Kidderminster) or his driver where it was tipped from the lorry in through the doors for making concrete. As we were doing a substantial amount of concreting and building in those days we used to have the cement delivered in 10 tonne loads. We all had to help unload this and it was very heavy work. There was a gang of around 12 to 15 men in those days and we all got along well together.

My bricklayers' mate was Jack MacDonagh and I well remember his handwriting was incredible. He wrote in copperplate and used to compile the time sheets and was equally efficient as a labourer. He continually had a broom in his hand and was so fastidious in keeping the workspace clear and safe it made my job much easier. Our work varied considerably and once per month we had to carry out boiler repairs which was a dreadful job as it necessitated physically climbing inside the boilers and underneath the boiler tubes to repair any brickwork. The repairs were carried out using bricks and pyruma cement which was both dirty and difficult work due to very limited space.

When the weather was fine we carried out many roof repairs and other times had to make good the damaged floors plus alterations to the sheds and offices. Jack Mac as we called him worked alongside me for many years, right up until I was promoted to Building Manager. After he retired he became unwell and I used to visit him at home. Opposite his house in Franchise Street there was an outdoor licence and he used to walk across with his jug many times during the evening for refreshment. This caused him to have his leg pulled as it was said he had formed a track between both ports from such regular use!

We had two well known residents at the Sling in the form of a tortoise shell cat called Tortie and her ginger kitten. Tortie had quite a reputation for attacking dogs who dared to approach her territory in the Sling. She would sit in the door way and pounce as soon as a dog approached and I well remember us having a complaint from one of the local dog owners that she had injured their pet! Weekends, they were fed by Harry Postins (who we nicknamed "Hagley Harry") one of the labourers for Fred Hunt and during holidays I brought them home to feed them while the factory was shut down. We had one of Tortie's kittens as a Christmas present for Des one year and placed it in a basket in the dining room as a surprise!

I spent a great deal of my time at the various Directors' houses – especially Mr Cecil Brinton's home "Yew Tree House" in Belbroughton which had large grounds and outbuildings of different types, including a swimming pool which was always leaking as a result of the tree roots! I remember there was an ornamental pool with a fountain in the lawn at the front of the house with a brick paved surround. The paving often perished in the frost which necessitated cutting the bricks out by hand to carry out repairs. It was quite a difficult task as it was easy to damage the good bricks in the process of removing the perished ones. In addition, someone made a stream from the swimming pool but this too was problematic due to the roots of the trees. The stream fed into a large fish pool and thankfully we did not have too many problems with this!

Either side of the entrance to the driveway of Mr Cecil's home was two brick piers which had been rendered in cement and on the top of each was a vase with a large sphere sitting inside. On one occasion one of the spheres was knocked off the vase by a lorry and broken and I was sent to execute the repairs. To achieve this I reconstructed the vase for which I had to have special tools machined. I placed a metal rod in the centre of the vase which also passed into the centre of the sphere. To make the ball on the top I used a large quantity of wire netting which I rolled up tightly to form a ball. This was pushed down on the rod and I had to build the ball in cement until I achieved the correct diameter. Each day he would bring Mrs Brinton down to inspect my progress and was delighted with the finished article!

Mr Cecil was picked up at 10 am each day by a chauffeur. This would be either Jack Beddoes or Reg. Holland (Harry Star's brother–in–law) who lived in Plimsoll Street, Kidderminster. The chauffeurs had to take us out each day to any Director we were working for and collect us again in the evening at about 4.30 pm. Mr Cecil only spent so much money each year on the upkeep of the estate and he would tell me around September time that his money had been spent so I would have to return to work at the factory.

On one occasion Mr Cecil (with the help of Mr Osborne) decided that he would like a gravity pump to be fitted to the main brook which ran below his fish pool with the idea of pumping water to the top of Yew Tree House. Unfortunately, however, despite exhaustive attempts this proved impossible due to the height of the house. The brook ran beside the lawns and fed into the fish pools. There was also a brook which ran alongside the road and continued into the village. Historically, during the previous century there used to be a company called Brades who made scythes for cutting grass, including other farm machinery and they used the water from the brook in the factory as part of the production process.

In the grounds of Yew Tree House was a cottage for the gardener who was called Mr Page and on the opposite side of Belbroughton Road was another cottage where the Butler lived with his family. There was also one further cottage which I believe was used for another gardener. In later years, however, Mr Julian Clist went to live here, just inside the grounds, when he first married. One of the last jobs I remember being asked to do was to rebuild a chimney on one of the outbuildings attached to the house. Mr Cecil's health was beginning to fail at this point and he had to take to his bed. Mrs Brinton asked me if I would like to visit him one of the evenings – this I did with Gladys and we discussed a few matters regarding his grounds and properties.

Another of the Directors I used to work for was Mr John Brinton. Mr John lived at Red Marley, Great Witley and Mr John Pilling lives there currently. This was a large farmhouse and orginally in front of the house was a well stocked pool with fish and wildlife. There were moorhens, coots, herons and ducks and it was a very pleasant place. The water supply to the house came from the hills at the back of the Police Station which fed into a large storage tank on the hill and then it was piped from the tank to another storage tank at the top of the house. We had a few problems with this in the wintertime due to burst pipes and freezing. Mr John had a monster of a boiler for central heating and hot water and Fred Hunt and I had to construct an area in the old kitchen to accommodate it. To achieve this in time we had to work over the weekend and Mr John asked us as lunchtime to go into the house for a drink but as I never drank I refused and carried on working but my other workmates spent most of the afternoon drinking with him!

In the grounds of Red Marley was a bungalow occupied by the gardener and quite soon after Mr John Pilling moved into the house I enquired about the possibility of purchasing the property but it was explained to me it was unfortunately not possible as it was intended for agricultural use only. My wife and I always liked this area and our good friends Tom and Vera Mills kept the post office at Great Witley so we would have quite liked to have settled there. However, this was not to be!

I remember doing quite a lot of work for Mr John after we did the boiler and sadly he developed throat cancer. I continued to carry out the work for him and we used to walk around the fields and woods and discuss future projects. After Mr John passed away the farm buildings were turned into dwellings which are where Julian Clist went to live and I believe this is still his home today. I also carried out a great deal of personal work for Mr Tolley Managing Director of Brintons, both during my time at Brintons and afterwards in my retirement. Mr and Mrs Tolley lived at Highfield on the Dowles Road and I have covered this under the section on "Dowles Road, Patchetts Lane and Bark Hill" earlier in this book.

Mr Jack Lemon was Mr Tolley's predecessor and lived for a time at Bridewell

Cottage on the banks of the river Severn by Bridewell Ford. Once again, he wanted an ornamental pool constructed in the grounds which would be fed by a small stream. This I did for him but he later moved on the Kidderminster to Stourbridge Road. The name of the house escapes me but the biggest job I was asked to do there was during the winter when his water main froze. This came across the field and we had to trace the pipe as it was buried very deep so we spent several days digging and thawing the pipe. Colin Wood came out with a car battery and attached a wire to either end of the pipe. This caused a current of electricity which steadily caused it to thaw.

Another Director I worked for was Alf Whadcoat, Works Engineer. He bought the public house in Button Oak which he ran for a few years. He then purchased a cottage on the opposite side of the road which is now part of the caravan site. At this point I was Building Manager and had to arrange for any building work he needed. He then bought another cottage on Pound Green Common that was not large enough for him. I did the plans for an extension which was carried out by Coopers the builders in Blackheath. He soon bought Cherry Cottage on the opposite side of the road for his daughter to live in but I was not involved in any renovation work with this. The next property he purchased was The New Inn, Arley and I was involved in arranging a large amount of building work here. Unfortunately Alf did not live long after completion of this work. He was buried at Kinlet church.

While I was a bricklayer I went to Wolverley Court to carry out some work for Sir Tatton Brinton. I had to take out the main wall between two large living rooms to make an even larger room in which he could entertain his guests. This meant propping up the walls at the very top of his house to ensure it was safe and after creating the opening it was necessary to make good the plaster. This took the form of ornamental plasterwork to match the existing design. It was very intricate and took three weeks to complete the entire job. He later moved to a large country farmhouse in Great Witley. I was Building Manager by this time and had to arrange for all the work to be done for him by Brintons personnel. This entailed work of several different trades in the process of altering the kitchen and general maintenance of the old buildings. He later moved to Tenbury Wells but I was not involved in any building works at this address.

During this period Sir Tatton also had a flat in London as he was a Member of Parliament for some time and I was involved with organising the alterations to the kitchen and bathroom by using labour from Brinton's staff. I therefore had quite a number of runs down to London which involved me setting off at 4 am in order to beat the traffic. I would aim to leave at around 3.30 pm, again to avoid the rush hour. Mrs Brinton insisted I took

Gladys down with me to visit as she felt I was always leaving her to carry out work for them in London. This I did on one occasion and we spent most of the time in Harrods. Both Sir Tatton and Mrs Brinton were kind to us and we had a very enjoyable time. While work was being carried out on the flat Sir Tatton always provided us with a hearty breakfast of bacon and eggs on arrival and also a meal at mid-day. He later purchased a house for his wife in Bournemouth and asked me to install a lift shaft but I did not see the completion of this work as he was taken ill and passed away soon afterwards.

While I was Building Manager I was asked by Harry Lowe to carry out any work required at Park Hall which had recently been purchased by Mr Michael Brinton. Various modifications were made such as provision of a new staircase at the rear of the house and all asbestos lagging had to be removed from the boiler house. Ray Bottomley painted the exterior of the building.

In 1974–75 Brintons Canteen was refurbished by William Cooper & Son. New kitchen equipment was installed incorporating a large serving hatch to the dining section and a bar and storage area was also built, together with a parquet floor for social evenings and dances. A meeting room/executive dining room was also created for other occasions and the new development was opened by Mr Terry Tolley on 16th May, 1975 at 5 pm. I was invited to this event.

The Sprinkler Tank House was in front of J Shed and this was maintained by Bill Hinton. (During the First World War J Shed was a jam factory and this is how it earned its name. It is now the Canteen and before modifications were carried out the rings where the jam kettles fitted into the floor were still visible!) The function of the Tank House was to supply water for the sprinkler systems in many departments around the factory 24 hours per day which were triggered off by heat in the event of a fire. If a fire occurred this would alarm the Night-Watchman in the house above Corporation Street Gate and he would make calls to the necessary staff (such as the Works Engineer) to attend to the problem.

There was also a sprinkler system installed at Nos. 5 and 6 Factory on Stourport Road, Kidderminster and we also took over the sprinkler system at the old Naylor's' factory when we purchased this from them for additional storage of carpets. During the August Bank Holiday maintenance of this system was often carried out as was a full schedule of other repairs while all the factories were shut down.

These included:
* Water tanks were cleaned and painted
* Dyehouse walls and roof trusses were repainted in all dyehouses
* River cleaning to keep it free of debris
* Stotts were employed to maintain all tea urns throughout factory

These were carried out every year but there was always a number of additional maintenance jobs carried out at this time when the factory was quiet.

Wintertime was always a problem with trying to keep the sheds warm, stopping the draughts and then in the summertime attempts to keep the sheds cool – particularly in the Picking Room! All roof lights and windows had to be summer shaded with a colour wash. Floods were another problem and attempting to control the flow of the river Stour which ran throughout the centre of the factory. The Dyehouse, Boilerhouse and A and B Sheds were mainly affected by this problem, especially when the carpets on the looms had to be raised from the floor level. Slingfield was also affected with Wool washing and Spinning Departments becoming flooded. A hole was cut through the wall to the canal side in order to allow the water to drain to the canal. The water was also channelled down the back of the Boilerhouse where a trap door had been put in the wall to allow water through into the canal. At times the Canteen also was affected, causing problems with the wooden–block floor where the water caused this to raise. When this occurred we had no option but to uplift the floor and relay it.

Another problem we experienced in the wintertime was sprinkler pipes becoming frozen and bursting. This was mostly at night and I would have to arrange for Len Castle (the foreman plumber) to assist me with these. I recall I was always in trouble with his wife Gladys for calling him into work during antisocial hours! This was one of the problems of being on the maintenance staff where you would quite likely be called out at any time during the day or night to keep the factory running. As Building Manager I was also responsible for all the Contractors engaged to carry out work for the Firm. William Cooper of Blackheath was the main contractor employed for building works and Arthur Faulkner was the Director of this company succeeding Mr Horace Cooper, their Chairman when he passed away. Mr Tim Clist (brother of Julian) was the designated Architect and the Construction Engineer at this time was Mr Brian Peplow, based in Kidderminster.

A new cantilever bridge was installed by William Cooper partly over the river through the main factory because the old wooden bridge was beyond repair and this was designed by Tim Clist with Brian Peplow as Structural

Engineer. A new building was erected to house the Machine Shop on the ground floor and offices for the Engineering Staff on the first floor. At this time the Maintenance Department moved into G Shed, having stripped out all of the Wilton looms to allow the Engineering Departments to move in, ie. Millwrights, Plumbers, Carpenters, Bricklayers and Painters, with the loom tuners in the next shed. This now brought all Maintenance Departments together.

When Brintons decided to use computers, they were delivered to Exchange Street yard and installed on the top floor of the office block. This meant the building gang had to rig up a hoist on the top floor and Bert Dalloway was in his element to take on this challenge which proved a very successful exercise. A bander room was also required for copying documentation and this was controlled by Sid Birch and a number of young girls, namely Alf Whadcoat's daughter and my own daughter Des. Unfortunately, the continual sitting down did not suit her, however, and she soon moved to other work at Stourport Road into the offices in the Packing Room. I later arranged with Fred Bond for her to begin work in the Picking Room and she remained in this job until she left to get married in 1972.

When Brintons decided to build No.5 Factory on the Stourport Road there was packing on the one side and weaving on the other. Alf Whadcoat was Works Engineer at the time the sheds were built and the weaving department was the largest single span roof constructed in the country. This was to suit the loom designed by Brintons without having any columns obstructing the space required for such large pieces of machinery as this was always a problem with the sheds in Kidderminster.

The roof had a slight fall on it which was covered with roofing felt and after a short time it proved to be troublesome. There were upright roof lights in the centre of the building to provide natural light and I remember one winter evening during bad weather conditions the wind blew off the felt at one end of the shed and we had to weight it down with whatever means we could to prevent rain from getting into the shed. We all had to work late into the night but it was almost a full-time job keeping up with repairs to this roof and within a few years the Contractors were called back to re-felt the entire roof at their expense. With this type of roof it would always present problems. Fortunately, the packing room shed did not have so many problems as it was a much smaller space.

No.6 Factory also contained looms and had its share of problems. The drains in Stourport Road could not cope with the amount of surface water from the area but as the Council would not enlarge the drains it would always prove to be a problem. Where the roof water came down for some strange reason the drain actually ran inside the shed which obviously caused flooding damage to the carpets and as the factory was about 4 feet higher than the building next door I installed an overflow pipe which allowed the surplus water to flow onto the road next door and to my knowledge such a simple diversion prevented this from occurring again! The same situation occurred with No.5 Factory during heavy storms so I repeated what I had done at No.6. Brintons purchased another small building at the side of No.6 Factory which was used to house the Design staff previously situated on the top floor of the main offices in Exchange Street. This was a huge improvement to the old Design Room.

When Oldington Sports Ground on the Stourport Road was purchased after the War Bill Whale was made Groundsman. He used to be a labourer in the Carpenters Shop and had a massive task to get things started as half of Oldington was a potato field and the remaining half was grassed. I was sent down to dig the foundations out for an old army Nissen hut. I prepared the ground and brickwork up to ground level and installed a concrete floor ready for the hut. It was split into two parts with a wall built to divide it, the larger part being used for the football and cricket teams to change and the other section was a shed for Bill to keep his tools and mowing machines in to maintain the grounds. Afterwards, a memorial pool was built for Mr Derek Woodward's father who was a Director of the Company before the War and it was aptly named The Woodward Memorial Garden. It was filled with water and many water-lilies but I do not recall seeing any fish.

Once the ground was in good shape a Sports Day was arranged in the late 40's or early 50's. There were tug-o-war and running races and I took part in the mile race and came second of which I won a clock and this is still on display in my home today! I could always run long distances as I used to run for the Worcesters during my army days, achieving 9 minutes 14 seconds for the mile. Gladys came with me to the Sports Day and a good time was had by all but I do not recall many of the names of those who took part. Wally Bunce was made Sports Representative for Brintons to arrange these type of events.

Many years later, while I was working in the office, I was asked to design a sports pavilion and this I did with large glass windows in the front with double glass doors in the centre as it faced the Sports Ground with the Woodward Memorial Garden at the side. It did not stay like this for very long, however, as it was turned into a club with a bar in the centre and the bar stools at the back. It was later decided to build a Squash Court at the rear which Tim Clist designed and it was constructed by Coopers the contractors. The ground then consisted of two football pitches, two cricket pitches – one covered with Brintons woven carpet (before Astroturf was invented) to try it out as an all weather pitch but it was not very successful despite great effort. There were two tennis pitches – one again being covered with Britons turf carpet and this was more successful. One of the problems was stretching it tight so we had to peg it down on all sides which was a difficult task but of course there was no need for mowing, it could be used in all weathers so it was worth the effort.

A bowling green was then laid and I believe it was one of the best in the area, although I never played myself. Now Brintons had teams in most sports. Before the War all Sports Days were at Spennells which was owned by the Woodward family. They had a swimming pool there for the swimming competitions and Bill Smith from the Carpenters Shop won majority of the races. When I went back to Brintons after the War I used to go swimming at lunchtimes in the pool in Castle Road in the summer. It was Bill who taught me to swim and we became good friends. He also used to pull in the tug-o-war teams at Brintons but after taking part in one of these competitions, he was taken home with chest pains and sadly passed away. I never took part in these again. Arnold Morris also pulled in the tug-o-war competitions and suffered with chest pains afterwards, therefore it was decided by the Sports Committee to stop this.

Brintons Telford

As Brinton's business expanded in Kidderminster the need for further space became apparent and so in 1970 it was decided to purchase two existing sheds at Telford for the wool spinning and carding. Philip Hales (who had been an electrician and then moved on to the Management side at Slingfield) was given the job of Manager at Telford. Peter Cashmore was made responsible to Derek Woodward for purchasing the wool. A staff of three electricians to cover the three shifts was arranged and as some people came from the Kidderminster factory, works transport was laid on to deliver them to the new premises each day by mini-bus driven by Colin (I do not recall his surname) who also did the running about for the factories in general. The building staff were also delivered and returned each day as they were involved in a great deal of work with the installation of the machinery. I had to make two or three journeys a week to arrange the building or installation work needed and Harry Betson (Manager of the Millwrights) was involved with quite a lot of work with the machines. Additionally, Eric Roberts (Chief Electrical Engineer) was heavily involved with the new installations.

After about two years Brintons bought quite a large area of extra land with the idea of installing a wool washing department from Kidderminster together with a section for wool blending/bulk dyeing. By this time we were having many, many meetings with Bob Powell who had been appointed the Director responsible for Telford and as such was in charge of arrangements for the extension work. As I was fast approaching Retirement I felt it would be better for someone else to attend these meetings as I would not be present up to the completion of the project. It was over two years work and I felt it would be more appropriate for   my successor to see this through but Harry Lowe asked me if I would stay on for two years to see the Telford job completed.

This was a major commitment and I discussed the implications with Gladys but she did not seem to mind. I agreed but on reflection I do not feel I made the right personal decision at that time as this would have been valuable time which we could have spent together. I was involved with a considerable number of meetings with Bob Powell and the contractors which resulted in very late finishes, often 9 or 10 o'clock in the evening.

At the same time as the construction of Telford I was involved with work on Sir Tatton's flat in London and I well recall leaving home at 4 am and had to be back at Telford for a meeting at 7 pm one evening, once again having a very late night! The gatekeeper at Telford used to ring Gladys and tell her she could put my meal on as I was on my way and it would take me 30 to 35 minutes to return home. For all this, I have to say I have always enjoyed being busy!

I also had to visit Yorkshire with Bob Powell to select a weighing machine to be installed at Telford for weighing the trucks of yarn when they came off the drying machine. Another time I went to see about an effluent machine to deal with the foul water discharged from the wool washing process. Towards the end of my two years I had words with my colleague as he was a difficult man to get on with. I decided to see Harry Lowe and tell him I wanted to finish work in December 1986. Topham Brinton came to see me afterwards but I had made up my mind to leave, so it was to no avail.

When the extension was completed at Telford, Sir Tatton asked Norman Tebbit MP to open the new premises. I was invited, together with other managers and directors of the Telford factory to show any guests around to explain the workings of the machinery. I was with Michael Brinton and afterwards Mr Tebbit and Sir Tatton gave a speech.

On 23rd December, 2011 I completed 40 years of unbroken service with Brintons Limited and the Board of Directors presented me with a gold watch to commemorate this. Sadly, while my wife and I attended a funeral service at Bewdley Methodist Church someone broke into our home and amongst the items stolen was a watch I had bought for Gladys during our courtship, another watch I had been awarded for building the scout headquarters and my gold watch from Brintons. Luckily, Woolworths of Wolverhampton found the Brintons watch in their store, reported it to Brintons and it was later returned to me. I was very relieved to have this returned but saddened to find the strap had been removed and replaced with the strap from the watch I had been given by the scouts. I would love to have this put back to its original state as it has never felt the same since it was tampered with. One day I hope to achieve this.

The day I retired I visited Telford in the morning with Keith Bayton who was to be my successor and on the way back we stopped and had lunch. I drove back onto the bridge in the main factory, dropped Keith off and then went straight home. Brintons had been a large part of my life, I had always been happy there, but the final parting, for me, had to be done quietly. About two weeks afterwards John Pilling asked me to call into his office and presented me with a book on Mountaineering which was a very kind gesture and I have returned to the Company a few times since.

I gradually adjusted to retirement by keeping myself very busy with various building projects and taking a day off each week on a Saturday to keep up my walking, often covering anything from 4 to 8 hours in duration. Gladys and I spent many days visiting places such as Birmingham, Gloucester, Hereford, Shrewsbury, Wolverhampton plus odd times we would go on day trips to Torquay to visit Gladys' friend Ruth.

ARMY LIFE

I was called up in 1941 and sent to Cleethorpes for my first posting in the Worcestershire Regiment to do my training with a number of Bewdley boys. They were Jack Bradbury, Colin Harrison, Bill Jakes and a person nicknamed Wockam Evans and they were all about two years younger than I. There was also someone called Les Tyler who came from Kidderminster and he worked at Brintons moving machines on a Lister Truck. Sadly he was killed during the War and Colin lost a leg. We carried out our training in the streets around Cleethorpes and Grimsby as we were billeted in houses. Also, Mike Young's cousin by the name of Les, who came from Dudley, was serving on a mine-sweeper moored at the docks at Grimsby. I sometimes saw him on Sunday afternoons when he was not at sea and had tea with him on the mine-sweeper and I remember the food was very good quality! My sister Florrie visited me once with her husband Charles while I was stationed at Cleethorpes and I found them rooms with a family by the name of Helgeson.

Before moving from Cleethorpes I was called to see the CO as he wanted to speak to me. At the time I was graded A2 due to an ankle injury I had sustained while playing cricket before I was called up. He asked if I would like to stay in the Worcesters and if so he would have me upgraded to A1, the reason being I had done quite a lot of cross country running etc and always done well. I refused, however, as I told him I wanted to get into the Royal Engineers. After four months training I was moved to the South Staffordshire Regiment, stationed at Mere near to Stoke on Trent to guard an aerodrome.

A short time later some of us were moved to Ditton Priors as this was a naval ammunition base and there were about 30 of us to guard this area. On my first day off I walked 16 miles to visit Gladys and returned on my tandem bicycle which belonged to Mike Young and I. This I found very useful as it enabled me to see Gladys regularly. Also, as Ditton Priors was quite a distance away from Bridgnorth and Bewdley stations and as we only had one truck to take the men on leave (sometimes this was out delivering food rations to other depots) I would use the tandem to take the men to Bewdley bus stop. Only one man was allowed leave per week and I recall on one occasion while delivering a soldier to the bus stop, the bus was in the process of pulling off as we arrived in the town and I caught it up on Bewdley Bridge and he jumped straight off and onto the bus. Fortunately, there was much less traffic about in those days! The officer in charge gave me a pass to enable me to stay at home for the night on these occasions.

My job was to go with the driver to Ludlow Racecourse to collect the rations three times a week. They were taken back to Ditton Priors where they would be split up into portions for depots based at Ditton Priors, Stottesdon, Cleobury Mortimer and Clee Hill. These were the points where Blue Cap soldiers were stationed, approximately 6 to 8 men at each site. I had to stay at Cleobury on one occasion for a week when the cook was on leave to carry out the catering as I was regarded as relief cook. I prepared a stew for them of vegetables and meat on one day and they commended me on the fact that it tasted more like a home prepared meal!

I took my 12 bore shotgun to Ditton Priors and as we were collecting rations from Ludlow I used to stand on the back of the truck and shoot the pheasants on Lord Boyne's estate as we passed by. I cooked pheasant for supper some Saturday nights if I did not go home and any birds I did not use I gave to some of the soldiers who would send them home to their families by post via Ludlow Post Office. As the post only took on average two days to be delivered, I only ever had one complaint about a bird being delivered unfit for human consumption! I believe the pheasant had more than likely been shot previously but it had not killed the bird. The lead shot had caused poisoning of the flesh and it must have been my shot which actually killed it outright but of course by this time the bird was inedible.

Dad's Certificate as First Class Signalman in Artillery

While I was at Ditton Priors, when I had my week's leave I used to work for Coldricks building Air Raid Shelters. One was for the Convalescent Home in Park Alley and the other was at the rear of Weatherheads shop in Load Street.

If my officer had guests he would ask the driver to take me to shoot a fresh pheasant in order to entertain. One time I returned from a day out at home at around 10 pm, parked my tandem and as I entered the sleeping quarters there was a commotion taking place. The officer had apparently burst into where the men had gone to bed and shot straight across the room, randomly between the beds and hit the wall opposite. The soldiers, understandably, were petrified and confused and the Sergeant Major arrested the officer. He was removed the next day never to be seen again. Soon afterwards we too were moved from Ditton Priors so I returned my tandem to our home at Winterdyne and I was sent to Aldershot to train for the Royal Engineers in 232 Army Troop Company. The Company was trained for building Bailey Bridges, mine-clearing and building work. It was while I was stationed here I had leave to get married to Gladys at St. Annes Church, Bewdley on 15th May, 1943 and I have covered this in detail later in my book under the chapter on family life and Gladys.

After my leave for the wedding I returned to Aldershot to complete my training. At the side of the training ground was where the rockets were tested at Farnborough. I well remember the noise was terrific and the fire from the explosion was immense. Our Company was then moved on to Kineton in Warwickshire which was an ammunition depot being constructed on the side of the Leamington/Banbury Road. The two sheds were built side-by-side and joined together with a roof. The floors were concrete and the walls were of brick construction. The rooves had concrete beams with a cement screed over the top to fill in the cracks and this was then waterproofed with felt and covered over with soil and grass seed to blend in with the surrounding countryside. The two sheds contained ammunition and there was a railway line running between them so that the trucks could be lined up out of sight.

The ammunition was delivered by train and unloaded into the sheds awaiting delivery to whichever destination was decided in preparation for D-Day. When we constructed these sheds I was part of a team who built from the foundation up to the damp course which consisted of two courses of blue bricks. We were allowed one week for our team to build one half of the shed up to the damp course and this work had to be carried out whether it was wet or fine weather. A minimum of 1,200 bricks had to be laid per day which entitled us to have a day's pass at the weekend. On my day off, after parade, I used to hitch-hike to Bewdley which was, of course, mostly via lorries going to Birmingham. I then had to catch the bus for the final part of the journey and Gladys would try and get some time off from work.

When I had to return at night I would catch a bus back to Birmingham and then the 9.30 pm train into camp. This was a passenger train until it arrived in Birmingham then it was converted into a troop train to take us back to camp. I could not always obtain a pass as there was only a few to be shared around and on the occasions I could not get one I had to dodge the Red Caps on Snowhill Station in order to board the train which was far from easy but I was never rumbled! I managed to obtain a supply of passes unofficially from the personnel office which my sister would sign for me – she called herself Lieutenant B. Smart as the official signatory and the system worked perfectly!

When I was moved from the ammunition sheds with two other 'Sappers' (the name given to the Royal Engineers) we were sent to build a church at the entrance to the camp which consisted of a bricked tower and Nissen hut and the back of the tower to form the church. During this time we had to go to Radway to complete a two-week refresher course in preparation for

D—Day and I met Gladys' brother John on the camp by accident. He was in the regular army and although I had never met him before, we became very friendly and when I could not get home we both used to visit his Aunt Rose at Aston in Birmingham. She was a very kind lady who brought both Gladys and John up before they went to the orphanage. While I was with John, during our visits to Birmingham to see Aunt Rose we sometimes went to watch Birmingham City play. Gill Merrick was their goalkeeper and also played for England at that time.

While I was at Kineton and did not manage to get home to visit Gladys I used to attend the Warwickshire Fox Hounds Meet in the village. I would follow on foot and on one occasion one of the ladies invited me back to her house and asked me if I would like a horse to ride but I never had the opportunity to take her up on the kind offer as we were moved not long afterwards.

After we moved from Kineton I never saw John again and the company started to prepare for the invasion of France. We were involved in more army training but I do not recall an awful lot about this time as I did not enjoy the army life or its training! I can remember all leave was cancelled and we were confined to camp but for the first time I went absent without leave so I could see Gladys before going to France. Everyone was surprised I had been granted leave when I arrived home in Bewdley but I never told them why. I stayed for three days before I returned (stays of longer than this would have been regarded as desertion which I did not want to do).

I was put on a charge when I went back and as I was a Lance Corporal at the time I was reverted to Sapper again. This only lasted until I arrived in France. Within a few days we were moved to Gosport, Southampton where we were in camps with chain—link fence around and were again confined to barracks. I managed to get out, however, and tried to phone Gladys but all the phone lines from public phone boxes had been cut. Although D—Day had already started we did not know anything about it until we left Gosport.

I kept a diary from the point where we left England on Saturday 29th July, 1944. The landing craft we sailed on had very high sides and we could not see anything. There was widespread singing and it was a very emotional time. When we landed in France the back section of the landing craft dropped down forming a ramp to walk down into the water and we made our way up to the beach. The following is an extract of my diary written at that time:

"Left Gosport, England at 2300 hours. A good voyage. Arrived Courseulles, France 1800 hours Sunday, 20/7/44. Disembarked at 2000 hours. Left

Courseulles at 0500 hours 21/7/44. Passed through Caen – it was smashed to pieces. We got lost in the Tille section and were shelled at the crossroads. Had a lucky escape and finally found the company at Le Mesnil. Immediately received orders to dig in. We stayed at Le Mesnil for 29 days during which time we did various jobs in Caen. Most of the time we were under gunfire and it was not pleasant."

We were stationed at a farm where the house had been made headquarters and we were put in dug-outs around the farmland where we stayed for several weeks unloading lorries bringing materials from the boats. Our first casualty was a Sapper having half of his finger cut off by trapping it between two RSJ's being stored for future use on a Bailey Bridge. Close to our camp was a company of Blue Caps and one night the US Air Force bombed them but I do not know how many casualties there were as a result. The British bombed the enemy in front of the lines at night and the US carried out their attacks in the daytime. The account in my diary at this time reads:

"Our dug out was not waterproof. Every time it rained we were swamped out. We were also at Le Mesnil soon enough to witness the "big push" and now we started our travels in earnest."

We stayed at the farm until we broke through the Falaise Gap between 12th to 21st August, 1944 and reverting back to my diary account I wrote:

"On 29/8/44 we left Le Mesnil and went to Caen and stayed there for bridge maintenance. On 1/9/44 we left Caen and joined our headquarters at Clee Champs. Stayed there the night and left at 0500 hours the following day for Rouen. The journey could not be made in one day owing to the amount of traffic on the road. We stayed the night at Elbeuf and eventually arrived at Rouen on 3/9/44 where we stayed for 4 days during which time we helped to put a bridge across the Seine."

We built one side of the bridge and the Canadians built the other. In order to complete the task as quickly as possible we challenged one another! We started early in the morning and by evening the first tanks were going over the bridge. After we built the bridge over the Seine our next one was a lifting Bailey bridge and four of us designed this in Aldershot, England and the same four were sent to build this in France. The bridge was over a canal and was designed to lift to allow barges to pass underneath and then be lowered again to form a road. Charles, my brother-in-law, who was in the RAF said he went over the bridge and I believe this was the last one we built until we arrived in Ostend.

Reverting to my diary, on the 5th September, 1944 we were on the move again, destined for Abberville:

"Reached Abberville the same day. We spent 7 days there in a field and it rained nearly all the time. We were thoroughly fed up by the time we moved again on 12/9/44, this time for Inxent. We arrived the same day and once again the stay was short. We had two days training, much to our disgust and left on 14/9/44 for Ostend in Belgium.

We arrived in Ostend, Belgium on 14/9/44. We were the first British troops to enter the town and had a very good welcome" (Gladys wrote and told me later this was published in the Daily Express). "Most of us liked the Belgians far more than the French. The people were so different. My job in Ostend, to start with on 16/9/44, was clearing mines and booby-traps but our party of 4 were satisfied as it was the job we were trained to do. Had a break on 26/9/44 for 3 days to help mark a road on the beach for the LTC's (landing craft) to unload.".

We stayed in Ostend quite a few weeks as we cleared the mines from the beaches. The mines were fitted on the top of poles sunk into the sand as obstructions to stop landing craft. We then had to clear shops and hotels along the seafront as quite a number had booby-trapped mines put in them. We also had to put in a temporary ramp from the sea to the main road for men arriving from the landing craft before progressing to the Arnhem Battle area. Reverting back to my diary now:

"Although a few small boats were beginning to land in the docks, one of the first got blown up by a mine. We were soon called back to the platoon again working on bridging and road-making. We carried on checking houses, although they were pretty clear as the sea had exploded most of them but on 9/10/44 we came to a finish and had to join our platoon on the road. They had just started so that broke our little gang up as a working party because being in different trades we do different sorts of jobs. The road we started was to the bridge the company had built. I was helping on this job until 16/10/44 when I was moved with 4 others out of our platoon to help No.1 platoon on a bridge which the army had blown in 1940.

We started off by stripping it as the idea was to have a Bailey bridge put across the centre and leave the two ends as they were not damaged at all but after 3 days we were recalled to our own platoon as they had got another road to do and so we started that on 13/10/44 and finished on 5/11/44. On 6/11/44 we began clearing the beach of mines on the west side of Ostend but on 10th I was taken off to fetch some timber from Holland for Bailey Bridging. I transferred into 2 platoon, which meant a move to Knokke and we started to get ready for the Bailey bridge on 15/11/44 over the Leopold Canal. After getting the site ready we started to repair a bridge over the second part of the canal. Then on 3/12/44 we put the Bailey bridge across. We completed the bridges on 13/12/44 and on 14/12/44 we started to repair hotels that were going to be used for hospitals and convalescent depots."

A lifting Bailey Bridge

At this point we were sent to clear road mines which involved 2 or 3 of us digging a hole at the side of the canal. We had to reach a drum which was filled with explosive, locate the detonator and defuse this to make it safe. While we were doing this some of our colleagues were clearing the actual road mines. On one particular occasion, a mine blew up killing Sapper Gibbs (a bricklayer from Coventry). Also, Sergeant Reynolds, with whom I had become close friends, was killed by the same mine. He had been in the 8th Army in the Middle East and a few weeks before had the news of a new baby daughter and I felt his loss deeply. He had experienced a very difficult time in the Middle East and survived so it seemed dreadful he lost his life doing something he had successfully carried out many times before. After this I went to Brussels and my account of this from my diary is as follows: "On 7/1/45 I went to Brussels on 48 hour leave where I had a nice time visiting places of interest such as the Unknown Warriors Tomb, The Palace of Justice and one of the best canteens was The Montgomery where there was everything for comfort. The only thing that was not good was the weather as it snowed most of the time. Then on 9/1/45 I returned to my platoon at Knokke. On 28/1/45 we left to go to a village close to Bruges for the purpose of building a prison camp in Zedelgem. It was a place where the Germans had a lot of ammunition sheds so we had the job of laying on water and light and different tasks of a similar nature. The amount it was to hold was 50,000 prisoners. When it was finished and the first batch arrived from Germany (on 15/2/45) on 25/3/45 I was posted to 665AW Company at Ostend but on 26/3/45 I returned to 232AT Company to carry on with the Prisoner of War Camp.

We stayed until 17/4/45 when we went to headquarters at Ostend to start our travels again but on arriving I got details to go on a Werewolf Training Course with 3 NCO's at the west side of Ostend as A company going into Germany. So many men trained on various things so the company moved off on 18/4/45 leaving us behind to catch up with them at a later date. We finished the course on 19th May and on 20th May we started off to join our company in Hamburg. The first day we arrived at Dieste in Belgium where we spent the night with some Belgian people and had a very nice time. The second day we crossed the border into Germany for the first time. Everything was alright except for the roads which were terribly knocked about by tanks and bombs. Then we crossed the Rhine where the RE's were putting a Bailey bridge across at Xanten and travelled to Holland where we stayed the night with some Dutch people.

The house belonged to a Dutch gentleman (who was a Bank Manager) and his wife and two young daughters. When we got up to have our breakfast next morning (which was supplied to us by the army as a 14 day ration pack) and began eating we noticed the two daughters were crying. We asked what was the matter and their father explained it was because they had never seen white bread before. There was a shortage of food everywhere and when we left we gave them the remains of the ration pack and the white bread and it was like giving them the world. We left their house after breakfast.

Taking up this position in my diary now, it reads:

"On the 3rd day we started off at 9 am back into Germany along very bad roads, through towns and cities that had been bombed terribly. We arrived at Brennan at 5.30 pm, went along the by-pass so we did not see much of the city as we got onto the autobahn which was a treat to ride along and at 6.30 pm we stopped at a REME workshop for tea and decided to stay the night. Then on the fourth day we started off at 8 am and got to Hamburg which we were told had been bombed terribly with incendiary bombs but these were not all military objectives. We travelled through the other side of the city where our company was stationed in a school and I think the best billet I had ever been in.

The company had German civilians working for them and I became friendly with the tailor who lived close by. He carried out all the alterations to uniforms and any repairs that were needed. On several occasions he invited Sapper Sidebottom and I to meet his family and we went along one evening, although as we were not supposed to fraternise with the German people, we had to be careful and were told when it was clear to enter or leave. When we were chatting generally with these people they told us that two members of their family were in the forces stationed in Russia. I believe the youngest daughter's husband was in the navy as he was in a submarine and they had not heard from either of the men for two years.

The second daughter worked in a women's clothes shop and she gave me a pair of stockings for Gladys which I took home when I next went on leave and promised to bring them some ground coffee in return. This I did and they were very excited as they had not been able to obtain any for years. When we left their home the daughter married to the submariner would go down the stairs and tell us when the coast was clear to return to barracks. Other times I would walk around the park in Hamburg and the officers used to have horses to ride around the grounds and the local Germans would try and make conversation. It was difficult but a great many of them spoke broken English. I was soon posted back to Rippon in Yorkshire, however.

On my way back to England by train we saw many towns which had been bombed. Essen was nothing but rubble. After I arrived at Rippon to start my Military Foreman of Works Course, the War in the Far East had finished so I did not complete it and became posted to Halifax where I was stationed in a school for a short time to carry out repairs that were required to any of the buildings. I was then moved to South Oram into Nissen huts and this I found very boring as there was nothing to do but guard duty once or twice a week. The days I was free I used to go for walks quite frequently and on Sundays I attended the church service in Brighouse which was three or four miles walk from South Oram. Brighouse had a famous brass band, although I was not aware of this while I was stationed there but I have seen it perform on television several times since.

While I was in South Oram I met a family by the name of Mr and Mrs Carter and their daughter called Edith who was about 16 years old. This was quite by accident as I was travelling from Halifax to South Oram on the bus and struck up a conversation with Edith who was sat next to me. We chatted and she invited me to visit them at their home. They had a son who was also in the army and made me very welcome.   I used to visit some evenings when I was free and as I was working in the Cookhouse, sometimes I managed to take them a half-pound of butter which they were very pleased to receive! They were very hospitable and I enjoyed their company.

I also attended evening classes at Halifax College where I took up stone dressing which I found quite interesting at the time. Yorkshire was noted for its stonework so it was appropriate to learn this art and proved to be valuable knowledge throughout my working life. I was in the area approximately nine months and was then posted to Egypt. We left England and sailed for four days, during which time there was a terrible storm as we passed through the Gulf of Lions in the North–West Mediterranean. The swell was so great I vividly recall seeing the wall of the waves rising far higher than the side of boat which was very frightening and caused mass biliousness! After a few hours the storm subsided and the sea became quite calm and at that point I have fond memories of the sight of flying fish all around the boat and a school of porpoise swimming and rising in the wake.

When we eventually arrived at Alexandria, Egypt and were unloaded onto the lorries I well remember the Lieutenant sitting on the back of the truck with his coat slung over his arm. As the lorry moved off one of the Egyptians sprung from nowhere, stole the coat from him and was out of sight within a few seconds! We made our way to where I was stationed which was close to the Suez Canal. On my first morning there, when I looked out of the tent, I saw a ship which appeared to be travelling across the sands and this peculiar sight I will never forget!

During my stay here I worked in a Drawing Office with very little to do. The small amount of drawings I carried out were engineering ones of mechanical components of army vehicles and we developed the blue prints in a glass frame using the sun. While I was in the Drawing Office I was offered "B Release" but turned it down as I was very close to being de–mobbed I considered it a waste of time. With the benefit of hindsight this was a mistake as I was later called up for "Z Training" after being de–mobbed regardless and I will go into greater detail on this later in my book. In my spare time I played quite a lot of tennis and used to get up early before the weather became unbearably hot and also played the occasional game of cricket. The pitch consisted of a concrete slab with closely woven coconut matting on its surface.

I recall I once went to Alexandra for a week's leave and spent majority of my time swimming in the sea. It was from here I was sent to England to be de–mobbed but a short while before I returned home I recall one night the CO's car was stolen from the car pound. The wire enclosure had been cut and the car had been pushed approximately 200 yards to the road where it was loaded onto a lorry and stolen by the Egyptians. This was not an uncommon occurrence and we followed the footprints and the track of the car where it had been pushed across the desert and put on the lorry. As I left the area for France within a few days I do not know if it was ever located but very much doubt it would have been found.

The morning I was due to leave early to catch the train the guard who was given the task of waking us must have overslept and consequently I missed the army train. A vehicle was laid on to take me to the station and the driver tried to catch up with the train but it was too late so I had to wait for the next which was a civilian one. This arrived a few hours later and during my journey where several other soldiers were coming from Burma for de-mobbing, one of the Egyptian beggars was sat on the floor of the carriage asking people to buy chapattis. Two or three of the Burmese soldiers picked him up and threw him through the window while the train was moving. I was so shocked at this but later realised the soldiers had a dreadful time in Burma with the Japanese witnessing many atrocities and the beggar bore the brunt of their tortured state of mind. The most shocking fact is no one showed any emotion or protest at what occurred and it was a very distressing experience to witness.

When we arrived at the de-mobbing depot in Toulon, France we spent approximately one week there and it was very boring and frustrating as we were very impatient to get home! We then took a train across to Calais which was a very pleasant journey with wonderful scenery and took three days travelling time altogether. We crossed from Calais to Dover and were taken to another de-mob centre where we collected our suits which fitted where they touched! Upon arrival in UK we then had to make our way across London to catch the train to take us home. I then made my way from Kidderminster station to Parkfield in Chester Road, Kidderminster to continue my life with Gladys. She had no knowledge of this until I arrived at the front door!

MY PLACES OF WORSHIP

I was between the age of 10 and 12 when I first joined the choir at Ribbesford Church after being asked by Gerald Clee. Mr Stevenson was the choirmaster at the time and he lived at Severnside South. Fellow choirboys were Gerald Clee, Harrold Gillam, and John Gardiner. The male choristers were Frank Ashcraft, Harry Gillam, Fred Gardiner from Acacia Avenue (Uncle to my friend John Gardiner), Mr Smith from Lax Lane, Jim Davis from High Street (my Uncle), Sam Page (unofficially used to play the organ and I used to pump up the bellows for him to play while the other lads kept watch outside and told us when Mr Stevenson was on his way so we could close it down before his arrival!). Once a year we used to go to Longbank Church for the Harvest Thanksgiving Service. This church closed long ago and is now a domestic dwelling.

While I was a choirboy at Ribbesford I attended Confirmation classes with the Reverend Gunner. I was Confirmed at St Annes Church on February 28th, 1934 and my first Communion took place on Mothering Sunday in 1934. Notable members of the congregation at Ribbesford at that time included Mr Machiness and his family of two children (a Dentist who lived at

Cleobury Road and I mentioned this under the history of this road) and Mr and Mrs Geoffrey Sturt and family of three boys Anthony, Phillip and Evelyn also attended when they came to Winterdyne on their holidays around four times each year.

When my voice broke I could not sing very well and still can't! I attended St Annes Church in the evening and was asked by Jack Coldrick if I would like to be a Sidesman and I accepted and became very friendly with Mike Young. We remained good friends up until he passed away and it was during these times I met Gladys Timms who later became my wife. I have spoken about this in greater detail under the chapter on Gladys. The bell ringers at St Annes Church were George Bishop from Acacia Avenue, Alf Moule from Severnside South and Wilf Bishop from the Anchor Pub in Welsh Gate. Sadly I cannot recall the names of the others and knew these people well as they also worked at Coldrick's.

Gladys and I used to attend Callow Hill Methodist Church on a Sunday evening with Mr and Mrs Busy and Auntie George. Gladys' Foster-Father, William Busby, was Superintendent of this church and also conducted the services at Frith Common Methodist Church six miles away. On 9th January, 2011 this church was sadly closed and the very last service was performed. This takes me back a long, long time. I used to talk to Gladys about when she was living at Pleasant Place, Longbank with the Busby family. Her foster parents had taken her from an orphanage at Marston Green, Birmingham at around the age of 13 years of age. Gladys lived in Lichfield Road, Aston, Birmingham before becoming an orphan.

Mr and Mrs Busby were very strong Methodist people, visiting Callow Hill Methodist at least three times a day on Sundays. When Mr Busby preached at Frith Common on certain Sunday evenings he used to cycle but when he took Gladys with him they used to have to walk a round trip of approximately 12 miles! I do not know how many attended the service but one family in particular always visited and in later years it was for this family the church was kept open. I took Gladys in the car to visit the church many years later when she was alive, especially when there were problems with the church building whereby the existing wall on the roadside collapsed and had to be reconstructed. Unfortunately, we never found time to attend a service before its closure due the commitment to Bewdley.

It was a very sad time for me to attend the last service at Frith Common on 9th January, 2011. I spent most of my time thinking of the occasions Mr Busby and Gladys had been there and I considered it a travesty to close it as in my time I had seen Callow Hill almost closed but it was revived again. Also, Bewdley Methodist had seen some lean times but they have survived.

I feel sure, however, with Desiree being a member at Callow Hill Methodist Church Mr and Mrs Busby and Gladys would be very proud of her. I have never been a member of the Methodist Church but have regularly attended since 1938 with Gladys at Callow Hill and Bewdley when she was alive and have continued this to date since my retirement.

When I came out of the army in 1945 I did not go to church very often as I was working most weekends. While we lived in Kidderminster Gladys attended George Street Methodist Church for about two years and joined Bewdley Methodist Church around 1952 after we moved to Spencer Avenue and was a member for more than 50 years. At that time they had a choir led by Mr Cliff Jones from Stourport. He used to cycle over to take choir practice on Tuesday evenings and the services on Sunday, both morning and evening. I can remember the people in the choir at that time were Nancy Sollom, Phyllis Cross and Lilly Bridgman (all of whom were sisters), Phyllis Dalloway and Gwen Hughes (also sisters), Mrs Christie, Eric Finch, Hux Jones and Gladys. In those days I only went to church occasionally as I had to work quite a number of Sundays at Brintons or elsewhere!

Des attended Sunday School at Bewdley Methodist every Sunday and received an award for her constant attendance. Once Des had her own car she and Pat Dalloway used to collect the children from home to take them to church and return them home afterwards. Although I am not a member, I frequently used to help and was made Property Steward with Hux Jones. I also assisted Eric Finch when he wanted to locate a suitable site on which to construct a new church. We visited several sites, the most suitable being in The Park on the way up to Tickenhill but it was not possible to obtain planning permission. Soon afterwards, however, Eric left Bewdley to spend his retirement in Wales and the plans were forgotten. I used to go when I was not working and we attended evening services until they were discontinued.

At Bewdley it was suggested we ought to do something about the heating as it was so cold in the winter so I suggested we installed a partition at the rear of the church and put in a false ceiling, including over the organ. This I put forward at a meeting in the church which was attended by most of the members, including Phyllis Cross, Phyl Dalloway, Nancy Sollom and many others who thought it would be a good idea. Two members, however, were against this, Philip Powell and one other (a Bank Manager at Cleobury Mortimer whose name escapes me as he did not attend very often). It was not long afterwards part of the false ceiling and partition was put in but to my mind this was never completed as it still loses a great deal of heat above the site of the organ. With all the ups and downs I still attend Bewdley Methodist Church to be with Gladys in my thoughts on alternate Sundays and I firmly believe it was wrong to close Frith Common Methodist Church just to appease a certain few.

We helped on many occasions with raising funds such as Rummage Sales in St Georges Hall with Nancy Sollom and also cleaning the church with Phil Dalloway, plus any other projects if I was asked as the church was Gladys' enjoyment in life. There was a period of around five years, however, where we could only attend church when Gladys was well enough. After she died I returned to Callow Hill for a short time where Des is now a member and attends every Sunday. I also attend St Marys, Abberley where Gladys' ashes are interred in the churchyard and alternate my attendance every week, visiting Bewdley Methodist one week and Abberley the following, then occasionally I go to Callow Hill Methodist. In the past I have done a sponsored walk for Stourport, Bewdley and Callow Hill Churches to raise funds for different projects.

FAMILY LIFE WITH GLADYS AND DES

Gladys was born 5th May, 1919 in Aston, Birmingham, nee Timms. She lived in an orphanage in Marston Green until the age of 13 when she was fostered by the Busby family with another girl from Birmingham by the name of Betty Stanley. I remember Gladys joining Lax Lane School but only as a new girl starting in my class and she lived at Pleasant Place, Longbank. As previously mentioned, Mr Busby was superintendent at Callow Hill Methodist Church and Gladys had to attend church three times on Sundays. Morning Service, afternoon Sunday School and again for the Evening Service. Some Sundays, when Mr Busby was preaching at Frith Common Methodist Church she would walk the considerable distance from Long Bank with him to attend the service. She was a member of Bewdley Methodist Church for over 50 years and received a plate in 1995 to commemorate their bicentenary 1795 to 1995.

Mr Busby was extremely strict and even though her Foster Mother, Mrs Busby, was quite the opposite, the religious discipline had an influence on her for the rest of her life. Also living with the family was Mrs Busby's sister, known as Auntie George, a very kind lady who kept house for them and there were two sons by the names of Harry (who lived at Edgbaston) and Stan (who lived in Sutton Park Road, Kidderminster). Betty Stanley also attended Lax Lane School but after she completed her time there she returned to Birmingham where both she and Gladys were born and she lost contact with her from then on.

Mike Young, a fellow classmate at Lax Lane School took a liking to Gladys and bought her a box of Milk Tray chocolates during our schooldays and she told me years later she did not actually eat them and gave them to the other classmates! That is about all I can recall about her in my schooldays. When Gladys left school the Busby family said she had to go into service so they found a job for her doing housework at Dr. Lawrence's in Wribbenhall where she made friends with Marjorie Woster and remained close to her for the rest of her life. In her spare time she helped Marjorie with her family as she was always very fond of children.

After a short time at Dr. Lawrence's she left to work for Dr. Miles (Snr.) as a housekeeper and receptionist. She worked very long hours. Breakfast had to be cooked for 8 o'clock and then she had to carry out all the housework, plus answering the telephone and door to people who wanted to see the Doctor privately. Gladys was in contact with a large number of people in the district during the course of her job and she became very well known.

The next time I recall seeing Gladys was in 1937 while I was out with some of my scout friends, Les Evans, Jim Tolley, Harry Purcell and Mike Young. We were selling programmes for the Coronation of George VI so we visited the Miles' home in the hope they would purchase one. Gladys opened the door and was met by a degree of light-hearted banter from the other boys! I remained quiet at the back of the crowd and it is one of the occasions when it paid me to do so as she noticed this fact and agreed to purchase one of the programmes if it was from, and I quote, *"The quiet one at the back!!"* This was the beginning of what turned out to be a union in excess of 65 years.

When I started work I never thought of her again until one day when I was working on some houses in High Street opposite Dr Miles Senior's House at No.42. Gladys spoke to me on several occasions from the kitchen window as I worked on the houses nearby for a period of about 6 weeks. Gladys told me how she used to watch me walking along High Street on Saturday mornings on my way to violin lessons at Harry Oakes' on the Stourport Road. These cost 2 shillings and sixpence per hourly lesson! After I completed the work on High Street, Gladys sometimes would be looking out of her bedroom window just before 8 am and we would stop and have a few words with one another before I went on to work. A short while later, while I was working on one of the houses in Lax Lane she brought me a jug of tea each morning when Mrs Miles was away from home and it was from this point our friendship began to develop!

Other occasions I saw Gladys was at evening service at St Annes Church where Mike was in the choir and I was Sidesman. (I was not in the choir as my voice was not good enough and in later years Gladys often reminded me of this!). By this time Mike and I had become great friends and after the services we would always go for a walk before returning to my home at Winterdyne. Gladys only had every other Sunday off work as Mrs Miles was a very hard task-master. On some Sundays, when Gladys was allowed by Mrs Miles to attend St Annes Church, after the service we would stand chatting outside Tommy Timmis' the butchers. One particular time Mike asked her if she would like to go for a walk with him so I returned home. After about an hour Mike arrived at my home and I asked him why he was back so soon. He stated he and Gladys had walked down Stourport Road and when they arrived at the part where there was no street lighting she refused to walk any further. As a result, he and Gladys did not go on any more walks together!

I used to cycle to work, arriving at Coldricks at 8 am and she would sometimes be at the kitchen window of the Miles' home and now Gladys and myself were getting friendly I would stop and have a few words with her before starting work. After a short while I asked her if she would like to go to the Central Picture House in Kidderminster and she agreed. This was on my 19th birthday and I have to confess I cannot remember what we actually went to see but I know we walked home afterwards. From then on I used to see her every Friday as it was her half day from 3 o'clock until 10. We would visit some of her friends, Joan Purcell and Marjorie Woster and as Gladys had every other Sunday free from 2 pm until 10 pm we would go to tea with Mr and Mrs Busby, served by Auntie George and attend Callow Hill Methodist Church for the evening service.

Continuing with our life on Friday evenings and Sunday afternoons, we used to meet when I finished work at 5 o'clock, sometimes at my home at Winterdyne, and we used to walk around the grounds in the summer when the weather was nice. We liked to sit on the Drying Green (so called as it was where the washing was taken to be dried) which had a lovely view over the River Severn. In those days people used to swim in the area opposite the Bewdley Schools which was called Deep Splunts and we could see this clearly from the Drying Green. We had some very good times together at Winterdyne.

During one of our chats I asked Gladys what she would like for her 19th birthday. She used to do a large amount of needlework and told me she would like a sewing box. I went to Kidderminster on the day of her birthday and found a wooden sewing table which fitted the bill perfectly. I walked all the way back from Kidderminster with it and took it straight to Gladys at the surgery at 42 High Street. This was kept throughout our entire married life and after Gladys' sight failed her we used this to hold all our important documents. I still have it today and have very fond memories when I polish it each week!

On Sundays after church we would visit the Purcell family in Park Lane until it was time for Gladys to return to the Miles' home at 10 pm. Gladys was very friendly with Joan Purcell – Harry had been in the scouts with me and we were always made very welcome there. However, in 1939 there was major change when World War Two broke out which upset all our lives for some considerable time. Most of my friends were in the Territorial Army and were called up straight away. I tried to join the Royal Engineers with Dad's help but as I was an apprentice bricklayer they refused to accept me. I was instructed to go back and complete my apprenticeship and they would contact me later. I continued with this until I was 21 years old and was, therefore, able to continue to see Gladys on Friday evenings and Sundays as usual.

I recall on one occasion in 1939 Gladys wanted a present taken to her sister called Doll in Tamworth so I took it on my bicycle and returned back to Bewdley the same day. It was a Sunday as I remember and there was very little traffic in those days thankfully!

Mrs Miles Senior was a very unkind person to Gladys and I because I had not gone into the army, although we got on well with the rest of the family. I considered her to be an unpleasant woman but other than this we were fortunate to not be badly affected by the War at this point. One night, when we were at Marjorie Woster's home the air raid siren sounded. As we were not allowed out after hearing the siren we had to stay at Marjorie's and Gladys went to bed while I stayed on the settee all night until 6am when we went home to change before starting work.

Gladys and Marjorie always remained good friends until Marjorie sadly passed away on 31st March, 2003. Gladys kept in close contact with her daughter Margaret (with whom she spent a great deal of time while she was growing up). Margaret later had a daughter of her own called Hayley and I recall we were invited to Hayley's wedding in the Manchester area around thirty years ago. She also has children of her own now – time passes by so quickly!

In 1940 when I moved from Coldricks to Brintons although I was working long hours I was seeing Gladys as often as I could. I was called up by the army in 1941 and as the remuneration for working on munitions was good at Brintons I asked Gladys if she would like to work there. I took her around the factory to see what it was like but she was not impressed at all! I think one of the reasons for this was because the Busbys did not want her to return to Pleasant Place to live, therefore, she would have needed to lodge somewhere so she decided to remain at Dr Miles' despite the fact she was not happy with the treatment she received from Mrs Miles. She was, however, very fond of Dr Miles as he was always kind and by the time Dr Bob Miles joined the practice (Dr Hubert Miles' son) she had a very busy life looking after the extended family.

As mentioned under my army days, while I was stationed at Aldershot I obtained 7 days leave for Gladys and I to get married and this took place at St. Annes Church, Bewdley at 2 pm on 15th May, 1943. The service was conducted by Reverend Hollis, Harry Bishop was the Best Man, the Pageboy was Brian Woster and Pamela Busby was Bridesmaid. Gladys arranged for us to stay at Winbrook Cottage for the week while I was on leave.

This was owned by Nora Mynard whose husband was in the army and this is where we spent our honeymoon. Reverting back to our wedding, two of our guests Mr and Mrs Churchill (a former Bewdley policeman and his wife who were good friends of Gladys) attended from the Black Country. On the day of the wedding they had to return home and we walked them back to the

station to catch the train for their return journey. I remember it was a dreadfully cold day and the wind along the riverside was bitter. We were glad to make our way back to Winbrook Cottage.

There was a second time when I had leave and Nora allowed us to stay in her home again. It turned out to be a working holiday for me, however, as a fire developed under the hearth which was tiled over the floor joists. necessitating replacing the hearth and wooden floor and I had to obtain all the building materials from Coldricks and carry out the work before returning to the army.

After the wedding I returned to Aldershot to complete my training and then onto an ammunition depot in Kineton, Warwickshire. Next I was posted to France and wrote to Gladys every day but of course we were not allowed to disclose where we were stationed so I had pre-arranged with Gladys that the initial letter in the first word of my correspondence would be the first letter of where I was posted and subsequent letters would gradually spell the remainder of the place in which I was located. This is why Gladys always knew where I was within days of being moved!

Gladys now had a marriage allowance and I sent an extra amount from my pay of one shilling a week from which she managed to save and started accumulating items for our home. She purchased a dining room suite of which she was very proud and the two Miss Westley sisters in Lower Park kept it in their home until we had our own house when the war ended. Sadly, this had woodworm from the old house and although we kept it a number of years and treated the problem we eventually had to part with it.

I had several periods of leave where I came home to visit until I was sent to Egypt which prevented this, but I well remember the day I returned home after the War ended. It was not really like going home at all as by this time Gladys had found a job as housekeeper for a Mr and Mrs Gordon-Smith at Parkfield House in Chester Road South. They were a very pleasant couple and this was where we lived for a short while.   It was not really the home I wanted for us, however, but they made us very welcome. Mr Gordon-Smith had been a Judge somewhere in the Far East and his wife was a very pleasant, meek type of person.

It was not very long before Gladys became pregnant with Desiree and it was then very important to me to find our own home. This was very difficult at that time as rental and purchased properties were in very short supply so we decided upon renting a room with a Mr and Mrs George Millward at Habberley Road, Bewdley.   Gladys went into Sunnyside Nursing Home in Kidderminster to have our baby daughter. She was in the private nursing home for approximately one week where she was attended to by Dr Bob Miles. It was while she was in the nursing home I registered our daughter's birth as Desiree Allana. 'Desiree' had been mentioned several times as she knew a girl in the orphanage with this name and I liked it because it was unusual but when I told Gladys what I had done she was not very pleased with me. She had changed her mind and wanted the name Joan after her friend Joan Purcell but by then it was too late.

I took Gladys and our new baby back to the rented rooms at Habberley

Road and it proved to be rather an unpleasant time for us there. Within a few days Gladys had an accident while she was preparing Desiree for a bath and this had to be done in the kitchen as there was no bathroom. As she

Desirée at 4 years

was mixing the water for the bath she suddenly slipped with a basin of boiling water which unfortunately caught Desiree. I was informed at Brintons as Gladys was in a state of extreme distress and I biked back home to Habberley Road straight away. Desiree was taken to hospital and due to the panic of what happened I do not recall how she got there but she was very ill and Gladys had to supply her own milk for her to sustain her throughout this period. I do not know how long Desiree was in hospital as time did not register but thankfully she recovered and came home.

After this I was even more driven to find a home of our own but houses did not come up for sale very often. One was advertised for auction in Welsh Gate, Bewdley but we did not have the funds as being in the Forces there had never been sufficient to save. I went to the sale with the idea I could maybe have a mortgage so I bid up to £700 but had to drop out as it reached more than I could afford.

A short time afterwards In 1948, while I was working at Brintons, I heard on the grapevine there was a house advertised for sale in the Shuttle at No.62 Lorne Street. I immediately visited Phipps and Pritchard estate agents to enquire about it and met David, their Auctioneer at the time. Almost immediately, a person I knew who worked as a milkman for the Co-op arrived at their offices and he was also interested in purchasing the same house! In an effort to be fair to us both, David said we could either bid or toss for it. We chose the latter and I won the house on the toss of a coin for the princely sum of £700. I had not seen this property and took the risk due to the housing shortage either for rental or purchase. Our daughter Des was a baby in her first year and when we went to view the property Gladys was so upset at the prospect of having to live in a house in such bad condition she cried bitterly.

I made a promise to her that I would put the house in good order for us and it would only be necessary to keep it for five years as I would earn enough money in that time to build our own house. We moved into Lorne Street and I began the process of renovation. A new fireplace was installed in the lounge together with a sliding door at the foot of the stairs. Dick Keightly (who I have mentioned earlier in this book) came and did the decorating and painted the outside woodwork in a wood-grain effect which was popular at the time. I also re-built the kitchen and toilet at the rear of the property with a wooden clad passage from the back door to the kitchen. Bill Smith, the carpenter at Brintons carried out the woodwork modifications to provide a new passageway which saved Gladys needing to go outside in bad weather. Gladys became friendly with the neighbours, especially Kate Dorrell and Mr and Mrs Walker and we were a very happy family. Des started at Lea Street School and Gladys joined St Georges Methodist Church.

After we had settled in Lorne Street Mr and Mrs Gordon-Smith asked us if we would go back to Parkfield for two years as they were returning to work in the Far East. This we agreed to do and as it had a nice garden we thought it would be good for Desiree to play in. They paid for a person to visit to mow the huge lawn when required and Dad would come down on Sunday mornings to amuse Des. We allowed my brother Geoff and his wife to use Lorne Street until he purchased a house in Chester Road North so now I had to think about raising the money to build a house for Gladys as I had promised.

Detached houses then were costing £2,500 to £3,000 to purchase which was a great deal of money to us. My first opportunity came when Jack Morris (who worked in the Machine Shop at Brintons) asked me if I could help him out as his daughter and husband (Bill Lewis) were building a house in St John's Avenue, Kidderminster and they were having difficulties. I discussed this with Gladys and told her with a little luck this would enable us to raise the money to build a house of our own in five years added to the income from the overtime I earned at Brintons, plus the extra jobs I used to pick up in those days. This meant, however, that I would not be at home with Gladys and Des very much.

I do not recall the exact date but I think it was around 1949 when I started work on St John's Avenue. The work on this house progressed well with Bill being an electrician and a friend of Bill's by the name of Dick Garbett was a carpenter and we became great friends. Dick bought a piece of land next door to Bill as he intended to build a semi-bungalow on it (a bungalow with bedrooms upstairs) as he was unable to obtain planning permission for a bungalow. Reg Perrin, the Architect did the drawings for this and Harrold Lane, brother-in-law to Dick carried out the plumbing work with the electrical work being completed by Bill.

After I completed the brickwork on Bill's we started to dig out the foundations for Dick's and I completed the brickwork, helped him to put the roof on and then tiled this and laid the drains. At this time I was training for running in the sports day at Oldington and used the sports field at Harry Cheshire School which was at the bottom of Dick's garden. I climbed the fence onto the school field and Dick would ride his motorbike around the track as a pacer for me! Although I had gone past my best in running (in my army days I managed to run the mile in 4 minutes and 19 seconds) I achieved second place and won a clock.

During the time I commenced work on Dick's home, Harry Bishop also approached me asking if I would do the plans for the 3rd Bewdley Scout Headquarters in Wribbenhall but as I was still working in St John's Avenue it meant I would not be able to spend so much time on Dick's semi. I was, therefore, working Monday, Tuesday and Wednesday evenings for the Scouts and Thursday, Friday, Saturday and Sunday for Dick. As this was part of my five-year scheme I knew I would be pushing myself somewhat but I soldiered on. I began organising myself to a schedule for the two building jobs. Gladys visited most Saturdays on whichever job I was working with exception to when I worked at Brintons on Saturday mornings. On my building jobs in those days I used to ride a bicycle to work on which I had a baby seat fitted at the back and often took Des where she used to play at St. John's Avenue in the sand and later Gladys would come to be with us both. After Dick had completed the second fix on his home I did the plastering for him which completed my involvement with Dick's house.

I approached Len Thomas to buy a piece of land at the top of Spencer Avenue as I now had the money for this. He would only allow me to purchase part of it, however, and although it was not very big I decided to go ahead at a cost of £75. When I first came to the Avenue there were no cars and it was lined from top to bottom with Lime trees. There was a grass verge on both sides of the Avenue where people used to sit outside their homes. At the bottom of the Avenue next to the Parish Room was a tennis court but this is now used as the car park for the club room.

The first house beside the tennis court (No.1) was occupied by Mr and Mrs Lake followed by Mr and Mrs Millward (he was a Carpet Designer for Carpet Trades) at No.3. Miss Gardiner and her nephew Stan lived next door at No.5 and Miss Gardiner owned the next three houses too, Nos. 7, 9 and 11. Mr Nash and his son rented No.7 and Mr and Mrs Page (he was a weaver at Brintons) rented No.9. Stan Murray and his daughter rented No.11. This house was rented by my grandparents many years before and as previously mentioned, my parents lived with them for a time when my mother worked in the factory at Kidderminster and this was where my sister Florrie was born.

On the corner of Wheatcroft Avenue lived Mr and Mrs Danby and their daughter Winnie. They lived there for a large number of years, even after her parents passed away and she brought up her two sons there. Next was a piece of land owned by Mr Bert Stokes who lived in New Road. He used this land for growing vegetables and fruit trees and also kept poultry. He sold the land to my parents shortly afterwards and it was upon this land I built a bungalow for them which was No.15 Spencer Avenue. Next was a piece of land owned by Dick Lambert, Group Scout Leader of 1st Bewdley Scouts and he worked at Brintons. He also used the land for growing vegetables and I later purchased this and built the bungalow for my daughter. This brings us to the top of the Avenue where I built The Glen.

Covering the right-hand side of Spencer Avenue now which begins from No.4 belonging to Mr Ted Bath, this was originally built by his Father who was a carpenter by trade. Ted worked at Brintons in the front offices and lived alone as he had lost his wife previously. At that time he owned the land to the left which has now been built upon as No.6 Spencer Avenue. A bungalow has been built on the corner (No.8) which was occupied by the late Mr and Mrs Glazard and now John and Julie live here. The next bungalow (No.10) was a wooden home constructed by George Wallis, the carpenter and undertaker. This was lived in by Mr and Mrs Virgo (Mr Virgo was a Miner) and after they both passed away I dismantled it and built a brick bungalow in its place.

The next four houses (numbers 12, 14, 16 & 18 were built by a local builder by the name of Mr Farmer. Mr and Mrs Drew and her son Reg lived at No.12. Mr Bill Drew was a carpenter at Brintons and Mrs Drew lived to the grand age of 104! Mr and Mrs Wilkes (Mr Wilkes was Verger at the Church) and their daughter Gladys lived at No.14. Gladys used to clean the church and was responsible for the flower arrangements. No.16 was lived in by Mr and Mrs Birch (no relation) and she was a school teacher. Next door (No.18) was the home of Mr and Mrs Hunt (Ernest was a bricklayer and he worked for his cousin, Hunts the Builders).

There was a spare piece of land next to which was built upon by Mr and Mrs Millward, the designer at Brintons who lived at No.3, followed by No.22 which was owned by Mr and Mrs Thompson and their two sons, Mr Thompson being the owner of Thompson and Parkes the builders' merchants in Kidderminster. Mr Haynes lived at No.24 and he was a retired person who did not live there very often and it was then sold to Mr and Mrs Cliff Hancox until they passed on. I worked with Mr Hancox (who was a painter and decorator) on a number of occasions when I was an apprentice at Coldricks and helped to care for him until he passed away. Gladys and I took care of Mrs Hancox also when she became blind and she kindly left the bungalow to me when she passed away.

Covering Wheatcroft Avenue now, (which crosses both the left and right of Spencer Avenue), first taking the left hand side spur, the first house on the right was Mr and Mrs Thomas and they had a son and daughter. Mr Thomas was an Engineer who worked at Muller in Cleobury Mortimer. The next house was occupied by Mr and Mrs Thomas Rickets who was a wheelwright and blacksmith from Stourport Road. Later Styles the corn merchants moved into that building but it is now residential houses known as Rickets Place. The following property is a wooden bungalow lived in by Mrs Edwards and her two sons, one of which is called David and he still lives there. The last bungalow was occupied by a retired butler but I do not know his name. The field next to this property used to belong to Spring Grove and is called Cordle Marsh.

Passing to the right-hand side of Wheatcroft Avenue now, there were no houses in this section in my younger days. This was in fact the only right-of-way for a property situated in Maypole Close and allowed the family access to the church. I owned the land in this road together with No.10, the bungalow on the corner which I rented to Mr and Mrs Virgo at that time. I later took a piece of land off the back of the gardens and built a bungalow on it called "Charlcote" for my sister.

Reverting back to my preparations to build The Glen now I drew up the plans for the house and Trevor Jones out of the Drawing Office at Brintons agreed to re-draw them and take some prints for me. I raised sufficient money to build The Glen and started constructing it in 1951 and this is still my home today. It took me five years to raise the funds and complete the construction, by working an average of 13 to 14 hours a day, seven days a week over that period whilst also building the two houses in St John's Avenue and the Scout Room on a voluntary basis. It was close to the bus route for Gladys to go to Kidderminster or Birmingham as she liked looking around the shops there and she could get to Aston to visit her Aunt and Sister called Rose.

Gladys said she would not move to a house on this site unless I attached it to the main sewer so I went to see Mr Rowe the Bewdley Surveyor, and, of course, he was fully supportive on condition I installed large enough pipes to put the entire Avenue, including Wheatcroft Avenue on the system. If I agreed to do this he would bring the sewer across the road to the bottom of the Avenue for a charge of £14 which was worthwhile to me so I did as he asked. The Council connected the Parish Rooms to the sewer so they managed to avoid paying.

Harry and I decided upon a charge of £25 per connection and once I had completed each interested household to the sewer I was now ready to dig out the foundations of The Glen. I discussed the plans with Sid Beddows, one of the bricklayers at Brintons who suggested it looked too much like a council house so I should install a bay window in the front, which I did. The window frames and woodwork was carried out by Dick Garbett. I used Hopes Windows which were supplied to me at cost by Harry Busby, Gladys' brother who was a Manager there. I seemed to be getting help from everywhere! Harry and Ruth lived at Edgbaston, Birmingham at the time and when he later retired they moved to Torquay to live.

Harry and Ruth had two daughters called Nina and Margaret. Nina lived in flats at Lea Bank, Birmingham and Margaret moved to Torquay to be close to her Mother. Gladys and I went down to visit several times and stayed with them but sadly Harry passed away leaving Ruth alone so Gladys and I spent several summer holidays with her. After I retired I used to take Nina down to spend time with her Mother and would return the same day. I would later collect her again when she was ready if she needed transport as sometimes she returned by bus. Nina moved to Churchill, Redditch and I used to collect her to take her to Callow Hill Church Anniversary as she always attended this church when she stayed with her Grandparents during holiday time.

While digging out the foundations of The Glen, due to the slope of the ground, I decided (to Harry's disgust) to put a coal cellar under the dining room. This took me four days hard work as I had to remove approximately 4 feet of sandstone but it was worth it as I later made it into a boiler room and workshop when I later removed the coal fires. I then completed the brickwork up to the damp course. The bricks I used were second-hand and came from Bantock's Stables on Station Hill in Kidderminster which was being demolished at the time. It was from here the horses were taken to collect carpets from the local manufacturers to deliver to Kidderminster Station.

I decided I would suspend the concrete floor over the site as it would be warmer and would avoid any damp problems. I covered the area with galvanised sheets before laying a depth of approximately 6" over the ground floor. The concrete was mixed by hand with help from a few friends and with this completed I decided I would start installing the sewer in the avenue. This was quite a task as the depth was approximately 3 feet at the bottom of the avenue up to Wheatcroft Avenue where I made it around 6 feet deep as one person said he would like his bungalow in Wheatcroft put on the sewer. As this would bring in extra cash I said I would consider it and the sewer finished at the top of the avenue at about 3 feet deep. Des used to come with me at weekends on the back of my bike, often playing with Sandra Thomas who lived locally – I recall them sitting on my saw bench which doubled up as their horse!

The water supply for the Glen was connected to the pipe which fed the Scout Room. Arthur Goodwin carried out the connection for me as he had put the Scout Room on from the mains outside No.22. I now began putting the other houses on the sewer and Harry Bishop made arrangements with the owners for the connections. The first pair of houses (No.1 and 3) said they did not want to go on as in those days they were rented properties and the landlord refused to pay for it. Then came Miss Gardiner who owned the next four houses (Nos. 5, 7, 9 and 11) and she agreed to the connection. Ted Bath who lived on the opposite side of the avenue refused and the residents at No.8 asked to be included. Winnie Danby at 1 Wheatcroft Avenue agreed and there were no further properties on this side of the road at that time. On the opposite side, Eric Thomson lived at No.8 and asked to be connected and the last resident was Mr Haines who also said yes.

I returned to Wheatcroft Avenue to speak to the residents and all agreed with exception to Len Thomas whose son Stan lived in his property and felt he should not be expected to pay as I was making enough money so he offered me another piece of land at the rear of The Glen which I accepted. After all the connections to the houses were made I could concentrate on The Glen. During the summer months I worked 13 to 14 hours each day, including weekends and in the winter I borrowed a floodlight from Brintons so I could keep the work going. I worked most evenings on my own but Dad helped me a few evenings when he could. My brother Geoff came one day but it was not really his line of work. Harrold Lane did the plumbing with Don Williams installing the electrics. The scaffolding consisted of oil drums and planks which would have given health and safety a field day!

Although it was approximately two years hard work, Gladys and I felt it had been worth all the problems. She soon made friends with Stan and Pinky Thomas who lived in Wheatcroft Avenue and Des soon settled down to the area, having the Rutter family as friends together with Sandra Thomas. Gladys and Des joined the Bewdley Methodist Church and Des attended Sunday School, attending three times a day and was presented with a medal for not missing the three Sunday visits for 52 weeks of the year. I helped out at church when necessary but had to work most Sundays. In fact when Des had her first car many years later she used to collect the local children from around Bewdley to take them to Sunday School. When the time came for naming the house, Gladys discussed this with her friend, Mrs Muir (the vet's wife from Imperial Avenue in Kidderminster) and as she was from Scotland, Gladys decided our house should be called The Glen.

Now with most of the work completed we had to move from Lorne Street, Kidderminster. I believe it was November, 1953 and it snowed that day! We had Jimmy Douglas (a haulage contractor through Brintons) to bring our furniture as I did a lot of business with him at work. As we were leaving Lorne Street Des asked the driver to pass by Lea Street School so she could wave goodbye to her friends! In total, the cost of building The Glen amounted to £1,000 and this I achieved without any loans or mortgage. During the building process I won £100 on the Harriers Grand Slam which paid for the roof tiles. I had several wins on the Brintons Tote and Ray Ferris who administered the scheme began to tire with me winning so many times! With overtime and the profit from the sewer I paid for the entire build with my own resources!   It was now time to do the garden. I built a rustic four-sided shed for Des to play in, plus my own shed at the back to house my tools. Des called her area The Little Glen!

After we settled in Harry Bishop asked me to go in shares with him to purchase house numbers 12, 14, 16 and 18 in Spencer Avenue, which I did and as it was £200 each to buy these properties Harry persuaded me, against my will, to borrow £200 from Bewdley Council which incurred 2.5% interest. I paid this back in two years and then a few years later Harry asked me to go in shares with him again to purchase a wooden bungalow (no.10 Spencer Avenue). The cost was £700 and we decided to go ahead but when I told Gladys she was not very pleased as she said it was more work and worry for me.

It may be interesting to note the rents we charged in 1956 for these houses ranged from 8 shillings and sixpence to 13 shillings (for a three bedroom, with kitchen, dining and living room – no bathroom at this stage). In 1961

Mrs Birch at No.14 died and Eric Bishop (Harry's son) took over the house at a rent of £2.14.10 per week and in 1962 the rent on the bungalow was £1.2.0 per week, all these charges being inclusive of rates!

We later decided to install bathrooms in all of the houses so I drew up the plans for one at the rear of the kitchen on each home as this was the easiest option without causing too much disruption to the tenants. When the plans had been passed I immediately began building the extensions which took several months as I had to put them all on the sewer and also a new water pipe had to be installed from the water main in Spencer Avenue.

Des at 17

Now most of the large building jobs were completed, Harry Bishop (who was Chairman of The Old Pals in Bewdley) bought a shed and room previously belonging to the old Convalescent Home in Lower Park and as covered previously in my book under Park Alley (off High Street) I became involved with the conversion of this building.

Sadly, in 1964 my friend Harry Bishop was taken ill and passed away with cancer and I was not allowed to go to the funeral. No one but his son Eric attended but this was possibly his father's wishes. I know Harry took his wife's death very badly and was against religion but I was very upset as Harry, Gladys and I had been good friends for a number of years. He was best man at our wedding and we had been through a lot together over the course of time. After Harry died the Old Pals finished sadly and the Scouts had the room in the grounds of the old Convalescent Home for a short time

188

afterwards but today it forms part of a private dwelling. Harry's share of the houses passed to his son Eric and I now had to collect the rent. In 1967 Eric and his family went to live in Canada where he was a teacher. I would bank his share of the rent at the Midland Bank in Bewdley and he could then access this from Canada. In 1968 I purchased Eric's share of the properties and gradually sold them all off as they became empty. I regularly receive telephone calls from Eric who still lives in Canada and we keep each other posted with current news!

When the occupant of the wooden bungalow passed away by the name of Mrs Virgo, I dismantled the structure, erecting a brick built bungalow in its place and sold it as soon as it was complete. In 1960, after we had been living in The Glen for two years I asked Gladys if she would like Mother and Dad to live in the Avenue to which she replied "not at all!" but Dad bought the two plots of land next to Winnie Colley from Bert Stokes, a weaver at Brintons Limited. I did the plans for their bungalow (No.15 Spencer Avenue) and it took approximately two years from plan to actual erection. I later built "Charlcote" in Wheatcroft Avenue for my sister Florrie and also No.10 Spencer Avenue which I later sold.

Gladys loved to go on the bus to look around the shops in Birmingham and the position of The Glen being so close to the bus route made this very easy. She used to go to Fellowship on Tuesday afternoons and it was after one of these meetings she came home and asked me if we could foster a baby boy. I immediately agreed to this and she said it was to be a black child to which I was in complete agreement. When Gladys asked Des if she would like a black baby brother she was very excited and said she did not mind what colour he was! The following day the lady arrived from the fostering agency at Stourbridge with the baby and we called him David. His name beforehand was Spancho. Gladys immediately went to buy bedding for Des' old cot and clothing for David, which was quite a task as he had arrived so quickly! As he grew up Gladys took great delight in dressing him nicely as she had always done with Desiree.

This was such a happy time and we took him everywhere. I can remember the time we took him to Wales with Mother and Dad – people always made a fuss of him everywhere we went. We were amazed at how much attention he was given by all, even in the shops and David always had a smile for everyone. We had many humorous times with him. He set about picking all the heads off the flowers in the garden one day at the age of two and took them to Gladys. Des still recalls David's reaction when he was told he really should not have picked them. He said "Daddy will not be very pleased!"

We had thought of trying to adopt David against the advice of many of our friends and I feel we should not have listened. His Mother never came to see him but his Father came bringing several friends with him each time. It was not easy to make conversation with them and each visit became more difficult. His Father eventually wanted him back and so we decided we had no option but to go ahead with this. We had to take him to Redditch where he was put on a coach with his cousin Primrose to take them to the airport in readiness for their return to Jamaica to live with his Granny. When the coach pulled off Gladys was hysterical. Mother came with us and tried to console Gladys but I can honestly say this was the worst journey of all our lives and we missed David terribly.

This affected us profoundly for a long time afterwards. Dr Miles decided Gladys should have a job to distract her from her grief and obtained a position for her at Kidderminster hospital looking after aged people for a time and she later moved onto the wards. Gladys worked at the hospital for a number of years. She was now getting over the loss of David a little – I say a little because she never really recovered from the emptiness. He came to visit us a number of years afterwards when he returned from Jamaica and he used to ring Des quite frequently but it is some years since we last heard from him.

It was during the time Gladys worked at the hospital that she met Richard Mills who had sustained a broken leg in a motorcycle accident, resulting in rather a long stay in hospital and she also met and made good friends with his parents, Tom and Vera from Great Witley. This friendship was to last for many, many years until they all sadly passed away.

Tom and Vera had the Post Office at Great Witley which Vera ran, together with a general store attached while Tom was the Postman for the Great Witley area. At the back of the Post Office Tom had a large shed where he repaired farm vehicles belonging to all the local farmers. He also carried out repairs to some properties in the local vicinity. We visited the shop several times and met an Aunt who lived with them. There was a large cherry orchard at the back of the shop and Tom wanted a bungalow to be constructed on this land. I prepared the plans for this and he had the property built, while I constructed a septic tank for him and set it up before they moved in. They sold the Post Office and shop and we made regular visits to them and they often called to see us at The Glen.

Tom asked me if I would go to Abberley Church where his parents were buried to repair their graves and we did this work together. There were two graves, one for his parents and another for his Aunt Agnes. Historically, Tom's parents owned The Manor Hotel at Abberley when he was young and after they passed away, Agnes took over and lived there until she died.

Tom also owned several properties in Abberley Village, including a piece of land. I surveyed this for him and drew plans to enable him to obtain planning permission. He then gave this land to relatives but to this day it remains undeveloped. Close to this there is a row of houses which Tom owned and I recall helping him to sort out a problem he had with some of the tenants. His brother also had a bungalow built in the village where he lived until he tragically died there in a fire. Tom and Vera were laid to rest in the Aunt's grave, together with Richard who sadly passed away before his parents and Tom's brother who lost his life in the fire.

Shortly after Tom and Vera's death Gladys became unwell and she asked if anything happened to her would I always take care of Des. I have done my best to this end since Gladys died and decided I would build a new bungalow for her on the land next to The Glen. This I achieved with the help of Bewdley Builders and I feel Des is happy in her home. When she moved into the bungalow majority of the members of Callow Hill Church came to the House Blessing which was carried out by Paul Booth, the Vicar at the time.

Gladys and I loved our time spent in Abberley as it was very quiet and peaceful until the rooks were breeding in April and May time when the chatter from them was incredible! Gladys always said she would like to be buried in Abberley Churchyard but Tom and Vera said it was only possible for Abberley people so we gave up hope. Fortunately, I later obtained permission for Gladys' ashes to be buried there after talking to Alan Norkett the Vicar of St. Marys, Abberley at the time so she had her wish.

Our 40th Wedding Anniversary on Concorde

MOTHER AND DAD

As I mentioned under the section on Wyre Hill, Dad was born at No.14 on 24th May, 1891, the second eldest of a large family of seven children. They were named Ernest, and then my Father William, Allen, Ethel, Gertrude, Edith and the youngest was Cyril.

Dad was educated at Wyre Hill School but the younger ones attended Lax Lane. Wyre Hill later became the Junior School for those children living locally but sadly this was knocked down soon after the Second World War. One of the places Dad worked after first leaving school was for his Uncle who was a contractor for drain laying. There was a lot of work in this area at that time to insert land drains across farms and various other properties as there were no road drains in those days. All waste water flowed into ditches and eventually into the River Severn. One of the places he carried out this work was at Abberley where he had to walk there and back each day regardless of the weather. His Uncle, however, spent a great deal of his time drinking in the pub!

Dad later went to work at Horsehill farm in Light Lane where he used to tend the cattle. He would start very early to milk the cows and the owner at that time was Mr Chapman. He then moved to take up employment in the Dyehouse at Carpet Trades as his Father had done before him. During this time he met and married my Mother who also worked in the carpet industry as a picker at Mortons which was situated in New Road, Kidderminster.

After their marriage they lived for a time at 11 Spencer Avenue with my maternal Grandparents, the Westons, which was why Florrie (being their first child) was born there. My parents later moved to Porthcawl in the district of Bridgend, Wales and his brother Ern also went with them. They both worked on the railway as track layers there. Uncle Ern frequently used to take Florrie paddling in the sea as a small toddler as they lived within walking distance of the beach.

It was during this time they moved from one house to another in the same district. When they arrived at the new house they discovered it was infested with bugs so they moved back to the old house in the same day. The landlord at the first house did not even know they had left! However, shortly after the War began they returned to Bewdley to live at No.35 High Street. Dad and Ern both joined the army to serve in the First World War at that time. Ern joined the Infantry where he was sadly killed in France having both legs blown off and Dad was a Signaller in the Artillery. I remember Dad telling me he had only met up with him two or three days beforehand so it was a terrible shock.   When Dad came out of the army he took the job at Winterdyne as a labourer but after a short time was made up to the position of Coachman. It was at this point we all moved to Winterdyne above the stables.

My Mother Elizabeth was born at Westbourne Street on 14th April, 1892, the eldest of three girls, and attended Wribbenhall School with her sisters Florence and Harriett. She told me that when she started work after leaving School at 14 years old she used to walk to Mortons Carpet Works as there were no buses in those days. Employers were very strict on timekeeping and if they were not there for 7 am the doors were closed and they would have to wait until breakfast time to enter their workplace. For this they would lose what was known as "a quarter." She also said *after* she married and stopped going to work the first of the buses began running from Bewdley to Kidderminster. She never said much about what type of bus they had but I can remember a double-decker with an open top in my childhood.

My Mother also told me about her Father called John Weston who worked at Kidderminster in Pitts Lane at a Printers as a Compositor. Her parents also lived in Wribbenhall as their first home was a bungalow called The Lodge at the bottom of Spadeful Lane along the Stourport Road, Bewdley. This was a former Toll House and when they went to live there they had no furniture, just a few boxes to sit on and a tea chest for a table. After this property they moved to the cottage in Whispering Street, now known as Westbourne Street and I have mentioned this earlier in my book. Later in life they went to live in Greatfield Road in Kidderminster where Florrie used to go on holiday for a week each year to stay with them. I only went once, however as I did not like it. Although Greatfield Road was just a sandy lane bordering a farm in those days and there were none of the houses we see today, I missed the fields to play in as it was so different to Winterdyne and found Granny to be very strict. I have a photograph of the occasion showing me standing with Granny outside the front door of their home with their dog named Floss.

I spent majority of my time with Dad when I was growing up as we often used to go riding and rabbiting together and he would tell me all about his life experiences. When we moved to Winterdyne Mother spent all her time looking after the family and was very strict. I was always teased about being Mother's favourite but I did not think so as I always had to behave myself! There was one occasion when I had done something she did not like while we were living in the rooms over the stables at Winterdyne. To go outside I had to go down the stairs and I recall her chasing after me and threw a broom at me while I was making my escape. Despite this I was very fond of her and used to help her with the shopping in Kidderminster on a Saturday plus I ran many errands.

Also living with my grandparents was my Aunt Flo and her husband Bert who worked in the Black Country in the ironworks. Although he seemed to talk in a strange accent to me with the strong Black Country lilt he was a very kind person. He used to like a drink of beer which they fetched from the Outdoor Licence at the bottom of Greatfield Road. On Sunday afternoons I very often went with Mother to visit her parents and when we got off the bus there was an iron gate we would pass through to cross the fields to Greatfield Road. Where we crossed is now a housing estate and as previously mentioned the sandy lane we walked along to reach Granny's was part of Greatfield Road at that time. Sutton Farm estate in those days was a working farm and I remember seeing cattle there as we passed. There were also allotments on the farmland and Granddad and Uncle Bert had one of these where they used to grow all their own vegetables.

My Grandparents other daughter was called Harriet and I referred to her as Auntie Al. She was married to Uncle Tom who worked in the building trade. I believe he was a bricklayer working for Vales of Stourport and they had two daughter's named Vera and Hilda who often visited us at Winterdyne. I remember Uncle Tom being involved in the building of the new Co-op in Oxford Street, Kidderminster. When Dad wanted me to go into the building trade he tried to arrange an apprenticeship with Vales but they turned me down as work was short in those days. On one occasion, while I was an apprentice   working on the Vicarage wall in Habberley Road for Coldrick's, a bricklayer bearing the tools of his trade on his back, had walked from Wolverhampton in an effort to find work and asked me if I knew of anything. They were difficult times and sadly there was no work to offer him.

MY RETIREMENT

When I was approaching my 65th birthday Ron Keight, Divisional Manager of Works Engineering at Brintons said he had been asked by the Directors if I would like to stay on for a further two years. This was the time when Brintons were building a further extension at Telford and so after discussing this with Gladys we decided it would be a good idea, although in hindsight I believe I made the wrong decision as it was two years less I was able to spend with her. At the time I enjoyed my job although it meant I worked very long hours as we had two or three progress meetings a week in the evenings while the extension at Telford was underway. When I finished at the meetings, the Gatekeeper would ring Gladys and tell her to begin cooking my tea as I would soon be home! I also had a considerable amount of work to do for Sir Tatton Brinton in London at this time which meant leaving home at around 3 am to avoid the rush-hour traffic.

After the two years I felt I was ready to retire fully and spend quality time with Gladys who was very pleased at this decision and I recall she put balloons outside The Glen for when I returned home on my last day! I certainly found it difficult at first with so much time on my hands so I decided I would work on No.24 Spencer Avenue which had been left to me by Mrs Hancocks for the time Gladys had spent looking after her. The bungalow was in a very poor condition with asbestos walls inside and out so I decided to prop up the roof and remove the walls below. I began this work on the occasions when Gladys did not want to go out anywhere and it took me approximately two years to complete, after which we decided to rent it out to a couple. Tony McGrath had his own business with an office in Bridge House, Bewdley and Carina worked on the Birmingham Road, Kidderminster in a water purification works. They stayed for approximately two years and another couple then rented it for six months while they found a property to buy in Stourport.

Gladys and I spent a great deal of time driving around the countryside during afternoons and evenings and she also enjoyed looking around the shops so we visited Birmingham, Hereford, Worcester and Ludlow. We also frequently travelled to Torquay on holiday where we stayed with Ruth Busby, widow of Harry Busby who were members of her adoptive family from when she lived at Pleasant Place, Longbank. Ruth was a very kind person and had always treated Gladys well in her childhood. She was getting older and we used to drive to Torquay for the day until she became infirm and spent her remaining days in a nursing home in Devon. It was after this that I decided to start walking every Saturday, which included treks around the Wyre Forest, Arley and Trimpley.

One day, when I was walking through Pound Green (by Harbour Farm) I saw Phil Hales who was Manager at Telford when we worked at Brintons. He invited me in for a cup of tea where I met his sister Eve and his nephew Philip who all lived at Harbour Farm. I was made very welcome by the family and we became good friends so I always call in when I walk by. When Gladys was unwell, Phil (ex-manager of Telford and brother of Eve) and Phillip (Eve's son who worked the farm) came down to see her and try to cheer her up but since then Phil passed away. Unfortunately Gladys' health deteriorated and I had to stop going on my walks so I could look after her as she was not able to be left alone.

Approximately five years later, sadly my wife passed away on 15th March, 2003 which I found extremely difficult to deal with but having Des living close helped me to return to normal life and I gradually started my walks again but I still think of Gladys and of the time she would be getting up and preparing dinner for us at about 1 o'clock. I leave in the morning at about 6 o'clock

Whatever the weather. I always enjoyed my hikes in the Venture Scouts and had been in the forest night hiking with Rob Williams and the remainder of the Venture Scouts as Rob (who lived at Beau Castle on Long Bank) knew the Wyre Forest quite well. I therefore decided my Saturday morning walks would incorporate the Forest. To begin with I was not that familiar with the many routes but with compass and map I have become very used to it. I often use the sun now to gain directions but losing my way sometimes is part of the fun of walking in the forest! I walked 20 miles plus in those days and there was a great deal more deer about. Now I sadly seldom see them.

My favourite walks of all are definitely in the Wyre Forest away from all the noise of the traffic. I also enjoy the route walking through the Forest following the Dowles Brook as far as Sturt Common where I leave the Forest at the bridge at Furnace Mill and walk along the lane passing Wyre Forest Station on the left, meeting up with the Cleobury Road at Far Forest. I then pass The Plough after approximately two miles and walk 200 yards, taking the turning on the right called Pound Bank. Walking past the council houses at the top of this road, I cross the Clows Top road taking the lane immediately in front towards Bliss Gate. This brings us out on the Bliss Gate Road, passing through part of the Estate, taking the turning on the left leads to a gate in the field.

I next climb over the gate and walk across the fields, past a house on the right, which then brings me out onto The Lakes Road. Crossing over and passing Pounds Portable Buildings on the right-hand side, continue past the greenhouses on your left and another house on your right; this leads into the Forest. By taking a turning to your right, after approximately 200 yards you arrive at Chapman's Forest. Crossing over a small brook, continue walking through the wooded area brings you out to a lane beside the Golf Course. Take a turning to your right and this takes you past Chapmans School Camp onto the Heightington Road. Walking for approximately 200–300 yards brings you to a footpath which follows along the side of the Golf Course. Opposite is the Ash and Layes ancient wooded area. Walking beside this until we arrive at a style and climbing this I cross the fields which brings us out to the log cabin belonging to 3rd Bewdley Scouts. This is now used by the Far Forest Scouts run by Peter Johnson.

Continuing across the fields, we pass the Well on your left where the Scouts obtain their water for cooking and washing purposes in the cabin. This is the Well from which Winterdyne and Kateshill used to obtain their all their water in times past and as explained earlier in the book this was cut through to allow the by-pass to be constructed. I then walk past Park Farm which was owned by Mr Wilkes in the past but now the sheds and pig sties have been converted into dwellings, one of which is lived in by Dr Prince. I now take the road which joins up with Light Lane, past the bungalow which used to be lived in by Mr and Mrs Leek and after 200 to 300 yards I take the footpath to a gate into the field, with the Golden Valley on your left. I cross the field which used to be owned by Mr Charlie Ife, you arrive at Bewdley Park path. Taking the left turn, past the monkey tree on your right (this is actually an oak tree, and we then continue along past the Convalescent Home into High Street which completes my journey.

Another of my favoured walks incorporates visits to Arley and Pound Green. During my journey across Pound Green Common on a regular basis, I have made several friends who I call on as I pass. Firstly, Godfrey who has a small holding with chickens and sheep and a little further along David who I often share a conversation with as he leans over his stable door while I am making my way through to Harbour Farm!

For many years I would call in to see Eve and Phillip at Harbour Farm and, of course, Phillip later married Sue, to have a chat and cup of tea with them. Eve's daughter Roz also lives in Arley with her family at the local Post Office and keeps the coffee shop next door. I often used to meet her on my walks as she was delivering newspapers around the surrounding area. Eve sadly passed away on 28th November, 2010 and I have many fond memories of her kindness. At Christmas she had a pig killed for the festive season and always sent Phillip with a joint for our table.

During one of my recent walks Andrea and I called at Harbour Farm, Pound Green, Arley to find Philip and Sue altering the farmhouse kitchen and old dining room. They were in the process of exposing all the original ceiling beams when they came across an old letter written by a Mr John Partridge who resided at The Harbour, Near Bewdley. The letter is concerning travel arrangements by coach from Worcester to London and is addressed to a Mr Potter. They also found an invoice from Mr Potter to Edward Bodenham dated 1802 for tailoring services carried out on May 22nd, 1802 detailing the cost of all the components used in the making of a coat for Mr Bodenham, totalling £2.5.0. It is fair to assume both documents related to the same Mr Potter who was a tailor and stayed at Harbour Farm.

When Philip and Sue uncovered the old fireplace in the dining room they uncovered the original baking oven on the left hand side and planned to renovate this to its original state as Philip had fond memories from his childhood when there were seats set either side. It will be a very interesting journey to watch their project develop. After visiting the farm I then often make my way down into Arley Village, passing the Severn Valley Railway Station on my left, over the footbridge, turning right to follow the river along to Eymore Woods. I then either return to Bewdley via Trimpley or continue following the river back home to Bewdley.

As Gladys asked to be buried at Abberley Church I make a point of incorporating walking at Abberley, climbing to the trig point at Abberley Top where I stop and think about Gladys and say a few silent words to her. For me this is the highest point I can reach to be near to her. I also do this when I climb Clee Hill and the summit of Snowdon. This gives me the courage to keep going.

One of the things I started doing was Sponsored Walks to give me a purpose in life. The first walk I did was for Stourport Methodist Church to help them with their restoration funds. This was from Stourport to Bewdley, calling at Bewdley Methodist Church and back to Stourport. The walk was arranged by Reverend Paul Booth and I raised £200 for this cause.

The next walk I did was with a friend, Damien Chance, who had completed The Three Peaks Challenge and this was to climb Snowdon to raise money for the alterations to the kitchen and toilets at Callow Hill Church. For this I raised £1,561. Two years later when I was 88 I climbed Snowdon again and this time Damien and some of my old 3rd Bewdley Scouts, Peter Johnson, David Thomas and Andrew Franklin helped me. This time we raised over £2,000, £600 of which was given to the Scouts to help to pay for the school room for the scout Gang Show and the remainder was given to the Bewdley Methodist Church for installing a lift for the elderly people.

In 2009 when I was in my 90th year I decided I would like to climb Snowdon again and "the boys" who accompanied me previously came with me plus a friend of David Thomas' who once lived in the area of Snowdonia. His sister also lived in Snowdonia and belonged to the Snowdon Trust. I also asked Rob Williams who had been in the Senior Scouts with me and as he was still scouting he decided to take two Scouts with him to climb the ridge side of the mountain and meet us at the summit. In addition, David arranged for Don Williams to go up by train to meet us at the top but unfortunately the service had been cancelled on the day due to bad weather and he was not able to do this.

On Wednesday, August, 26th, 2009 I left home with Damien at 6 am and arrived at 9 am at the car park by the train station on the Llanberris route. We rang David to let him know we had arrived and waited for him on the Llanberris car park. We began climbing the mountain at 9.30 am and by this time it was raining quite heavily. In fact as we climbed further the wind speed increased to around 50 miles per hour. This did not worry me, however, as I have been in such winds before but it impeded our progress as it took us almost three hours to climb about $\frac{3}{4}$ of the way up but then the wind worsened and the rainfall became torrential. Peter, Andrew and myself braced ourselves together as if in a rugby scrum as the wind got up to about 70+ mph. A gust of wind blew us all over on top of one another. David was blown into a pool of water, by the wind. Damien was blown over and said David's friend was picked up and carried and dropped again after a short distance. He said he was unhurt fortunately, but after we gathered ourselves together it was decided it was too dangerous to carry on so we had to return to the cars.

During the descent, the heavy rainfall made walking very dangerous as it was similar to wading in a brook as the water was fast-running down the mountainside, up to our ankles and on occasions was over the top of our boots. Half—way down we stopped to have a drink and I discovered the waterproof covering my rucksack was filled with water and the entire contents of the bag was saturated despite my efforts to waterproof it before the expedition.

Here we all are now forty years later at the top of Snowdon.
It rained all the way that made it slower, we went on and on.
Allen wanted to stop to look at the scenery
We had to stop to make our breathing abit easy

Snowdon climb in aid of Kidderminster Hospital with Damien, David, Andy and Peter

I have to admit it was rather a struggle as I had hurt my leg during the fall. Damien brought the car closer so I did not have to walk too far. I changed into dry clothes for the return journey and drove to Llanberris Car—park to meet everyone and David said to go back to the hotel and wait for them. This I found strange at the time but it turned out they had arranged for Don and Hilda Williams to come up and meet us at the top but of course the trains had been stopped because of the weather. Don had returned home as he did not know which hotel we were staying at.

When the boys returned to the hotel we cut a celebration cake Des had made for us to mark the occasion and had a cup of tea. David's friend's sister (who was a member of the Snowdon Trust) came to meet us and we talked of our experience of the day and in the safety of the hotel were now in a position to laugh about it! We then made our way home with Damien driving and as Peter had to be back at work the next day we were not late in leaving, returning home at around 8 pm. Rob Williams and the other two Scouts managed to reach the top of Snowdon as the side they climbed did not suffer from the winds we endured on our side of the mountain. Unfortunately, they did not meet up with us that day as we somehow completely missed one another but Rob came to see me the following day at The Glen.

This was not the end of the matter as it took Des, Andrea and I around three months to collect all the sponsorship money and it is fair to say we possibly walked more distance in this exercise than actually climbing Snowdon! Funds were obtained from Stourport, Kidderminster, Bewdley, Callow Hill (including money from Callow Hill Church Lunch Club), Far Forest, Rock, Pound Green, Arley, Button Oak, Clee Hill, and Bromsgrove. Damien Chance obtained donations from the Stourbridge area, Ray Bottomley also contributed, David Thomas collected sponsorship from Worcester and Andrew Franklin obtained donations from Stourport including Peter Johnson's and Rob Williams' contribution. In total we raised the grand sum of £6,713.84 including Gift Aid which purchased a Paxman Hair Loss System which is a cooling cap to prevent hair loss during chemotherapy treatment for The Millbrook Suite at Kidderminster Hospital.

The last charity walk I did to date was on 29th July, 2011 when Andrea, Damien and I climbed Snowdon again in aid of Help for Heroes. Damien collected us at 5 am and by 8.30 am we were preparing for the climb. We reached the summit at noon and marked the occasion by cutting the customary cake decorated by Des with Help the Heroes insignia on the top. It was a wonderful atmosphere as various people joined us in the celebrations and we shared the cake with them. There were people from Holland, Australia, Italy, Hungary and all parts of Great Britain and they were very interested to hear about my pursuits at the ripe old age of 91! One particular gentleman came back three times to congratulate me, even throwing his arms around me before we went our separate ways! There was also an 82 year old gentleman climbing that day and his son told me how old he was. They could not believe my age and called me Granddad from this point as I was the oldest man there!

It was perfect climbing weather that day in that it was cloudy, with a slight breeze, which made it the most comfortable and enjoyable walk I have ever had on Snowdon. We followed the Llanberris Route which is considerably longer and although visibility was poor at times due to the mist and fog, it was ideal conditions for the walk. It was a good mix of people and a very entertaining journey which made the time pass very quickly. I only wish that

Snowdon climb in aid of "Help for Heroes" with Damien and Andrea

David, Andy and Peter could have been with us after our experience last time we did the charity walk as the weather was far kinder to us! By 6 pm we were back in Bewdley and I was planning my next day's trip to Abberley Top. At 7 am I left home for my walk the following morning over Abberley Hills, calling at Gladys' grave on the way.

Once again it has taken far more effort than the actual climb to complete the lengthy process of collecting in all the donations for Help for Heroes which has brought me in contact with many different people. I am most grateful and extend my sincere thanks to all those who have generously donated and supported me over the years in my charitable causes without whom it would not have been possible to raise such worthwhile funds.

West Midlands Local Heroes Award at Molineux

This time we have raised the sum of £3420, bringing the overall total to date to £13,811 not including Gift Aid. It never fails to amaze me how much press interest my walks attract as it really is not such a big deal to me. I agree to the publicity purely to let the kind people who support me know when the walk has been completed successfully. This time I have been given an award by the Express and Star but to me, this award should be given to the real heroes who defend our country. Damien, Des, Andrea and I were invited to The Wolves Ground at Molineux where we were wined and dined and entertained by the football team and I was presented with a Local Hero Award together with other local heroes around the Midlands area. It was a lovely day.

I was recently contacted by Bewdley Town Clerk, Stephen Inman with an invitation to attend a further ceremony on Thursday, 22nd March, 2012 to receive the Bewdley Civic Award from the Mayor Dr. Janette Adams at the The Guild Hall. I was accompanied by my daughter Des, Andrea Clarke and Peter Johnson and was asked by the Mayor to say a few words on my charitable pursuits. Our photograph was taken with the Mayor between the famous pair of Bewdley Maces. These are one of only two pairs in England given by Queen Anne. They are solid silver, Hallmarked 1710 and are priceless. The maces are symbolic weapons to remind the people of the sovereign's power. They carry the initials "A.R." relating to Anne Regina. A very pleasant evening was had by all with a buffet and refreshments to follow. At this event I was also invited to meet Stanley Baldwin's grandson in May during the unveiling of an important photograph of our famous past Prime Minister.

Civic Award at Bewdley Guildhall

Civic Award with guests, Peter Jackson, Andrea Clarke, Pam, who kindly nominated me and Jill Stone

Mayoress Dr. Janet Adams presenting me with Award

Presentation to Lord Baldwin, Stanley Baldwin's Grandson

MY VISIT TO BUCKINGHAM PALACE

On 10th May, 2010 I received an invitation from the late Mr Michael Brinton, Lord Lieutenant of Worcestershire, to attend a Garden Party at Buckingham Palace. The visit was scheduled to take place 22nd June, 2010 which I had great pleasure in accepting with my daughter Desiree. This prompted an urgent shopping trip to provide a suitable outfit for Des and new suit for myself. We made some enquiries about the trains and Des spoke with my grandson, Christopher, who kindly offered to take us directly to the Palace by car which was a great relief as it was much easier than having to catch the train.

When the day arrived the weather was absolutely beautiful. Christopher arrived at 10.30 and we left home at 11am and had a pleasant journey to the city. As Christopher knew London very well we had no problems with the traffic. We arrived at Buckingham Palace at approximately 1.30pm but the parking was very difficult. We were issued with a permit which had a letter written on it leading you to your parking area which was situated in The Mall. There were hundreds of cars there already by this time which was a good mile away from Buckingham Palace gates. Des would have had problems walking this distance so Christopher dropped us at the gates of the Palace and parked the car more than a mile away!

Christopher was hoping to meet us before we entered the Palace in order to take some photographs but unfortunately did not return in time as we had already gone into the grounds. Fortunately, he was able to take some pictures of the beefeaters marching and the Palace itself but sadly not us in our finery! Then we had to wait in a queue for around 45 minutes and show our driving licence and either domestic bills or bank statements to prove identity. After we had passed through Security we were directed to the gates into the Palace grounds which is where the Queen's coaches pass through when she and her family return following official engagements. As we entered the archway we were greeted by scouts and police who took our official visiting cards and we then walked around the lawns. It was extremely crowded as there were at least 8,000 guests present!

We next made our way to the refreshment tent but could not find a seat as they were all occupied. The tea consisted of egg or cucumber sandwiches and various cakes and tiny pastries. I chose one of the famous cucumber sandwiches, Des selected egg and I sampled a piece of fruit cake and a truffle with the Royal Crest iced on the top. We drank a refreshing apple juice to quench our thirst but had to stand throughout this time as all the chairs were occupied. There was a 6 foot long by 18 inch wide table and a dozen of us used this on which to place our food. As soon as a plate was emptied it vanished as the service was extremely efficient and they seemed well prepared for the routine! After we had taken tea we made our way across to the pools. There were quite a number of birds such as coots and moor-hens but sadly I did not see any swans.

At 2.30 pm we made our way to stand at the entrance where the Queen would eventually pass through. At 4 o'clock she came out of the Palace to meet various chosen guests so we had a long wait but during this time we had the opportunity to have some interesting conversations with other people around us. One lady belonged to the CID and carried out duties for royalty on many occasions and she had brought her partner with her as it was his birthday. She showed a great of deal of concern about me standing when she was told of my age! Also stood near to us was another couple, the lady of which also became worried about me having to stand for so long, offering to fetch me a chair. I was absolutely fine and was more concerned about my daughter although she was well prepared and had brought a walking aid with a seat attached which proved invaluable.

At approximately 4.30pm we had our first sight of the Queen and she was wearing a striking two-piece outfit in yellow. About two dozen beefeaters marched into the area and stood to attention. The soldier in charge then marched them four at a time and stood them in front of the crowd until they had all taken up position with their backs to the people. He then gave the order to about turn so they we were facing us, with their staffs horizontal in order to push the crowd back. They organised the gathering to provide a large area where the Queen could meet a group of assembled chosen guests.   This was a very serious, controlled manoeuvre until they were told to stand at ease and became far more relaxed, chatting to those of us waiting. The soldier in charge was the most humorous and kept us all entertained with his remarks!

There were about 8 or 10 aides dressed in morning suits walking in front of the Queen and these were responsible for choosing those who would be personally presented to her. One of these approached me and asked why I was there and I explained I had climbed Snowdon with some of my old scouts and raised £6,000 to purchase a Paxman Hair-Loss System at Kidderminster Hospital for local cancer patients and had done this climb every other year for different charities. He also asked me how long I had been in the scouts and I told him majority of my life, since I was 7 years old. He said "you had better come and explain all that to the Queen!" He took Des and I into the circle where she was talking to the other selected guests.

Unfortunately, just before it came to my turn to be introduced to the Queen, (at which point she was approximately two feet away) one of her aides approached me, apologising profusely, and explained the Queen had run out of time as Prince Philip was approaching and was eager to take tea. She was unable to talk to me as everything is strictly run to time with military precision. We then made our way back towards the fellow guests we had been chatting with earlier when I was again approached by the same aide who originally selected me to meet Her Majesty, saying how very sorry he was that the Queen had not managed to speak to me personally, but he was very impressed with what I had done and said *"you are a star in my eyes!"* I have to admit I was very disappointed – both for Des and I but it did not spoil the day and was just the luck of the draw!

The Queen then went for tea, followed by her husband, where there were two marquees, one for the royal family and special guests and the other for dignitaries. While the royal family had tea the marching bands played for everyone. Des and I decided we would make our way out of the grounds to avoid a huge rush at the end and so said goodbye to the people we had met having had a lovely day.

We rang my grandson, Christopher, who collected us from the gates and made our way back home. We left the Palace at 5.15 pm and arrived home at approximately 8.15 pm Christopher had to return home straight away due to work commitments and did not arrive home until 11.30 pm. Next morning he had to be up at 6.30 am to return to London as he had work at the Old Bailey in the City. The following day I paid a visit to Monica Brinkworth, Michael Brinton's secretary, to tell her about my experience and asked her to thank Michael, who she advised me had also been at Buckingham Palace that day.

This brings me to the end of my book and I can honestly say I have enjoyed what can only be described as a very full and eventful life. I would like to take this opportunity to thank my daughter Des for all her help and support in my charity work and to publicly apologise as I never intended to cause her so much worry! Thanks also to Andrea for helping me with this book. We have enjoyed both the many walks and carrying out all the research together. Lastly, I would like to extend my gratitude to everyone who has supported me in my charitable causes, without which this target would not have been achievable. Thank you all!

Allen's in peak form for charity

Allen Birch with Ian Baldry, the Worcestershire county co-ordinator for Help for Heroes and Andrea Clarke, who joined Mr Birch on a Mount Snowdon trek

SPRIGHTLY 91-year-old Allen Birch has handed over more than £3,000 to armed forces charity Help for Heroes after walking up Snowdon. The great-grandfather, a former soldier in the Royal Engineers, was congratulated on his "tremendous effort".

It is the fourth time Mr Birch, of Wribben hall, Bewdley, has tackled the 3,560ft mountain since his 86th birthday. Previous outings have raised thousands of pounds for Bewdley Scouts, the town's Methodist Church and Kidderminster Hospital.

This time he generated £3,320 in sponsorship and is planning his next climb in 2012, which will be in aid of the Midlands Air Ambulance. Mr Birch said: "I think it is a really important charity."

He served during the Second World War in Hamburg and Egypt, building bridges and clearing mines.

Ian Baldry, Worcestershire county co-ordinator for the charity, visited Mr Birch's home to collect the cheque and thank him.